BUSINESS INTERRUPTION INSURANCE:
THEORY AND PRACTICE

Business Interruption Insurance : Theory and Practice

Edwin H Gamlen FCII
and
John H P Phillips FCII

Buckley Press Ltd
London

First published in 1992 by

Buckley Press Ltd
58 Fleet Street
London EC4Y 1JU

A member of the Timothy Benn Publishing Group

Text © Edwin H Gamlen and John H P Phillips

All rights reserved. No part of this publication may be
reproduced, stored in a retrieval system or transmitted,
in any other form or by any other means, without the
first permission in writing of the publisher, or be otherwise
circulated in any form of binding or cover other than that
in which it is published and without a similar condition
to this being imposed on the subsequent purchaser.

Typeset in Ehrhardt by TecSet Ltd, Havelock House,
Blenheim Gardens, Wallington, Surrey SM6 9PL.

Printed in Great Britain by Biddles Ltd, Guildford, Surrey

Business Interruption Insurance: Theory and Practice
ISBN 0 900236 46 2

THE AUTHORS

Edwin H Gamlen is a Fellow of the Chartered Insurance Institute. He spent his working life in the Fire and Survey Departments of the Guardian Assurance Co Ltd, becoming Fire Superintendent of the City Branch following the merger of the Guardian with the Royal Exchange Assurance. On retiring, he joined the College of Insurance as a Senior Fire Tutor, subsequently as a consultant, positions he has held for over 18 years. He was for many years a Senior Examiner for the Chartered Insurance Institute examinations and has lectured for a number of overseas Insurance Institutes.

John H P Phillips is a Fellow of the Chartered Insurance Institute. He has spent his working life in the Fire, Survey and Consequential Loss Departments of the Northern Assurance Co. Ltd. On the merger with the Commercial Union, he became a Consequential Loss Underwriter to the new Group. On retirement, he became a Consultant in this specialised subject. He was for many years an Examiner for the Chartered Insurance Institute and has lectured both at the College of Insurance and to local Insurance Institutes. He is a Past President of the One-Fifty Association, which is an association of practitioners in Business Interruption insurance.

Contents

Preface   xvii

1 **WHEN FIRE OCCURS, WHO WILL KEEP THE WOLF FROM THE DOOR?**   1

    1.01   Title   1
    1.02   The Effect of a Fire on the Business   1
    1.03   What does a B/I Policy seek to do?   3
    1.04   How a Business Interruption Policy operates   4
    1.05   Losses not covered by the Policy   7

2 **LOOKING AT THE ACCOUNTS**   8

    2.01   Accounts   8
    2.02   Trading Account   8
    2.03   Profit and Loss Account   10

3 **THE PRINCIPLES OF BUSINESS INTERRUPTION INSURANCE**   11

    3.01   Turnover   11
    3.02   Variables   11
    3.03   Standing Charges   12
    3.04   Payroll   12
    3.05   Net Profit   13
    3.06   What needs to be insured   13
    3.07   Variable or Standing Charge?   14
    3.08   Semi-Variables   15
    3.09   Partial and Total Losses   16
    3.10   V.A.T. and Current Cost Accounting   16

3.11	The Indemnity Period	17
3.12	Factors involved	19

4 IMPORTANCE OF SUM INSURED — 21

4.01	The Sum Insured	21
4.02	Gross Profit	21
4.03	Difference Basis	22
4.04	Definition of Gross Profit	24
4.05	To arrive at the Basis for the Sum Insured	24

5 PROJECTION OF THE BASIS FOR THE SUM INSURED — 27

5.01	Basis for Sum Insured	27
5.02	The Projection	27
5.03	Provisional Premium	29
5.04	"Declaration Linked"	30
5.05	Reinstatement of Sum Insured	31
5.06	First Loss Gross Profit Policy	32

6 THE COVER PROVIDED BY THE POLICY – PART I — 33

6.01	Recommended Wording	33
6.02	Summary	34
6.03	The Preamble	34
6.04	The Perils Covered	35
6.05	Fire	36
6.06	Lightning	37
6.07	Explosion	37
6.08	Operative Clause	39
6.09	Material Damage Proviso	40
6.10	Material Damage Proviso (continued)	41
6.11	Material Damage Proviso Waiver	42
6.12	Limitation of Liability	42
6.13	One Contract	43
6.14	Signature	43
6.15	Collective Policies	43

7 THE COVER PROVIDED BY THE POLICY – PART II — 45

7.01	Legal Contract	45
7.02	Definition of "Consequential Loss"	45
7.03	General Exclusions	46
7.04	Riot, Civil Commotion, War and Kindred Risks	46
7.05	Radioactive Contamination and Explosive Nuclear Assemblies	46
7.06	Terrorism in Northern Ireland	47
7.07	Pollution	47
7.08	General Conditions	48
7.09	Utmost Good Faith	48
7.10	Alteration	49
7.11	General Condition 2(a)	50
7.12	General Condition 2(b)	50
7.13	General Condition 2(c)	51
7.14	Claims Conditions	52
7.15	Discontinuance of the Business	54
7.16	Fraud	55
7.17	Contribution	56
7.18	Subrogation	57
7.19	Arbitration	58
7.20	Premises not in the Occupation of the Insured	59
7.21	The Schedule	59

8 WHEN FIRE TAKES PLACE – PART I — 60

8.01	Notification	60
8.02	The Loss Adjuster	60
8.03	When a Loss takes place	61
8.04	Increase in Cost of Working	61
8.05	The Role of the Accountant	62
8.06	Final Settlement	62
8.07	"Collective" Settlements	62
8.08	Summary	63
8.09	The Loss Assessor	63
8.10	The Specification	64
8.11	Demonstration Loss Settlement	64
8.12	Data Sheet	65

8.13	Loss of Gross Profit	66
8.14	Reduction in Turnover	67
8.15	Shortage in Turnover	71
8.16	Increase in Cost of Working	72
8.17	Economic Limit	75
8.18	Circumstances under which the Economic Limit might be exceeded	76
8.19	Alternative Trading Clause	77
8.20	Additional Increase in Cost of Working	78

9 WHEN FIRE TAKES PLACE – PART II 80

9.01	Savings	81
9.02	Proportionate Reduction	82
9.03	How much will be paid?	83
9.04	Final settlement	84
9.05	Assembling the figures for the claim	85
9.06	Professional Accountants Clause	85
9.07	Payments on Account	87
9.08	Alternative Basis of Settlement	87

10 WIDER COVER 89

10.01	Special Perils	89
10.02	Explosion	92
10.03	Aircraft	93
10.04	Riot and Malicious Damage	93
10.05	Earthquake	96
10.06	Subterranean Fire	97
10.07	Spontaneous Fermentation	97
10.08	Storm and Flood	97
10.09	Escape of Water	98
10.10	Impact (Third Party)	98
10.11	Sprinkler Leakage	99
10.12	Explosion and Collapse and Overheating	100
10.13	Subsidence, Ground Heave, Landslip	100
10.14	Notifiable Disease, Vermin, Defective Sanitary Arrangements, Murder and Suicide	101
10.15	Theft	103

	10.16	Fines or Damages	103
	10.17	Deterioration of undamaged stock	104
11	MISCELLANEOUS		105
	11.01	Departmental Clause	105
	11.02	Salvage Sale Clause	106
	11.03	New Business Clause	107
	11.04	Accumulated Stocks Clause	108
	11.05	Damage Occurring to Office Premises	109
	11.06	Insurance of rent	109
	11.07	Property Owners	109
	11.08	Property Developers	110
	11.09	Where the Letting is not the Main Business	110
	11.10	Tenants	111
	11.11	Rating	111
	11.12	The Fire Basis Rate	112
	11.13	Consequential Loss List of Rating Adjustments (CLORA)	112
	11.14	The Maximum Indemnity Period	113
	11.15	The Sum Insured	114
	11.16	Payroll	114
	11.17	The Range of Perils	116
	11.18	Extensions	117
	11.19	The Underwriter's Judgement	117
	11.20	Discounts	117
	11.21	Specimen Premium Calculation	118
12	DAMAGE AWAY FROM INSURED'S PREMISES		120
	12.01	Extending the Cover	120
	12.02	Suppliers	121
	12.03	Suppliers' Suppliers	123
	12.04	Unspecified Suppliers and Storage Sites	124
	12.05	Motor Vehicle Manufacturers	124
	12.06	Property Stored	125
	12.07	Patterns etc	126
	12.08	Transit	126
	12.09	Motor Vehicles	127

	12.10	Contract Sites	127
	12.11	Prevention of Access	128
	12.12	Public Utilities	129
	12.13	Professional Insured – Documents	132
	12.14	Specified Customers	132
	12.15	Unspecified Customers	133
	12.16	Bomb Scares	133
	12.17	Reminder	134
13	**SPECIAL COVERS**	135
	13.01	Increase in Cost of Working Only	135
	13.02	Additional Increase in Cost of Working	137
	13.03	Advance Profits	137
	13.04	Book Debts	139
	13.05	Research Establishments	140
	13.06	Engineering Business Interruption Insurance	141
	13.07	Computers	143
	13.08	Exhibitions	144
	13.09	Exhibition Proprietors	144
	13.10	Exhibition Organisers	144
	13.11	Exhibitors	145
	13.12	Stand Fitters	145
	13.13	Caterers on Exhibition Premises	145
	13.14	Car Park Lessees	145
	13.15	Gross Revenue	145
14	**INSURANCE OF WAGES USING "DUAL BASIS"; AND "ALL RISKS" INSURANCE**	146
	14.01	Background to Dual Basis Wages	146
	14.02	Arrangement of Cover	148
	14.03	Definition of Wages	149
	14.04	Operation of Dual Basis	149
	14.05	Consolidation	150
	14.06	Increase in Cost of Working	152
	14.07	Summary	152
	14.08	Payroll on Dual Basis	153
	14.09	Loss settlement	153
	14.10	"All Risks" Insurance	153

15 EMPLOYING A BROKER 156

- 15.01 Brokers and their Duties 156
- 15.02 Initial Discussion of the B/I Insurance with a Broker 158
- 15.03 Completion of the Proposal Form 159

16 BRIEF THOUGHTS ON RISK MANAGEMENT 161

- 16.01 Introduction 161
- 16.02 Risk Identification 161
- 16.03 Risk Analysis 161
- 16.04 Physical Risk Control 162
- 16.05 Pre-loss – Risk Avoidance 162
- 16.06 Pre-loss – Risk Reduction 163
- 16.07 Post-loss Risk Control 164
- 16.08 Financial Risk Control 164
- 16.09 Risk Retention 164
- 16.07 Risk Transfer 165
- 16.08 Summary 165

17 INSURANCE CONCEPTS AS APPLIED TO BUSINESS INTERRUPTION INSURANCE 166

- 17.01 Introduction 166
- 17.02 The Law of Contract 167
- 17.03 Fair and Equitable Premium 167
- 17.04 Insurable Interest 168
- 17.05 Utmost Good Faith 168
- 17.06 Indemnity 169
- 17.07 Proximate Cause 170

AIDE MEMOIRE 171

- A.01 Gross Profit and Revenue cover 171
- A.02 Indemnity Period 171
- A.03 Gross Profit Sum Insured 172
- A.04 Payroll 172
- A.05 Perils to be included in the cover 172
- A.06 Extensions to be considered 173
- A.07 Deposit Premium 173

A.08	Clauses to be considered with the Insurer or Broker	173
A.09	Premises and Business	174
A.10	Other covers	174
A.11	Deductibles and LTA	174
B.01	Action to be taken following an Incident	174

APPENDICES 175

1	Standard Fire Policy (Business Interruption)	176
2	Standard "All Risks" Policy (Business Interruption)	181
3	"Gross Profit" Wording – Sum Insured Basis	188
4	"Gross Profit" Wording – Declaration-Linked Basis	191
5	Wages: "Dual Basis" Wording – Sum Insured Basis	194
6	"Dual Basis": Example of Loss Settlement	196
7	Fines or Damages; and Premium Adjustment Clauses	206
8	Special Perils	208
9	Special Clauses	219
10	Business Interruption Extension Wordings	222
11	Book Debts Insurance Wording	228
12	Research Expenditure Wording	230
13	Gross Revenue Wording – Declaration-Linked Basis	232
14	Collective Policies	235
15	*City Tailors Ltd v. Evans (1921)*	237
16	Overseas Wording: Model Fire and Special Perils Policy	239
17	Standard Policy (Pre-October 1989)	246

Index 251

Preface

Whether or not you are in insurance, most people regard Business Interruption insurance as a difficult subject and a mental portcullis seems to be lowered when the subject is broached.

Buying a building or buying a machine, a tangible object, demands time and trouble, thought and judgement. A specification will be studied and only when the prospective purchaser is satisfied will the purchase go ahead.

Buying insurance, on the other hand, is buying a promise that in the unfortunate event of a fire, a boiler explosion or any other catastrophe, the Insured will be compensated. But how ? What is the measure of the loss ? What are the stages to achieving a fair level of compensation ?

In just the same way as there is a specification to guide a purchase of the building or the machine, so there is a specification attached to the business interruption policy, setting out the terms under which compensation will be provided.

Naturally, it is technically worded, but so is the machine specification. The difference is that the purchaser may be familiar with the machine specification, whereas the insurance specification leaves him cold!

Computer manufacturers claim their machines are "user friendly". We, the authors of this book, hope that this, too, will be regarded as a user friendly volume.

We shall take you, the reader, step-by-step through the accounts to the sum insured, through the cover provided by the policy and the stages of a loss settlement.

Thank you for inviting us into your sanctum; we shall be perfect guests and not interrupt. We shall just express the hope that, should you be involved in a claim, you will have cause to be thankful that the insurance was properly arranged and full compensation resulted.

Over the years, the title for this class of insurance has undergone several changes. To start with, it was known as "consequential loss" (a title still used by many practitioners); later this became "profits" or "loss of profits", and then our transatlantic colleagues introduced the term "business interruption". But a rose by any other name . . . , the insurance remains the same.

For the sake of consistency, we shall use the title "Business Interruption", shortened to B/I for ease and to save repetition; the word "incident" will be used to represent the result of the operation of an insured peril.

The material in this book is based on our experience of the market in the United Kingdom and the wordings used and included in the Appendices are those published in October 1989 as Amendment Issue No. 2 and March 1991 as Amendment No. 3, and recommended for use in this country by the Association of British Insurers. We are aware that a number of countries overseas use the same or similar wordings and we hope that this book will be helpful to insurance people worldwide. (The "recommended" overseas wording is included as Appendix 16.)

Learning is a fundamental human exercise, whether it is learning to read, learning to walk or learning one's job. It is something that no-one else can do for us. But given good colleagues in a working environment the job is learned more easily and in greater depth.

Both of us have enjoyed that environment during our working life, wherein we have had the benefit of colleagues prepared to show us the ropes and we, in our turn, have had the privilege of guiding others towards a better understanding of this subject. There is no doubt that the best way of exploring a subject is to undertake to teach it.

So we would like to pay a tribute to all our friends in the business who have helped us acquire the skill of handling this type of insurance and who have encouraged us to undertake this project. We hope we have met the need for a book designed to be readable and useful to insurance and non-insurance readers alike.

We gratefully acknowledge permission given by the Association of British Insurers to reproduce the "recommended" wordings published in October 1989 and subsequent amendments, and for permission from the Chartered Insurance Institute Tuition Service to reproduce various diagrams in the book.

Our acknowledgements would not be complete without a big "thank you" to Clive Pick FCII, previously a Senior Tutor and now a consultant at the College of Insurance, for his help and encouragement during the preparation of this book and to our wives, who have indulged our whim to see ourselves in print.

E. H. Gamlen
J. H. P. Phillips

1 When Fire Occurs, who will keep the Wolf from the Door?

Title – The Effect of a Fire on a Business – What does a B/I Policy seek to do? – How a B/I Policy operates – Losses not covered by the Policy

1.01 TITLE

This book uses the term "Business Interruption Insurance". If, however, your Insurers use the term "Consequential Loss Insurance" or "Loss of Profits Insurance", the three titles are all referring to the same type of insurance and no difference in that cover will arise as a result of the change of title. We shall use "B/I" for "Business Interruption".

In October 1989 the Association of British Insurers (ABI) published the "recommended" Business Interruption wordings, replacing those which had been in use for many years. The result is policy documents, specifications and clauses which are more readily understood, without affecting the level of cover provided. A further amendment was published in March 1991, completing a major task and these new wordings will be used in this book.

A comparable wording for use overseas has also been published, following traditional overseas lines. Again, the level of cover has been maintained while the regrouping of the Conditions renders the document readily understandable. (See Appendix 16.)

1.02 THE EFFECT OF A FIRE ON THE BUSINESS

Cash flow – the life blood of every business – must be maintained if the business is to survive. Without a steady flow of cash inwards from goods sold or services rendered, there will be inadequate funds to meet the continuing cost of maintaining the business and of having to pay the wages of employees even when their services cannot be used. The cost of replacing goods or materials will, of course, be met by the material damage insurance. When it becomes apparent to suppliers of goods and services that the business has developed into a "slow payer", credit may be restricted, even when the reasons are well-known, and a vicious circle commences.

Borrowing to survive may be possible, but interest charges impose a further burden on a business already in difficulties and survival becomes even more problematical.

The effect of fire on a business, interrupting production or sales and the inevitable delay in fulfilling orders, is to jeopardise the life blood, the cash flow. While money may be received for a short while after the fire for goods already despatched, there will be a further period when the result of unfulfilled orders is a much restricted cash flow.

The cost of operating a business does, however, continue and the serious situation is further compounded as customers are compelled to turn to competitors to maintain their own business. This, in turn, leads to the problem of winning back their custom when production re-commences, especially if they have had to sign extended contracts to obtain supplies.

Three other serious aspects of the effect of a fire on the business must be considered.

Firstly, the effect on the employees, both the office staff and the factory workers. A serious fire immediately raises the question as to the likely survival of the business, even if it is possible to resume production. Will the fire be the catalyst which triggers a scheme for rationalisation and the relocation of production and the consequent closure of the damaged premises? Will there be a large number of redundant workers who cannot be relocated and who will be legally entitled to a redundancy payment?

Every employee will be considering his or her own future in the light of events. Employees with skills can find alternative employment and may well decide to join a competitor, rather than risk eventual redundancy if the business fails to survive, either as a result of failure to recover from the fire or as part of the rationalisation programme.

Money invested in training is lost and the previous restraint of pension rights is no longer available, as "portable pensions" are now on the Statute Book.

Secondly, if, after the fire, production is to be maintained, either on the fire damaged premises or elsewhere, considerable ingenuity and cash will be required. Few firms are willing to maintain sufficient funds in liquid form to meet this eventuality and most firms would be reluctant to capitalise assets to provide the much needed cash, even if they were able to do so.

Thirdly, the net profit, the heart of the matter, will disappear rapidly when production is interrupted and a net loss may have to be carried forward in the balance sheet.

To summarise – after a fire the business will be faced with
– shortage of funds;
– bills for the cost of maintaining the business;
– salary and wage payments to retain staff, without the equivalent production;
– notice and redundancy payments if staff have to be dismissed for lack of work;
– increase in cost of working in an endeavour to maintain production;
– disappearance of net profit;

altogether, an unenviable situation.

1.03 WHAT DOES A B/I POLICY SEEK TO DO?

Subject to the insurance having been properly arranged, the policy will meet the shortfall in cash needed, but which has not been earned,
– to pay the bills to maintain the business (rent, rates, interest payable, insurance, etc.);
– to meet the cost of employees who remain, but who are not fully productive;
– to meet the cost of notice and redundancy payments for employees who have to be dismissed or laid off;
– to fund the increase in the cost of maintaining the production after the fire or the extra cost of continuing production elsewhere (subject to an economic limit);
– to restore the net profit.

All of which sounds almost too good to be true. But, as the survival of many businesses after a serious fire, where there was adequate insurance, testifies, the policy can indeed prevent the collapse of the firm. Thousands of businesses have cause to rejoice that their insurance cover, properly arranged, saw them through a very difficult time.

1.04 HOW A BUSINESS INTERRUPTION POLICY OPERATES

Let us begin by examining the accounts for the year before a business suffered a fire; for the purpose of this short introduction, we shall assume that there were no changes in the operating expenses in the following year.

Accounts for the year prior to the year in which the fire occurred

Cost of production	100 000	Sales	200 000
Overheads } i.e. 50% {	90 000		
Net profit	10 000		
	200 000		200 000

Fig. 1 Turnover represented by production costs, overhead costs and net profit.

In B/I insurance, the cash received from the sale of goods or from services rendered in course of the business at the premises is termed "Turnover". Every £1 of Turnover earns a proportion of the cost of production, the overheads and the net profit; let us assume a ratio of 50%, 45% and 5% respectively.

In the event of a fire, there will be a reduction in the production or sale of goods, leading to a reduction in the money received – the Turnover; and the cost of production or purchase of raw materials – the prime cost – will fall in line with the level of output.

The overheads will, however, largely continue and the net profit will be much reduced or, more probably, disappear, to be replaced by a net loss.

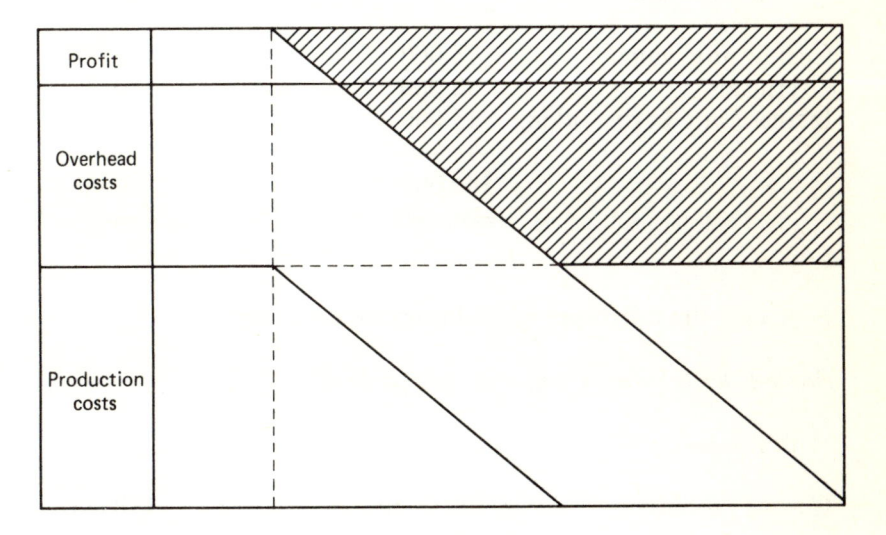

Fig. 2 After an interruption in production: production costs fall in line with the reduced level of production; overhead costs continue; profit is lost. The hatched area shows the loss resulting from reduction in turnover.

The proportionate reduction in the cost of production will mean that the manufacturer will suffer no loss under this heading, but there will be a loss under "Overheads" and "Net Profit", equivalent to 50% (45% + 5%) of the shortage in turnover due to the fire.

6   *Business Interruption Insurance: Theory and Practice*

If, therefore, the policyholder receives a payment equal to 50% of the turnover lost, the policyholder will be able to meet the full cost of the overheads and the net profit in the accounts will be restored.

In addition, increase in cost of working to regain the level of pre-fire turnover will be met, so long as the Insurers are not asked to pay more in increase in cost of working than they would have paid in loss of overheads and net profit had the increase in cost of working not been incurred. (This is known as the "economic limit".)

The following set of accounts show this operation:

Accounts for the year in which the fire occurred

With no insurance

Cost of production	75 000	Sales	150 000
Overheads	90 000	Net Loss	30 000
Increase in cost of working	15 000		
	180 000		180 000

Now note the difference when insurance cover applies.

Accounts for the year in which the fire occurred

With insurance

Cost of production	75 000	Sales		150 000
Overheads	90 000	Insurance Claim –		
Increase in cost of working	15 000	50% × 50 000 reduction in turnover	25 000	
Net Profit	10 000	Increase in cost of working	15 000	40 000
	190,000			190 000

The measurement of the turnover lost in consequence of the fire and the Economic Limit will be explained later.

.05 LOSSES NOT COVERED BY THE POLICY

Perhaps at this point – and to prevent euphoria! – it would be as well to point out some of the losses consequent upon fire damage which are not covered by a B/I policy.
- (1) *Deterioration of undamaged stock* after damage has occurred.
- (2) *Failure to recover debts* of pre-fire damage trading, owing to destruction of records.
- (3) *Fines, damages and/or penalties* under contracts arising from breach of contract in consequence of the damage.
  Cover is available either by a special policy or as additional items in respect of (1) (2) and (3) above.
- (4) *Third party claims* other than fines etc (except as mentioned in 3 above).
- (5) *Loss of goodwill.* Provided a suitable indemnity period (see later) is chosen, there should be no loss of goodwill, since the indemnity period under the policy is to place the Insured, so far as possible, *in the same financial position as he would have been in* had the fire not occurred.

2 Looking at the Accounts

Trading Account – Profit and Loss Account – Opening and Closing Stocks – Work in Progress

2.01 ACCOUNTS

Every business has to maintain a day-by-day record of receipts and expenditure. The expenditure is broken down into convenient headings, so that it is possible to budget and control the amounts spent.

At the end of the financial year, the various headings are brought together to form the Accounts.

For B/I insurance purposes, our attention is concentrated on the Trading Account and the Profit and Loss Account, examples of which are shown opposite.

2.02 TRADING ACCOUNT

The Trading Account carries the items relating to the DIRECT cost of making and/or selling the articles marketed by the firm – the cost of raw materials etc, wages and the outlay on lighting, heating and power.

When a business has been operating for more than a year, at the point when the Accounts are closed, say midnight on 31 December, there will be Raw Materials not yet taken into use and Finished Stock not yet sold. There will also be Work-in-Progress, some just started, some nearly finished. All of these items represent Working Capital in the form of Stock and Work-in-Progress and as such will be brought into the Accounts.

So, in the Trading Account – top left hand side – will be found the value of the stock in hand and the Work-in-Progress on the first day

TRADING ACCOUNT

Opening Stock	40 000	Sales (Turnover)	1 500 000
Work in progress	10 000	Closing Stock	36 000
Raw Materials	500 000	Work in progress	9 000
Packing	46 000		
Carriage	30 000		
Wages	420 000		
Lighting	10 000		
Heating	20 000		
Power	10 000		
Gross Profit	459 000		
	1 545 000		1 545 000

PROFIT AND LOSS ACCOUNT

Directors' Fees	65 000	Gross Profit	459 000
Salaries	80 000	Interest receivable	25 000
Office Expenses	20 000	Rent receivable	15 000
Rent/Rates	25 000		
Interest payable	10 000		
Advertising	20 000		
Depreciation	25 000		
Insurance	8 000		
Bad debts	3 000		
Net Profit	243 000		
	499 000		499 000

of the accounting year and the last items on the right hand side are the Stock and Work-in-Progress when the Accounts were closed.

The difference between the two sides of the Account – 459,000 – is shown as Gross Profit at the bottom of the left hand column and this amount will be carried down to the Profit and Loss Account.

2.03 PROFIT AND LOSS ACCOUNT

The Account is opened by bringing down the Gross Profit from the Trading Account as shown.

On the left hand side are listed the items which are usually known as 'Overheads', since they do not form part of the direct cost of manufacture.

On the right hand side, extraneous items of receipt are shown, in this case, Interest receivable from some form of investment, and Rent receivable, say from a building owned but not occupied by the business.

The difference between the two sides of the Account will be shown as Net Profit and the amount of 243 000 will be carried forward to the Balance Sheet.

Interest from investments will not, however, be included in the B/I sum insured, although the Rent receivable can be included either as part of the Gross Profit covered or as a separate item.

B/I insurance is concerned with the trading of the business, so the Balance Sheet will not be involved.

In a business which sells a service – the accountant, lawyer, insurance broker – this account is usually referred to as the Revenue Account.

3 The Principles of Business Interruption Insurance

Turnover – Variables – Standing Charges – Payment of Wages and Salaries – Protection of Net Profit – V.A.T. – Indemnity Period

3.01 TURNOVER

The income of the business – usually shown in the Trading Account as "Sales" – is, for B/I insurance purposes, known as TURNOVER.
"Turnover" is defined in the policy as

> "The money paid or payable to the Insured for goods sold and delivered and for services rendered in course of *the Business* at *the Premises*."

Note. The items in italics are important. As will be seen later, it may not be desired to ask for cover in respect of all the business activities or possibly all the premises.

Turnover, then, is all the money coming in from the business activities and does not include, necessarily, rent receivable for, say, a building on the site, owned by the Insured and occupied by a tenant. Rent should, preferably, be insured by a separate item. Neither does the term "Turnover" include interest receivable on investments, since the interest will be received independently of the fortunes of the business.

Let us take "Turnover" and break it down into four main headings.

3.02 VARIABLES

The manufacture of any saleable commodity involves the purchase of **raw materials** or, if the business buys in goods from other manufacturers, the purchase of items of stock. These may range from sheet or strip metal, rough timber to finished components which the Insured assembles. The Insured will also require **packing materials** and despatch of the goods will involve **carriage**. (If the carriage is by vehicles belonging to the business, this item will not usually be a variable.)

The purchase of raw materials, packing materials and carriage will be closely linked to the level of production (except when carriage is by own vehicles). If production increases, additional purchases of these items will be necessary. By the same token, a fall in production, as, for instance, following interruption due to a fire, will lead to a lower level of purchasing.

These items are known as **Variables,** since expenditure on these items will normally vary DIRECTLY with the level of production.

3.03 STANDING CHARGES

Apart from items mentioned later, most of the other costs of running the business will continue to have to be paid either in full or in part, IRRESPECTIVE of the level of production. These costs will include Directors' Fees, Rent payable, Rates, Interest payable, and Office expenses.

The level of expenditure on these items does not vary directly in line with the level of production and they are accordingly known as **Standing Charges.** They are the expenses referred to in ordinary speech as "the overheads", in the sense that they are the unavoidable expenses of running the business.

3.04 PAYROLL

The days of "hire and fire" have virtually gone and payment of wages to factory staff and salaries to office staff no longer follows the level of production. Legislation defines the period of notice and the redundancy money to which an employee is entitled, if circumstances require that service with the firm must terminate. (It is not proposed to go into detail as to the amount of these items, which are well known to any employer and which can vary according to specific Trade Union agreements.)

Alternatively, although production may be impaired or at a standstill, nevertheless it will be sound economic policy to retain skilled staff, even if there is little to show for their labour, especially if the interruption is likely to be limited in time.

It would be foolish to lose the investment that skilled staff represent and few manufacturers would relish their skilled staff being employed by competitors. In addition, when the new machinery is delivered, they will need to be on hand to check and accept it, and subsequently to train new staff as production increases.

Legislation takes no account as to whether a person is a wage earner or a salaried employee. In the past, office workers might well have been retained in spite of little or no work to keep them occupied, but in today's economic climate, they will fare no better than the wage earners in the factory and the absence of work in the office means they will face lay off or discharge.

It is now customary, for insurance purposes, for all Wages and Salaries, including Directors' Remuneration or Salaries but not Fees, to be amalgamated under the heading of **Payroll** and included in full in the sum insured.

.05 NET PROFIT

This item in the Accounts represents the balance of receipts over expenditure during the year.

.06 WHAT NEEDS TO BE INSURED

Let us now look at these four headings – *Variables*, *Standing Charges*, *Payroll* and *Net Profit* – and see to what extent an Insured would suffer a loss in the event of, say, a fire interrupting production.

Variables. Since the level of purchasing of these items is in line with the level of production, it follows that in the event of an interruption of the business, the Insured will not suffer a loss under this heading. (No production, no purchases; 50 per cent production, 50 per cent purchases required.) This part of the Turnover is therefore not insured, since the Insured is unlikely to suffer a loss under this heading.

(Remember that the *physical loss* of stock etc will be covered by the material damage insurance.)

Standing Charges. These continue to fall due for payment, notwithstanding a drop in production and, therefore, cover for these items is necessary.

Payroll. A short stoppage involving loss of production will not necessarily mean any corresponding reduction in the payment of wages and salaries. The Insured would, therefore, be paying labour costs without a full return on this expenditure. It may be possible with a short stoppage that the loss in production can be made up later but at additional cost (such as overtime).

A serious loss involving lay off or dismissal of a section of the work force and the retention of the skilled employees will be an expensive operation and the Insured will be facing this expense at a time when income has been reduced.

Insurance for this part of the Turnover is therefore essential.

Net Profit. Any interference with the level of production has the immediate effect of lowering the level of Net Profit earned.

Protection for this vital element of Turnover is therefore required, especially if shareholders are concerned in the business and will wish to know why their dividend has been reduced and why their investment was not protected.

3.07 VARIABLE OR STANDING CHARGE?

Some items in the Accounts raise doubts as to the heading to which they belong.

Advertising. While, at first glance, it might be felt that Advertising is a variable, on the grounds that the firm might cease to advertise in the event of a serious loss by fire etc., further reflection will reveal that advertising is now no longer an *ad hoc* exercise except for a very small business, operating within a small geographical area.

Expenditure on advertising must be as cost effective as possible and most firms will now approach an advertising agency with a budget, to obtain professional advice and guidance. The agency will not only advise, but will also book space in the media and organise the campaign under a contract. In consequence Advertising is normally regarded as a standing charge.

Depreciation. This item in the Accounts is the writing down in value of the assets of the firm. By the same token, it is a reduction in the amount of Net Profit and constitutes the creation of a reserve for the future purchase of replacement assets.

Machines not only wear out, they become obsolescent and the obsolescence continues whether the plant is in operation or is idle owing to a stoppage in another part of the premises. Even if new machinery is installed as a result of a fire, it starts to depreciate in value from the time it is delivered. Accordingly, Depreciation is treated as a standing charge.

Bad Debts. Most businesses suffer bad debts. The amount outstanding will have appeared in previous accounts as "Sundry Debtors", but if there is now no likelihood of receiving the money, the decision to write off the debt will have to be taken. Insurers do not regard Bad Debts as a standing charge and this item must therefore be treated as a Variable. (But see the next paragraph.)

Bad Debts Reserve. When any level of trading is undertaken, bad debts will inevitably follow. Goods will be supplied but payment delayed and when pressure is applied, bankruptcy of the customer follows.

A prudent trader can create a Bad Debts Reserve by setting aside an amount against this item when completing the Accounts for the year. The Net Profit will be reduced in consequence, but a fund will be created from which money for bad debts can be withdrawn. Because this Reserve is a provision for the future, similar to Depreciation, Insurers regard this regular payment as a standing charge.

Accountants' and Auditors' Fees. An interruption in the business will make little impact on the level of charges made by accountants and auditors. Their annual remuneration should be treated as a standing charge.

This item must not be confused with the payment made to an accountant for work done in connection with a claim (see Chapter 9 – Professional Accountants Clause).

.08   SEMI-VARIABLES

Statements received from Gas and Electricity Boards (and Water Companies where the supply is metered) show a Standing Charge and a charge for the units consumed. The Standing Charge will not reduce with lower consumption and, in fact, may well increase. Depending on the use made of this energy, consumption may or may not be in line with the level of production.

In a simple clothing factory, power will be consumed virtually in line with production as current will be used only when machines are in use, but when they are run in an effort to maintain production, they may be used uneconomically.

In more complex risks, where electricity is used for space heating, refrigeration and/or operating lifts, the reduction in the level of consumption may be minimal, even though production is reduced.

Many machines require to be heated and kept turning over throughout the working day, even if production is intermittent, so that energy consumption will be only minimally reduced.

Much the same position applies where processes involve steam. It is difficult to gear steam production to demand, if machinery is in intermittent use. On the other hand, a total shut down could enable the boiler to be banked up and left for periods, or even have the fire drawn, if there is no requirement for steam at all.

This leaves the Insured with the difficult task of deciding if the cost of energy should be treated as a Standing Charge or a Variable.

A compromise solution is available by treating Lighting, Heating and Power as "Semi-Variables". The Insured can opt to insure these items as a percentage of the total cost. This does result in some saving of premium, but runs the risk that underinsurance could involve the Insured in meeting some of the cost. The decision to insure Lighting, Heating and/or Power as Semi-Variables should only be taken by the Insured in exceptional circumstances after discussion with their insurance adviser.

3.09 PARTIAL AND TOTAL LOSSES

Pictures of fires in the press and on television give the impression that a total loss will follow a fire on the premises. It should be emphasised, however, that while most losses are of a partial nature, a fire, a boiler explosion or a breakdown of machinery occurring in only part of the premises can result in an interruption in production out of all proportion to the material damage involved. Even though production is at a standstill or, at best, struggling through, the Standing Charges will have to be met. Without adequate insurance, the burden could lead the firm into liquidation.

3.10 V.A.T. AND CURRENT COST ACCOUNTING

All specifications carry the following notes –

> **Notes: 1** To the extent that the Insured is accountable to the tax authorities for Value Added Tax, all terms in this policy should be exclusive of such tax.

> 2 For the purpose of these definitions, any adjustment implemented in current cost accounting shall be disregarded.

3.11 THE INDEMNITY PERIOD

The Indemnity Period is defined in the Specification as:

> **Indemnity Period:** The period beginning with the occurrence of the Incident and ending not later than the Maximum Indemnity Period thereafter during which the results of the Business shall be affected in consequence thereof.

In the following paragraph entitled "Maximum Indemnity Period" is stated the number of months selected by the Insured.

The choice of the number of months for the Maximum Indemnity Period is of crucial importance.

1. *It governs the maximum cover under the policy*
   It should be noted that the Indemnity Period lasts as long as the results of the business are affected by the damage, limited to the maximum number of months chosen by the Insured.

   The cover does not cease when the buildings are restored and the machinery is functioning, but when the Turnover has reached the level at *which it would have been* had the damage not occurred. This could well be a number of months after restoration, when the production line is functioning properly and the customers are back or have been replaced. In some competitive industries it has been said by some marketing experts that if they were out of production for twelve months, it would take at least another twelve months to regain full sales.

While the level of Turnover is a good guide to the restoration to the "would have been" position, it must not be forgotten that the wording of the Definition of Indemnity Period is "... during which the results of the business shall be affected...".

The restoration of the level of Turnover may only be achieved if the Insured is buying in part-made or finished goods with the assistance of Increase in Cost of Working. Thus, while the Turnover may have recovered, nevertheless the business is still affected.

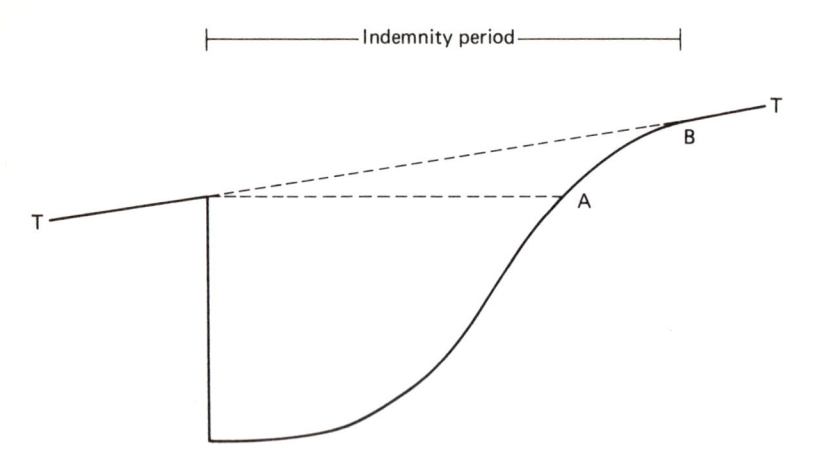

Fig. 3 Indemnity Period.
T = level of Turnover;
A = level of Turnover equal to level at date of the damage;
B = level of Turnover equal to the "would have been" position, i.e. end of Indemnity Period

Not every incident involving damage will involve the full period of cover. Liability for the loss ceases when the damage ceases to affect the results of the business. The period may be only four weeks or four months or the full Maximum Indemnity Period.

Notice that the Indemnity Period commences with the date of the Incident, so even if the policy is due for renewal the following day, the Maximum Indemnity Period will run from the date of the damage.

2. *The Maximum Indemnity Period governs both the sum insured and the rate payable*
   This will be discussed in detail later, but it is as well to emphasise that if a Maximum Indemnity Period of less than twelve months is selected, the sum insured will still be based on the annual Gross Profit but a lower rate (not reduced in proportion) is charged, recognising the Insurer's reduced liability. Insurers are, in fact, reluctant to issue a policy with an Indemnity Period of less than twelve months as experience shows that a combination of adverse

circumstances could prolong the time taken for the return of the business to the "would have been position".

3.12 FACTORS INVOLVED

The choice of the Maximum Indemnity Period requires very careful consideration, since failure to select a long enough period could involve the termination of the cover before the business has achieved the level of trading required.

Every business has its individual characteristics, but some of the principal factors for consideration are as follows:

(1) *Availability of alternative premises*
Many premises are purpose built or require modification before production can commence. Delay in starting up in alternative premises is inevitable and the necessary timelag must be taken into account in selecting the Maximum Indemnity Period. For instance, consider the problems involving a cinema, theatre or coldstore.)

(2) *The ease or otherwise with which the existing premises can be repaired or replaced*
A severe fire may be sufficiently serious to require the demolition of the structure, the removal of debris from the site and total reconstruction. This will usually involve planning permission before rebuilding can commence and delay can be expected if the factory is sited in a sensitive area.

(3) *The availability of raw materials*
Destruction of the stock of raw materials may impede the rapid resumption of production, if replacement stock is not readily available.

(4) *The timelag in the replacement of machinery*
A large proportion of machinery is "tailor made" for the factory owner. A generous estimate of the time required between placing the order for the machinery and its commissioning must be made, particularly if the machinery has to be imported. This is referred to as "lead time".

(5) *The possibility of manufacturing the product in another factory within the group should be explored*
This will be possible only if there is spare capacity or agreement can be obtained for overtime working or a second shift.

(6) *The estimated time required to "recover" customers* who have been forced to obtain their requirements from other manufacturers and who, in many cases, will have necessarily signed a contract for a certain period. Naturally, the level of competition in the market will have a bearing on this point.

(7) *For a seasonal business*, an Indemnity Period of twelve months should be regarded as a minimum.

4 Importance of Sum Insured

Basis for Sum Insured – "Difference Basis" – Example

4.01 THE SUM INSURED

The Sum Insured serves three purposes.
(1) It is the amount on which the premium is based;
(2) It is the limit of liability of the Insurer;
(3) If the insurance is "subject to average", too low a sum insured will result in the Insured receiving less than a full settlement of the claim.

It will be apparent, therefore, that care must be taken to select an appropriate amount, otherwise too much premium will be paid initially if the figure is fixed too high, or the Insured may receive less than indemnity if it is fixed too low. (There is provision for an adjustment after the end of the policy year when the actual results of the financial year nearest to the policy year are known.)

Because the amount has to be selected in anticipation of the trading results for the year, Insurers regard the premium paid at the commencement of the insurance year as a provisional premium and are prepared to accept an additional amount if the provisional premium was insufficient or repay any overpayment of premium. In each case, the additional or return premium will be subject to limitation.

4.02 GROSS PROFIT

The cover provided by the policy is known as **Gross Profit.** This is quite separate, distinct and different from the term which appears in the Trading Account, which is the accountant's understanding of the term.

From now on, unless anything is stated to the contrary, the meaning of the term GROSS PROFIT will *always* be that defined in the policy.

"Gross profit" refers to that part of the Insured's turnover which is at risk following destruction or damage at the Insured's premises by fire or by any other insured peril.

In Chapter 3 we saw that there were three elements of Turnover at risk, viz.
(1) Standing Charges;
(2) Payroll;
(3) Net Profit.

The other element, the Variables, is not included in the sum insured and no loss which occurred to these items would be paid under the B/I policy. (A loss related to the Variable items would not be expected, as has been discussed in section 3.06.)

One way of arriving at an amount to be insured would be to set out the items to be covered by the policy and to total the amounts from the Accounts. That method (which was originally employed and known as the "Additions" method) involves stating the headings – Directors' Fees, Rent, Rates, etc. – in the policy and, technically, anything not mentioned would be uninsured, although it was usual to include a "Miscellaneous" item of up to (say) 5% of the remainder of the Items specified to protect the Insured.

This somewhat unsatisfactory position, which required a constant check on the items included, was superseded by the adoption of the "Difference" basis, which is now almost universal.

4.03   DIFFERENCE BASIS

Instead of listing the items covered, Insurers approached the matter from the opposite direction. They say to their Insured, "Tell us your Turnover, tell us the items YOU DO NOT WANT TO COVER (the Variables) and everything else is automatically covered without the need for specifying it."

As will be seen from the diagram, if the Variables are withdrawn from the Turnover (represented by the full circle), then all the rest are fully covered, without the need to specify the items.

Importance of Sum Insuredured 23

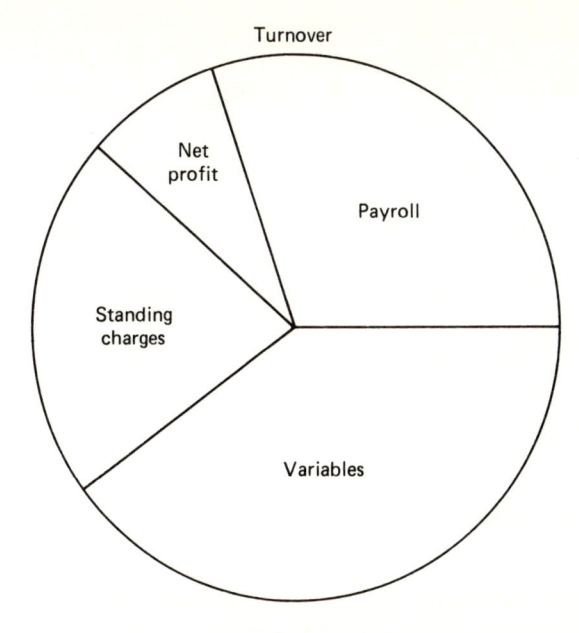

Fig. 4 Constituents of Turnover.

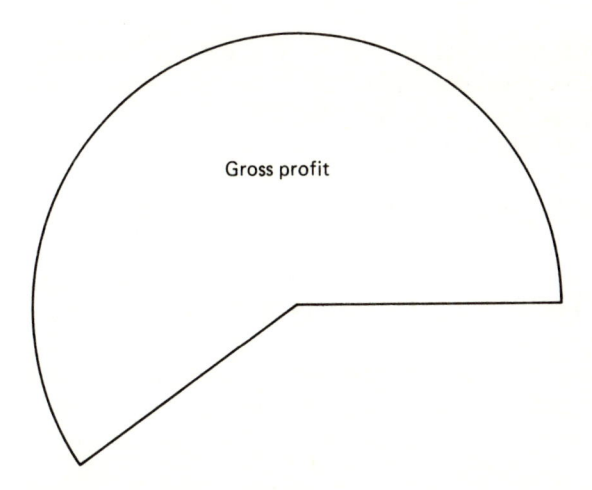

Fig. 5 If Variables are removed from Turnover, all that remains is covered without the need to specify the items.

In mathematical terms –

$$\text{Gross Profit} = \text{Turnover less Variables}.$$

4.04 DEFINITION OF GROSS PROFIT

The simplicity of the Difference Basis is slightly modified, because the trading result of the business will be affected by the difference between the stock and work in progress at the start and at the end of the accounting year.

The definition in the Specification (see Appendix 3) reads:

> **Gross Profit:** The amount by which –
> (i) the sum of the amount of the Turnover and the amounts of the closing stock and work in progress shall exceed
> (ii) the sum of the opening stock and work in progress and the amount of the Uninsured Working Expenses.
>
> **Note:** The amounts of the opening and closing stocks and work in progress shall be arrived at in accordance with the Insured's normal accountancy methods, due provision being made for depreciation.

There is then a further heading – **Uninsured Working Expenses** – (previously known as "Specified Working Expenses") and under this heading will be stated the items the Insured DOES NOT WISH TO COVER. These should be kept to a minimum.

4.05 TO ARRIVE AT THE BASIS FOR THE SUM INSURED

Let us assume that it is the month prior to the ensuing insurance year and the elements of Turnover are understood by the person proposing insurance – the proposer.

Following discussion with the insurance adviser or broker, the last set of completed accounts is obtained and the proposer decides that the Uninsured Working Expenses (the items which are *not* to be insured) will be –

100% Raw materials,
100% Packing,

100% Carriage,
100% Bad debts.

The proposer also decides that he requires insurance for 80% of his Lighting and Heating and he does not require any cover for his Power. (Note. The decision to limit the insurance on Lighting and Heating and ignore Power is one which an insurance adviser or broker would only recommend in exceptional circumstances. It is being used in this instance to demonstrate the insurance of Semi-Variables.)

We shall use the accounts in Chapter 2 and follow the definition.

We are told in section (i) of the definition to add together the Turnover and the Closing stock and Work-in-progress

Turnover	1 500 000	
Closing stock	36 000	
Work-in-progress	9 000	
		1 545 000

In section (ii) we have to add together the Opening stock and Work-in-progress and the Uninsured working expenses – the items which the proposer does not wish to insure –

B/F		1 545 000
Opening stock	40 000	
Work-in-progress	10 000	
Raw materials	500 000	
Packing	46 000	
Carriage	30 000	
Bad debts	3 000	
	629 000	

The proposer also said he required insurance for only 80% of his Lighting and Heating and no insurance for his Power.

This means that as Uninsured Working Expenses we must show 20% of the Lighting and Heating – the part which is not insured – and 100% of the Power.

	629 000	
Lighting (20%)	2 000	
Heating (20%)	4 000	
Power	10 000	
		645 000
Basis for sum insured		900 000

Because this figure of 900 000 will be arrived at from accounts for the previous year's trading, the figure is almost 12 months "stale". The way in which it is updated and varied according to the Indemnity Period chosen will be explained in the next Chapter.
(Note. Readers are reminded that the treatment of Semi-Variables as shown above should only be followed in exceptional circumstances.)

5 Projection of the Basis for the Sum Insured

Comparison between – when the sum insured is "subject to average" – when the insurance has been arranged under a "Declaration Linked" policy.

5.01 BASIS FOR SUM INSURED

In the last chapter, we saw how, by using the latest set of accounts available, the basis for the sum insured was calculated.

It is usual for the proposer to discuss insurance arrangements with his broker or insurance adviser some time before renewal, say in the month prior. Therefore, the latest set of accounts which will be available will be for the financial year prior to the year in which the discussion is taking place.

In the last chapter, the basis for the sum insured for the year of the accounts was 900 000.

5.02 THE PROJECTION

The broker will ask the proposer for an update on the trend of the business since the end of the previous financial year. Let us assume

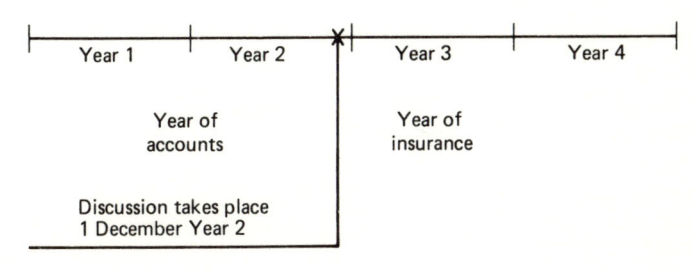

```
|————————+————————*————————+————————|
    Year 1      Year 2   |   Year 3      Year 4

                Year of      Year of
                accounts     insurance

            Discussion takes place
            1 December Year 2
```

Fig. 6 Time scale.

28 *Business Interruption Insurance: Theory and Practice*

that a combination of inflation and increased output has increased the turnover by 10% and that the proportion of Variables and other elements of turnover remain the same.

The figure of 900 000 must therefore be updated by 10%.

From the accounts	900 000
To bring up-to-date (+10%)	90 000
	990 000

The next question to the proposer is "What are your plans for next year?" Again, let us assume the reply was "Hopefully we will maintain the present rate of expansion".

So the table now reads –

From the accounts	900 000
To bring-up-to date (+ 10%)	90 000
	990 000
Insurance year (+ 10%)	99 000
	1 089 000

It will be recalled from Chapter 3 that the period after the fire is known as the 'indemnity period'. This period starts when the damage

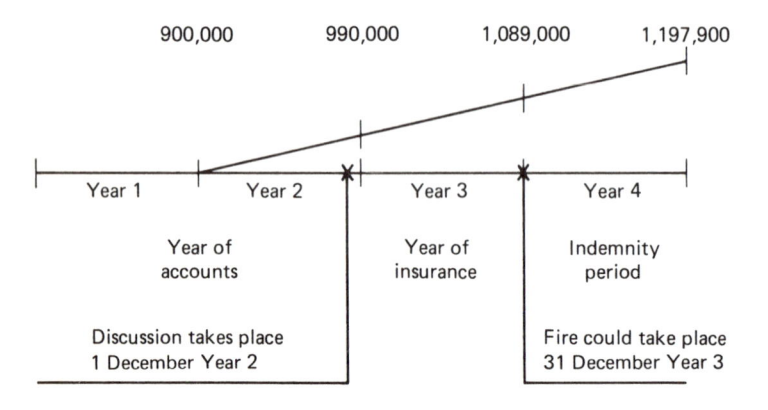

```
         900,000      990,000      1,089,000    1,197,900
                                                    |
                                          _____/
                                    _____/
                              _____/
                         ____/
                    ____/
        |_____|_____|_____|_____|
          Year 1     Year 2     Year 3     Year 4

                    Year of     Year of    Indemnity
                    accounts   insurance    period

                  Discussion takes place  Fire could take place
                  1 December Year 2       31 December Year 3
```

Fig. 7 Projection of basis for sum insured.

takes place and lasts until the business is fully recovered or the Maximum Indemnity Period is exhausted – whichever comes first.

So provision must be made for a fire which occurs on the last day of the policy year, and for the possibility that the Maximum Indemnity Period will be required.

So the table now reads –

From the accounts	900 000
To bring up-to-date (+ 10%)	90 000
	990 000
Insurance year (+ 10%)	99 000
	1 089 000
Indemnity period (+ 10%)	108 900
	1 197 900

The above figures presuppose that in the insurance year and the year following, the increase in turnover will be limited to 10%. But many firms are optimistic and their hopes frequently do materialise.

The amount shown above of 1 197 900 is, therefore, the absolute minimum sum insured and if the firm traded at a higher level, there would be underinsurance, the penalty for which is the application of "average" – in other words, the Insured will have to bear a share of the loss himself.

5.03 PROVISIONAL PREMIUM

Insurers are keenly aware that an unsatisfactory loss settlement does nothing for either party and, in a bid to prevent underinsurance, have made the following suggestion:
(1) Take a sum insured which is in excess of your minimum requirements.
(2) Pay a premium based on 75% of this enhanced figure.
(3) Supply details of the actual earned gross profit (as defined in the policy specification) when the accounts relating to the insurance year are published.

On receipt of these details, the true earned premium will be calculated. If there has been an overpayment, a refund will be made up to a maximum, which will usually be one-third of the 75% premium; if an underpayment, an additional premium will be charged up to the 100% figure i.e. one-third of the provisional premium.

In the example above, the broker could suggest:

Proposer
1. accepts a sum insured of   1 500 000
2. pays premium on 75%   1 125 000
3. supplies details of actual earned
   gross profit (say)   1 100 000
   and receives a return premium based on
   the difference   25 000

It should be noted that the proposer will enjoy the cover of 1 500 000 for the whole year of insurance and even if the business does greatly improve beyond the forecast, underinsurance is most unlikely. Should his prospects improve dramatically, he must advise the broker or the Insurer quickly, so that the necessary alteration to the sum insured can be made during the period of insurance. Once the damage has occurred, the Insured will not be able to amend the sum insured in respect of that claim.

5.04 'DECLARATION LINKED'

Whilst the provisional premium on 75% of an enhanced sum insured went some way to combating the problem of underinsurance, Insurers, nevertheless, found that policyholders were still "cool" to having a sum insured which appeared to be beyond their needs.

Insurers accepted that a more attractive scheme was required and "Declaration Linked Business Interruption Insurance" was successfully launched, under which the sum insured is not "Subject to Average".

Under this scheme, the Insured
(1) is asked to provide an estimate of the Gross Profit which will be earned in the forthcoming year of insurance (in our example earlier, 1 089 000);
(2) undertakes to provide details of the earned Gross Profit within six months of the end of the insurance policy year;

Projection of the Basis for the Sum Insured 31

(3) understands that failure to provide the figures will involve withdrawal of the scheme.

For their part, Insurers

(1) provide cover for 133.3 % (this figure may be 150% with some Insurers) of the estimated Gross Profit for the ensuing year (in our example, 1 089 000 + 33.3 % = 1 452 000);
(2) undertake not to apply average. This means that in the event of a loss, Insurers will pay *in full* up to (in our case) 1 452 000. This is the Insurers' "Limit of Liability". No payment beyond this amount will be made to the Insured.
(3) On receipt of details of the actual earned Gross Profit, Insurers will adjust the provisional premium, making a repayment or charging an additional premium as appropriate, with a maximum return of $\frac{1}{3}$ or $\frac{1}{2}$, depending whether the benefit of a 75% Deposit Premium has been given, but with no limit to the additional premium which will be charged on the actual earned Gross Profit.

5.05 REINSTATEMENT OF SUM INSURED

Under normal fire and B/I policies, the sum insured stands reduced by the amount of the loss until renewal, or earlier if instructions for its reinstatement have been given. This means, if instructions for reinstatement are not given, that in the event of a second loss in the course of the insurance year, the sum insured might be quite inadequate.

To avoid this problem, Insurers, under the "Declaration Linked" scheme, provide for the *automatic* reinstatement of the sum insured by the inclusion of the following paragraph in the Specification –

> (ii) in the absence of written notice by the Insured or the Insurer to the contrary the Insurer's liability shall not stand reduced by the amount of any loss, the Insured undertaking to pay the appropriate additional premium for such automatic reinstatement of cover.

Notice that both the Insured and the Insurer have the option to say "No" to the reinstatement of the sum insured. The additional premium will be based on the amount of the loss and charged *pro rata* from the date of the loss to the renewal date of the policy.

So important is this necessity to reinstate the sum insured after a loss, that many policies which are not "Declaration Linked" now carry a clause providing for the automatic reinstatement of the sum insured.

5.06 FIRST LOSS GROSS PROFIT POLICY

On rare occasions and in special circumstances, a few Insurers may be prepared to issue a policy on a first loss basis, that is, where the Insured chooses a figure for Gross Profit which is the maximum loss they think they could suffer after a fire. The premium would be more costly in proportion, compared with the premium charged for a full value Gross Profit insurance and, in the case of a large loss, would have to be paid again almost in full to reinstate the cover, as the sum insured may have been virtually exhausted.

6 The Cover Provided by the Policy – Part I

Examination of the Recommended Wording of the Business Interruption Policy – The Perils Covered – Material Damage Proviso – Limit of Insurer's Liability – Collective Policies

6.01 RECOMMENDED WORDING

Until 1985, the transaction of B/I insurance was guided by the Consequential Loss Committee, a sub-committee of the Fire Offices Committee. Those offices which were members of the Fire Offices Committee were known as "Tariff Companies" and were bound by the rules of that Committee. A large number of the leading Insurers subscribed to the Tariff.

The wordings produced by the Consequential Loss Committee, while being in many cases only recommended wordings, nevertheless were adopted by all Insurers (both company market and Lloyd's) and provided a standard wording.

Following the demise of the Tariff Committees in 1985, the work of providing market guidance has been continued by the Association of British Insurers (ABI) and the previous "standard" wording was continued as a "recommended" wording.

In October 1989 the ABI published revised recommended wordings. These improved the layout and involved small textual changes but did not affect the level of cover provided. Amendment Issue No.3 was published in March 1991.

Technically, Insurers are free to produce their own wording. But this would present a problem where the insurance has to be shared among several offices, as participants might not be able to agree as to the wording to be used.

The "recommended" wordings had the advantage that they had been in use for many years and had, in most cases, been found to be capable of providing the indemnity required and had rarely been challenged in the courts. The small changes are unlikely to alter this position.

A copy of the wording used when there is a single Insurer, has been used in this book and will be found in the Appendices. The ABI decided not to publish a "Collective" wording. Instead, guidance on the necessary changes to a "company" policy were published and will be found in the Appendices.

6.02 SUMMARY

The policy wording now consists of the following sections –
(a) Preamble with the perils covered, Operative Clause, Material Damage Proviso/Material Damage Proviso Waiver, and limitation of Insurer's liability;
(b) Definition of the words "Consequential Loss";
(c) General Exclusions;
(d) General Conditions;
(e) Claims Conditions;
(f) The Schedule.

6.03 THE PREAMBLE

> The Insurer agrees (subject to the terms, definitions, exclusions and conditions of this policy) that if after payment of the first premium . . .

Insurance premiums are payable in advance and are due on the first day of the policy year. When an insurance is being set up initially, and again, at renewal, when it is customary to up-date the insurance, it could well be that the premium due has not been calculated. Insurers may ask their client for a deposit in advance of the final figure, but once cover has been given and not withdrawn, a claim becomes payable even if no premium has yet been paid. (Note. It is possible that, in certain cases, payments by instalments will be accepted.)

> . . . any building or other property used by the Insured at the Premises for the purpose of the Business . . .

It will be seen from the Schedule attached to the policy document that space has been provided for the insertion of

(1) *the name of the Insured*
While the use of the words "and their subsidiary companies" is permissible, "associated company/ies" is too vague for a legal document. The expression "and/or" must not be used as this could lead to misunderstanding as to the makeup of the sum insured.

(2) *the description of the Business* – for example, furniture manufacturer, engineer, clothing manufacturer, restaurant etc.
This description must include all activities which are included in the sum insured. For example, if rent receivable is included in the Gross Profit figure, some such expression as "Property Owners" should be shown. The premium will have been assessed on the basis of the information supplied, or obtained following a survey, at the commencement of the insurance. If changes take place involving an increase in the risk of a fire starting or of the severity of the fire once it has started, the Insured must notify the Insurer or the Leading Office.

(3) *the address of the Premises insured*
The addresses of all the premises involved must be shown. This includes, for instance, the showroom in, say, London, even though the main manufacturing premises are away from London. The loss of the showroom could lead to fewer orders and there would be heavy additional expense in replacing the showroom as quickly as possible. It may be possible, if the Insured has many premises, to use a general term such as "All premises occupied by the Insured in the operation of his business."

The business may also be affected by a fire at the premises from which the Insured receives supplies of raw materials or packing, or to which he delivers his products. These are **not** included in the insurance unless an appropriate additional premium has been paid and the address(es) added by memorandum. (See Chapter 12.)

.04 THE PERILS COVERED

> ... be lost destroyed or damaged by ...

These words bring in the perils shown on the face of the policy.

6.05 FIRE

> 1. FIRE...

Fire is fire in its normal, everyday sense. The decisions of the Courts on a number of cases on this subject have provided a guide as to what is understood by this term.
(1) There must be ignition;
(2) There must be something involved in fire which should not be on fire;
(3) The fire must be fortuitous (accidental, by chance, unplanned) as far as the Insured is concerned.

> ... but excluding loss destruction or damage caused by
> (a) explosion resulting from fire...

Under the doctrine of Proximate Cause (see Chapter 17), all losses stemming **directly** from a peril specified under the policy are covered. Thus, the damage done to machinery and stock by water used in extinguishing the fire is payable as fire damage. By the same token, if a peril is stated to be excluded (as is "explosion" above) all losses arising **directly** from this peril would be excluded.

Fire can result from an explosion or an explosion could result from a fire.

Exclusion (a) makes it clear that fire, even if it results from an explosion (an excluded peril), will be covered and that damage caused by an explosion, even if it is the result of a fire, is excluded.

The intention of the Insurers is that there shall be an adequate premium received for the additional peril of explosion, which is then added to the policy to prevent a gap in the cover. Some Insurers are now adding the peril of explosion automatically and adjusting the premium accordingly.

> ...
> (b) earthquake or subterranean fire...

These perils can be insured on payment of an additional premium.

> ...
> (c) (i) its own spontaneous fermentation or heating...

The words "its own" limit the exclusion to the property which of itself spontaneously ignites. If the fire spreads from this property, then the exclusion will not apply to the spreading fire. Hay, jute, coal and certain chemicals, given the right conditions, may be subject to spontaneous ignition.

> ... (ii) its undergoing any heating process or any process involving the application of heat

The property undergoing a process (for example, goods in a drying oven) is not covered and any loss of Gross Profit, resulting from a loss of these goods, would not be covered. But if, as a result of the combustion of the goods undergoing a process, there is damage to surrounding property, and in consequence there is a loss of Gross Profit, then the policy would apply to this damage to surrounding property.

.06 LIGHTNING

The second peril is –

> 2. LIGHTNING

Although the peril of Lightning appears on a policy primarily concerned with fire, it is not necessary for fire to occur – loss of turnover due to any damage caused by lightning, would be covered.

.07 EXPLOSION

The third peril covered by the policy is –

> 3. EXPLOSION

In spite of what has been said earlier, this paragraph provides limited cover for the peril of explosion, the areas of cover being damage caused by the following types of explosions

> ...
> (a) of boilers used for domestic purposes only

That is, a boiler providing hot water for a low pressure hot water system and/or hot water for canteens and cloakrooms.

> ...
> (b) of any other boilers or economisers in the premises

Physical damage caused by the explosion of the Insured's boiler or economiser, both to the boiler and economiser, and to surrounding property belonging to the Insured, is covered by an engineering policy (separate from a fire policy). The engineering policy provides no cover for the interruption of the Insured's business due to loss of power or to the damage resulting from the explosion. This sub-paragraph (b) provides such cover, but it should be noted that it is limited to the explosion of boilers or economisers **on the premises**. If a neighbouring boiler, belonging to someone else, explodes, the only cover available is through the explosion extension (Chapter 10).

The explosion cover continues –

> ...
> (c) of gas used for domestic purposes only

The explosion of gas used in the canteen for cooking purposes and gas used for lighting or heating the building is covered, but not gas used for trade purposes, for example, raising steam in a clothing factory or a laundry.

"Gas" is interpreted in its wider sense – it would include natural gas and gas stored in gas cylinders.

> ...but excluding loss destruction or damage caused by earthquake or subterranean fire

This exclusion applies to the whole of the explosion section. Cover, if required, can be obtained on payment of an additional premium.

Full explosion cover (for example, explosion of petrol vapour) can only be obtained on payment of an additional premium and the endorsement of the policy. As mentioned earlier, some Insurers provide the wider cover automatically, amending the premium to correspond.

5.08 OPERATIVE CLAUSE

The next paragraph commences with

> ... during the period of insurance (or any subsequent period for which the Insurer accepts a renewal premium) and in consequence the business carried on by the Insured at the Premises be interrupted or interfered with then the Insurer will pay to the Insured in respect of each item in the Schedule the amount of loss resulting from such interruption or interference provided that ...

It is not enough that fire or lightning or explosion has occurred and perhaps caused damage – the Insured must demonstrate that the business has been interrupted or interfered with and a loss of turnover has resulted.

To sum up –
(1) Damage must be directly due to an insured peril.
(2) The damage has occurred to property owned or occupied by the Insured.
(3) The person claiming must be the Insured stated in the policy.
(4) The business being carried on is included in the description written in the policy.
(5) The premises where the damage occurred were included under the heading "The premises" in the policy.
(6) The Insured is able to demonstrate that the business has been interrupted or interfered with.

As we shall see in a later chapter, dealing with claims, the loss adjuster will check these facts before dealing with the claim.

Notice that the Insurer will "pay to the Insured". Cash payment is the method adopted to compensate the Insured for his loss and no other method is contemplated.

6.09 MATERIAL DAMAGE PROVISO

When the Insured has demonstrated that, through the operation of a peril specified in the policy, destruction or damage has occurred, in consequence of which his business has been interrupted or interfered with, the policy wording continues with

> 1 at the time of the happening of the loss destruction or damage there shall be in force an insurance covering the interest of the Insured in the property at the Premises against such damage and that
> (i) payment shall have been made or liability admitted therefor, or . . .

This paragraph is known as the Material Damage Proviso and is of the utmost importance to the B/I Insurer.

Let us look at the implications.

By setting out this Provision on the face of the policy, the B/I Insurer is seeking to establish that there will be a material damage insurance which will provide the cash needed to rebuild or repair the building, replace or repair the machinery and provide the necessary capital to purchase replacement stock.

Without this backup, the Insured might not be able to replace the damaged property and the B/I Insurer would be faced with a loss far in excess of that contemplated.

The Material Damage Proviso applies also in respect of the peril 3(b) on the face of the policy – "Explosion . . . (b) of any other boilers or economisers on the premises". There must be an engineering policy which will meet the material damage loss before the B/I policy will come into operation.

The Material Damage Proviso will not apply:

(1) when the policy is extended to apply to the premises of a supplier or customer, for whom our Insured has no responsibility or right to insure.

(2) when the insurance in respect of the business, for example an hotel, has been extended to include loss of gross profit following notifiable diseases, defective sanitary arrangements, murder, suicide (see Chapter 10).

3.10 MATERIAL DAMAGE PROVISO (CONTINUED)

The Material Damage Proviso has two further important features. Because the B/I policy is linked to the admission of liability by the material damage Insurer, there is:
(1) no necessity to insert Warranties in the business interruption policy. Breach of a Warranty would bar a claim under the material damage insurance and, in turn, the B/I Insurer could refuse to deal with the claim;
(2) no necessity for the B/I Insurer to investigate the cause of the loss. If the Insured is unable to demonstrate to the satisfaction of the material damage Insurer that the loss falls to be dealt with under the policy, the B/I Insurer is likely to take the same line and refuse to deal with the claim.

Circumstances sometimes dictate that the material damage Insurer is prepared to deal with the claim on an *ex gratia* basis – that is, a payment is made without admission of liability. The B/I Insurer will then have to decide whether or not to follow the material damage Insurer and to make a payment. It could be, of course, that the material damage is minimal, but that the effect on the business, due, say, to the loss of a key process, is quite severe. In this situation the B/I Insurer might take a different line, but this would depend on the reasons why the material damage claim was paid *"ex gratia"*.

All of the foregoing might lead the reader into thinking that the material damage Insurer and the B/I Insurer are different. In a sense they are, but when insurances are arranged today it is becoming increasingly rare for the two classes of business to be placed in separate markets. Not only does it avoid a conflict of interest which might arise if different Insurers or a different panel of Insurers held the material damage and the B/I insurances, but it is a positive advantage if they are the same, when it comes to payments on account, particularly payments on account under the material damage insurance.

Every day's delay in the restarting of production increases the liability of the B/I Insurer. A payment on account, therefore, to enable the rapid rebuilding or re-equipping of the factory could play a significant part in speeding up the process of returning to normality. A request for a payment on account under the material damage insurance is likely to be treated sympathetically, if it can be shown that this payment will be conducive to reducing the loss under the B/I insurance.

6.11 MATERIAL DAMAGE PROVISO WAIVER

> (ii) payment would have been made or liability admitted therefor but for the operation of a proviso in such insurance excluding liability for losses below a specified amount

A number of larger insurances carry a large excess, for which the Insured himself is responsible (known as a "deductible"), which can be of considerable size (say £50 000). A material damage loss of less than this amount would mean that there would be no payment under the material damage policy and therefore a claim under the B/I policy would be barred. It could be argued that the material damage Insurer could admit liability under the policy and advise the Insured that as the Insured is carrying this first amount of, say, £50 000 and, as the loss is below this figure, no payment is due from the Insurer.

However, to prevent a dispute in the event of a loss, the policy now carries the paragraph above – known as the Material Damage Waiver Clause. The Insured is thus protected should the loss fall below the level of the deductible.

6.12 LIMITATION OF LIABILITY

> 2 the liability of the Insurer under this policy shall not exceed
> (i) in the whole the total sum insured or in respect of any item its sum insured at the time of the loss destruction or damage

This sub-paragraph makes it clear that the liability of the Insurers is limited to the total sum insured, or to the amount stated against each item.

> (ii) the sum insured remaining after deduction for any other interruption or interference consequent upon loss destruction or damage occurring during the same period of insurance, unless the Insurer shall have agreed to reinstate any such sum insured

The earlier version of the policy form did not carry this reduction in liability following a loss. It was always understood in insurance circles that this was the situation, but, unless the policy carried a memorandum reinstating the sum insured after a loss (for example, Declaration Linked where it was included in the Specification), the sum insured stood reduced by the amount of the loss until next renewal. It was necessary, therefore, for the Insured or the Broker to take steps to reinstate the sum insured.

As has been pointed out in Section 5.05, the need to reinstate the sum insured after a loss is so important that many policies which are not Declaration Linked now carry a clause providing for the automatic reinstatement of the sum insured.

5.13 ONE CONTRACT

> This policy incorporates the Schedule, Specification and Endorsements which shall be read together as one contract. Words and expressions to which specific meaning is given in any part of this policy shall have the same meaning wherever they appear.

This paragraph emphasises the fact that the policy and the constituent parts form one contract and words and expressions used have the same meaning throughout.

5.14 SIGNATURE

A specific place is shown at the end of the wording for the signature of the person authorised to sign on behalf of the Insurer.

5.15 COLLECTIVE POLICIES

When the insurance is shared between two or more Insurers, it is normal to use a "Collective" wording. Only one policy document is issued and this will carry the list of Insurers with their respective proportions. All the "paperwork" in arranging the insurance will have been carried out by the "Leading Office" – usually the Insurer holding the largest percentage. The Co-Insurers – as the remaining Insurers are termed – will have authorised the Leading Office in writing to sign the policy document on behalf of all the Insurers.

The ABI decided not to publish a "Collective" wording. Instead, guidance is given to either:
(1) create a "Collective" policy form, using the "Company" wording with the amendments provided; or
(2) use the normal "Company" policy form and use a conversion page,
   for which the wording and layout is provided. (See Appendix 14.)

The word "severally" and the penultimate paragraph should be noted. Although all the Insurers appear on one document, this is an administrative convenience and the failure of an Insurer, through inadequate funds, to meet its share of the loss, will not involve the remaining Co-Insurers.

The person signing now does so as a representative of the Leading Office on behalf of all the Insurers.

7 The Cover Provided by the Policy – Part II

Definition of "CONSEQUENTIAL LOSS" – General Exclusions – General Conditions – Claims Conditions – The Schedule

.01 LEGAL CONTRACT

The B/I insurance policy is a legal document, expressing the contract between the Insured and the Insurer(s). It is therefore necessary to set out the terms of the contract, and these are to be found in the Exclusions and Conditions contained in the policy document. Although at first sight somewhat daunting, nevertheless important principles do need to be set out in such a document and an analysis of its wording will make this clear. A copy of the policy wording will be found in the Appendices (Appendix 1).

.02 DEFINITION OF "CONSEQUENTIAL LOSS"

Amendment Issue No.2: October 1989 introduced a new term – "CONSEQUENTIAL LOSS" (in capital letters). The definition reads –

> The words "CONSEQUENTIAL LOSS", in capital letters, shall mean loss resulting from interruption of or interference with the Business carried on by the Insured at the Premises in consequence of loss or destruction of or damage to property used by the Insured at the Premises for the purpose of the Business

The words are used in the General Exclusions and in conjunction with the Special Perils.

7.03 GENERAL EXCLUSIONS

> **GENERAL EXCLUSIONS**
>
> *This policy does not cover*

The four standard exclusions now follow.

7.04 RIOT, CIVIL COMMOTION, WAR AND KINDRED RISKS

> 1 CONSEQUENTIAL LOSS occasioned by riot civil commotion war invasion act of foreign enemy hostilities (whether war be declared or not) civil war rebellion revolution insurrection or military or usurped power

The perils of riot and civil commotion can be brought into the scope of the cover on payment of an additional premium but the remainder of the perils are beyond the scope of commercial insurance

7.05 RADIOACTIVE CONTAMINATION AND EXPLOSIVE NUCLEAR ASSEMBLIES

> 2 loss destruction or damage occasioned by or happening through or occasioning loss or destruction of or damage to any property whatsoever or any loss or expense whatsoever resulting or arising therefrom or any consequential loss directly or indirectly caused by or contributed to by or arising from –
> (a) ionising radiations or contamination by radioactivity from any nuclear fuel or from any nuclear waste from the combustion of nuclear fuel
> (b) the radioactive toxic explosive or other hazardous properties of any explosive nuclear assembly or nuclear component thereof.

Loss due to radioactivity from a nuclear risk is covered under the aegis of the Nuclear Installations Act 1965. Accordingly, the insurance market inserted this exclusion of cover on property and business interruption policies.

7.06 TERRORISM IN NORTHERN IRELAND

> 3 CONSEQUENTIAL LOSS in Northern Ireland occasioned by or happening through
> (a) civil commotion
> (b) any unlawful wanton or malicious act committed maliciously by a person or persons acting on behalf of or in connection with any unlawful association
>
> For the purpose of this exclusion
> "unlawful association" means any organisation which is engaged in terrorism and includes an organisation which at any relevant time is a proscribed organisation within the meaning of the Northern Ireland (Emergency Provisions) Act 1973.
>
> "terrorism" means the use of violence for political ends and includes any use of violence for the purpose of putting the public or any section of the public in fear.
>
> In any action suit or other proceedings where the Insurer alleges that by reason of the provisions of this exclusion CONSEQUENTIAL LOSS is not covered by this policy the burden of proving that such CONSEQUENTIAL LOSS is covered shall be upon the Insured

The Government and the insurance market agreed that in Northern Ireland losses due to terrorist activities should be borne by the Government. Accordingly, anyone who suffers a loss which is thought to be the action of terrorists, can apply to the Chief Constable for a Certificate and, using this, can obtain compensation from the Government. If the Certificate is withheld, the Insured can claim under his policy. The onus of showing that the loss is not due to terrorism depend on the Insured. This can be very difficult, but it will depend on whether the Chief Constable issues or refuses to issue a Certificate.

7.07 POLLUTION

> 4 Loss resulting from pollution or contamination but this shall not exclude loss resulting from destruction of or damage to property used by the Insured at the Premises for the purpose of the Business, not otherwise excluded, caused by

> (a) pollution or contamination at the Premises which itself results from a peril hereby insured against
> (b) any peril hereby insured against which itself results from pollution or contamination

This Condition took effect from 1 April 1988. In the wake of a number of serious fires, there has been considerable damage caused to the neighbourhood and environment by the escape of poisonous liquids and chemicals. The fire at the Sandoz factory which polluted the Rhine comes quickly to mind.

Endeavours have been made to claim on the material damage Insurers on the grounds of, for instance, removal of debris, and the wording is designed to limit the liability of the Insurers to pollution or contamination damage to the premises insured following CONSEQUENTIAL LOSS as defined by the policy.

7.08 GENERAL CONDITIONS

Two Conditions precedent are now stated under the heading of General Conditions, dealing respectively with the topics of utmost good faith and alteration.

7.09 UTMOST GOOD FAITH

> 1 **Policy Voidable**
> This policy shall be voidable in the event of misrepresentation misdescription or non-disclosure of any material particular.

The transaction of insurance of any kind has always been subject to the doctrine of "Utmost Good Faith". This means that the Insured and the agent of the Insured must disclose all particulars about the risk which may influence the judgement of a prudent underwriter (judges in several recent cases prefer to use the word 'reasonable') in deciding whether or not the risk is accepted and, if accepted, what premium is to be charged and what conditions are to be imposed.

The doctrine of Utmost Good Faith must, of course, apply to the Insurer as well. The underwriter may not mislead the Insured as to the extent of the cover he is prepared to offer or is provided by the terms of the policy

Notice the word "voidable". This means that the contract is void at the option of the aggrieved party, usually the underwriter. When a claim takes place and matters come to light which might have affected the acceptance or declinature of the insurance, the option whether or not to pay the claim will rest with the Insurer. If the new information is not crucial to the acceptance of the insurance, he may be prepared to pay the claim, subject to amendment of the terms of the insurance.

If the new information now disclosed is so serious that the decision is taken not to pay the claim, this will leave the possibility that the Insured will sue the Insurers for the amount of his claim. A decision to repudiate will not be taken lightly. Not only is it extremely expensive to defend such an action, but if the action be lost, the Insurers would be faced with paying the costs of the other party to the action and suffering the adverse publicity that would follow.

Nevertheless, Insurers are mindful of the fact that premiums paid to them are contributed by all their policyholders and payment of a claim which is outside the scope of a policy is paid at the expense of other policyholders.

The "Duty of Utmost Good Faith", as it is known, must be exercised up to the date the insurance becomes effective. During the currency of the policy General Condition No. 2 (see Sections 7.10 to 7.13) requires the Insured to notify the Insurers of any change "whereby the risk of loss destruction or damage is increased" and the "Duty" is revived at renewal, at which time, if there is any material particular which should be disclosed, the necessary information must be supplied to the Insurers (In re *Yager and Guardian Assurance Co.* (1912)

7.10 ALTERATION

> 2 **Alteration**
> This policy shall be avoided if after the commencement of this insurance
> (a) the Business be wound up or carried on by a liquidator or receiver or permanently discontinued or
> (b) the interest of the Insured ceases other than by death or
> (c) any alteration be made either in the Business or in the Premises or property therein whereby the risk of loss destruction or damage is increased
>
> unless admitted by the Insurer in writing.

The opening phrase of this Condition leaves no room for doubt. "This policy shall be avoided..."

The circumstances which bring the policy to an abrupt halt are set out in paragraphs (a), (b) and (c), but the policy may be continued if the Insurers so agree and signify their agreement by the issue of a memorandum, noting the change which has taken place. The inclusion of this condition has the effect of making the duty of disclosure a continuing warranty.

7.11 GENERAL CONDITION 2(a)

> (a) the Business be wound up or carried on by a liquidator or receiver or permanently discontinued or . . .

If the business is being wound up, there will be very little in the way of standing charges and payroll requiring protection. There is no prospect of future earnings and the cover accordingly ceases.

If the business is placed in the hands of a liquidator or receiver, it could be merely for the purpose of realising any assets for the benefit of the creditors, or it could be, given professional management, the firm is capable of being sold as a going concern.

If there is only a short term prospect, the Insurer will either:
(1) cancel the existing policy – the return premium forms part of the assets of the business – and issue a fresh policy in the name of the liquidator or receiver for such of the standing charges and payroll that remain outstanding; or
(2) if the business is being carried on by the liquidator or receiver, endorse the existing document to show the interest of the liquidator or receiver and adjust the sum insured as required.

The "permanent discontinuance" of the business will signal the end of the policy and a return of premium will be made if appropriate.

7.12 GENERAL CONDITION 2(b)

> (b) the interest of the Insured ceases other than by death or . . .

Business interruption policies fall into the category of "Personal" policies. The identity of the Insured will have been established when the insurance was arranged and the Insurers will have been satisfied with the credentials offered, particularly if a proposal form was completed. The conduct of the Insured can have an important bearing on the way the business is carried on and Insurers will not agree to transfer the insurance unless they have the opportunity of satisfying themselves as to the *bona fides* of the new owners.

This Condition does not apply when the owner of a private business dies. His or her executors continue to be covered by the policy until such time as they discharge their responsibility and the business is transferred or sold. The new owners will presumably make their own arrangements for a new policy to be issued by the current Insurers or some other Insurer.

7.13 GENERAL CONDITION 2(c)

> (c) any alteration be made either in the Business or in the Premises or property therein whereby the risk of loss destruction or damage is increased

The level of hazard, when the insurance was arranged, was assessed by the Insurers and rated accordingly. It follows that if, in the course of the insurance year, circumstances change – perhaps a new, more hazardous process is introduced – then the Insurers must be notified.

Interestingly enough, under the previous wording, it was an increase in the *level of hazard* which had to be notified. New machinery, more sophisticated and taking longer to obtain as a replacement, could have been substituted without infringing this Condition. The *level of hazard* may have been unaltered, but in the event of (say) a fire, there could possibly have been a much longer period of interruption, leading to a much greater loss. The revised Condition, introducing the word "loss" would appear to overcome this situation and the Insured is now responsible for notifying ALL alterations.

7.14 CLAIMS CONDITIONS

The conditions precedent to a claim are now set out.

CLAIMS CONDITIONS

1 **Action by the Insured**
   (a) In the event of any loss destruction or damage in consequence of which a claim is or may be made under this policy the Insured shall
       – notify the Insurer immediately
       – with due diligence carry out and permit to be taken any action which may reasonably be practicable to minimise or check any interruption of or interference with the Business or to avoid or diminish the loss.
   (b) In the event of a claim being made under this policy the Insured at his own expense shall
       – not later than 30 days after the expiry of the Indemnity Period or such further time as the Insurer may allow, deliver to the Insurer in writing particulars of his claim together with details of all other insurances covering property used by the Insured at the Premises for the purpose of the Business or any part of it or any resulting consequential loss
       – deliver to the Insurer such books of account and other business books vouchers invoices balance sheets and other documents proofs information explanation and other evidence as may reasonably be required by the Insurer for the purpose of investigating or verifying the claim together with, if demanded, a statutory declaration of the truth of the claim and of any matters connected with it.
   (c) If the terms of this condition have not been complied with
       – no claim under this policy shall be payable and
       – any payment on account of the claim already made shall be repaid to the Insurer forthwith.

This is, perhaps, the most important condition, since it governs the conduct of the Insured in the event of a loss. We shall study the Condition in relation to its lettered subsections and the itemised actions listed therein.

(a) In the event of any loss destruction or damage in consequence of which a claim is or may be made under this policy the Insured shall
    – notify the Insurer immediately

Insurers require immediate notification that a loss has occurred in order that the loss adjuster can visit the scene as soon as possible. The duties and responsibilities of the loss adjuster will be discussed later.

While the previous wording of the policy condition required notice in writing, Insurers accept that it is more usual for the Insured to notify his broker or agent by telephone and the message will then be passed on as quickly as possible. It is in the interests of both the Insured and the Insurers that the loss adjuster attends without delay and formal notification is no longer required.

> – with due diligence carry out and permit to be taken any action which may reasonably be practicable to minimise or check any interruption of or interference with the Business or to avoid or diminish the loss.

The doctrine of Utmost Good Faith requires the Insured to behave as though uninsured. This principle is emphasised here, where the Insured "shall *with due diligence* carry out and permit to be taken any action". In other words, everything necessary must be done which will lead to the prompt recovery of the business. An Insured who drags his feet for one reason or another will be reminded of this duty by the loss adjuster and failure to comply may lead the Insurer to withhold payment of the claim.

> (b) In the event of a claim being made under this policy the Insured at his own expense shall
> – not later than 30 days after the expiry of the Indemnity Period or such further time as the Insurer may allow, deliver to the Insurer in writing particulars of his claim together with details of all other insurances covering property used by the Insured at the Premises for the purpose of the Business or any part of it or any resulting consequential loss

The Insured is responsible for submitting his claim within 30 days after the expiry of the indemnity period. It will be recalled that the indemnity period is the period after the Incident during which the business is interrupted or interfered with, up to the maximum number of months chosen by the Insured when the insurance was arranged. So if the effect of the damage lasts for three months, the statement must be submitted within the month following. Of course, with a large loss, to submit a claim within the permitted time would be almost impossible and Insurers will usually exercise a wide degree of patience and extend the 30 days period.

It will be noted that the Insured must *at his own expense* prepare his claim as well as supply details of all other insurances covering the damage or any part of it.

> – deliver to the Insurer such books of account and other business books vouchers invoices balance sheets and other documents proofs information explanation and other evidence as may reasonably be required by the Insurer for the purpose of investigating or verifying the claim together with, if demanded, a statutory declaration of the truth of the claim and of any matters connected with it.
> (c) If the terms of this condition have not been complied with
> – no claim under this policy shall be payable and
> – any payment on account of the claim already made shall be repaid to the Insurer forthwith.

Not only must the Insured at his own expense prepare his claim, but also he must supply all other documents which may be required to support his claim.

As mentioned in Chapter 1 and as will be seen later, the cost of his professional accountants in producing the necessary particulars and details and reporting that such particulars or details are in accordance with Insured's books of account will be borne by the Insurers, but the Insured is responsible for all other costs which may be incurred.

A statutory declaration as to the truth of the information in the claim may, if necessary, be demanded by the Insurers and the Condition ends with the reminder that failure to comply will involve repayment of payments on account, if these have been made.

7.15 DISCONTINUANCE OF THE BUSINESS

The question is frequently raised – "What if the Insured does not wish to continue the business after a major loss?" or "what happens if the Insured finds that he will lose his market as a result of the fire and there is no point in continuing?" In the case of the Insured who does not wish to continue in business after a severe fire, it would be necessary to work out a compromise loss adjustment, recognising that remaining standing standing charges and obligations to employees will have to be met.

It might be thought that if the Insured were likely to cease to trade after a fire, that insurance is unnecessary. But a moment's thought will recognise that in the event of a partial loss, the claim payment could maintain the business as a viable concern and even if the decision were made to retire, there would still be a going concern to place on the market.

7.16 FRAUD

> **2   Fraud**
> If a claim be fraudulent in any respect or if fraudulent means are used by the Insured or anyone acting on his behalf to obtain any benefit under this policy or any loss destruction or damage to property used by the Insured at the Premises for the purpose of the Business is caused by the wilful act or with the connivance of the Insured all benefit under this policy shall be forfeited.

Fraud taints any commercial transaction; in insurance, where the Duty of Utmost Good Faith is paramount, any action by the Insured or anyone acting on his behalf to obtain benefit under the policy by fraud will bar payment of the claim.

Arson by the Insured or, at his instigation, by anyone else, may be suspected, but proving it to the satisfaction of the Court may be extremely difficult, as arson is a criminal offence and a high degree of proof is required. Withholding payment on the grounds of fraud could lead to the decision being challenged in the Courts. Loss of the action could prove expensive and damaging to the Insurers.

An alternative method was successful in the case of *S. & M. Carpets (London) Ltd* v. *Cornhill Insurance Co. Ltd* (1981), where the Insurers simply refused to pay. This left the Insured with only two alternatives – to sue for their money under the insurance contract or to accept the situation. The Insured decided to sue for their claim and it then became the burden of the Insurers to show, as this was now a civil case, that on the balance of probabilities the Insured was responsible for the fire – a less onerous task than the accusation of arson.

The judge said that on the basis of the facts submitted by the Insurers, the Insurers had proved to the requisite very high degree of probability within the general civil standard of the balance of probabilities that the fire had been deliberately started by the Insured's own managing director. The claim was therefore fraudulent and the claim under the policy was dismissed with costs.

The judgement for the Insurers is an important one inasmuch as a means of combating claims where fraud is suspected is now on record.

Notice that the Condition refers to "the Insured or anyone acting on his behalf" and also to "a wilful act by the Insured or with his connivance". This might bar a claim where, when the Insured is "on holiday", fire takes place in suspicious circumstances, but Insurers would need to be very sure of their ground before taking such action.

7.17 CONTRIBUTION

> 3 **Contribution**
> If at the time of any loss destruction or damage resulting in a loss under this policy there be any other insurances effected by or on behalf of the Insured covering such loss or any part of it the liability of the Insurer hereunder shall be limited to its rateable proportion of such loss.

If there is more than one insurance (a Collective policy is treated as one insurance) covering the interest of the Insured in the loss which has taken place, then all the policies must share the loss.

Because B/I insurance is a contract of indemnity, it is not permitted for the Insured to recover more than the loss and having two or more policies covering the same risk will not prove to be of any benefit unless there is some underinsurance. The existence of other insurances which might apply must be disclosed in accordance with Claims Condition 1.

At Common Law, it is open to the Insured to collect his claim money (up to the sum insured) from any one of the Insurers, but under this policy condition, the Insured can collect from each Insurer only a "rateable proportion". Fortunately, dual insurance is not very common. When it is found, the insurances contribute to the loss on the basis of their respective sums insured or independent liability.

7.18 SUBROGATION

> 4 **Subrogation**
> Any claimant under this policy shall at the request and at the expense of the Insurer take and permit to be taken all necessary steps for enforcing rights against any other party in the name of the Insured before or after any payment is made by the Insurer.

If the Insured suffers a loss due to the negligence of a third party, the Insurers, having paid the claim are entitled under Common Law "to stand in the shoes of the Insured" and exercise all the rights and remedies to which the Insured was entitled.

For instance, a plumber repairing a burst water pipe, sets fire to the factory roof with his blowlamp. The Insurers would be called upon to pay the claim for the damage and they can then take steps to recover their outlay from the plumber – normally, of course, the insurance company holding the plumber's public liability insurance will have to meet the cost if their Insured is found to be liable. If the plumber were not insured against such a liability, it would probably not be worth the Insurers' time and money going to the Courts.

As stated above, under Common Law, the recovery of the money paid for the claim can only take place *after* payment by the Insurer. If there is any delay in the settlement, it might be difficult to ascertain the facts when there is a time lag, so the policy condition, both here and in the material damage insurance, makes provision for the Insurer to take whatever steps are necessary *before or after* payment has been made. Investigation of the circumstances of the loss is thus rendered much easier, since steps can be taken immediately to obtain witness statements.

Recovery of the *economic* loss following a fire or other insurable damage caused by a third party is not so simple. The Courts have been fairly resolute in limiting the extent of the recovery of the loss to what is "foreseeable". An instance of this is *Spartan Steel and Alloy Ltd v. J. Martin & Co. (Contractors) Ltd.* (1972)(CA 557). Contractors were working on the road near the premises of Spartan Steel. One of the contractors' excavating shovels dug up the electric cable supplying power to the furnace in which metal was melted.

Because of the danger of the metal solidifying in the furnace, oxygen was poured in. This reduced the value of the "melt" and the anticipated profit on the melt was lost. In addition, Spartan Steel sued for the profit which was lost on subsequent melts. There was a delay of 14 hours before power was restored. In the Court of Appeal, judgement was given for the value of the melt lost and for the loss of profit on the melt, but their Lordships refused to award the profit on subsequent melts.

7.19 ARBITRATION

> 5 **Arbitration**
> If any difference arises as to the amount to be paid under this policy (liability being otherwise admitted) such difference shall be referred to an arbitrator to be appointed by the parties in accordance with statutory provisions. Where any difference is by this condition to be referred to arbitration the making of an award shall be a condition precedent to any right of action against the Insurers.

Disputes about the loss can fall under two headings –
1. The amount to be paid.
2. The liability of the Insurer to pay.

If the dispute is about the amount to be paid, the Insurers having admitted liability, the policy provides that the dispute must go to arbitration. The arbitration will be conducted in accordance with the Arbitration Act 1979, under which the parties agree on a person to act as an Arbitrator. Failure to agree will involve the Courts appointing an Arbitrator.

Arbitration has a number of advantages. It is normally speedier than waiting in a queue to appear before the Court, the Arbitrator appointed will be an expert in the particular field in which the claim lies, the hearing will be in private and, usually, the cost will be less. Unless the Arbitrator can be shown to have misconducted himself – legal language for making a mistake – the Courts will normally uphold an Arbitrator's award, on the grounds that he is an expert and both sides had the opportunity of presenting their case to him.

Where, however, the dispute is about liability, the UK fire and business interruption policies make no stipulation about arbitration and the Insured is free to sue the Insurer. This position does not necessarily hold good outside the UK. In a number of countries where insurance is conducted on similar lines to the UK, the

Arbitration Condition provides that all disputes – amount and liability – must go to arbitration.

7.20 PREMISES NOT IN THE OCCUPATION OF THE INSURED

The Note which follows the Claims Conditions sets out the amendments necessary to the policy wording where the insurance relates solely to premises not in the occupation of the Insured. An instance of this would be a policy limited to the rent of a building not in the occupation of the Insured.

7.21 THE SCHEDULE

The policy must, of course, carry details of the insurance to which the policy relates. These details are set out in the Schedule which is attached to the policy (see Appendix 1).

It will be seen that the headings comprise THE INSURER, THE INSURED, THE BUSINESS, and THE PREMISES, followed by details of the ESTIMATED GROSS PROFIT or the SUM INSURED as the case may be, the INSURER'S LIABILITY (a percentage has to be inserted), PERIOD OF INSURANCE and RENEWAL DATE, and the FIRST and ANNUAL PREMIUM.

The previous policy wording stated that the insurance terminated at 4 o'clock in the afternoon and the "insurance" year was shown as (say) 31 December to 31 December, the renewal date being 31 December.

Instead, the new schedule shows against the PERIOD OF INSURANCE heading the words "From" and "to" and as no reference to time is made in this current wording the assumption is that the cover will terminate at midnight on the "to" date, the policy being renewable on the following day.

The provision of the Schedule makes for easy policy preparation.

8 When Fire Takes Place – Part I

The Role of the Loss Adjuster – The Loss Assessor – The Specification – Demonstration Loss Settlement – Reduction in Turnover – Increase in Cost of Working – Alternative Trading Clause (Memo. 1) – Additional Increase in Cost of Working

8.01 NOTIFICATION

When destruction of or damage to the Insured's property by fire, or by any other peril insured against under the policy, takes place, the Insured must give immediate notice to the Insurers. If the policy has been arranged through a broker, notification through that office is customary.

On receipt of notification of damage and where it is expected that the loss will be more than a few hundred pounds, the Insurers will usually instruct a firm of Loss Adjusters to deal with the matter on their behalf.

8.02 THE LOSS ADJUSTER

Loss Adjusters will be members of the Chartered Institute of Loss Adjusters and, usually, are members of a firm of Loss Adjusters. Although their fee is paid by the Insurers and is not part of the loss settlement, their code requires them to act with strict impartiality between the Insurer and the Insured.

Normally, once a case has been placed in the hands of the loss adjuster, the Insurer remains in the background. Naturally the loss adjuster will provide regular reports on the progress of the loss settlement and, if in any doubt, will ask the Insurer to approve any recommendations, especially if there is any doubt as to liability. When the interruption ceases and he has determined the amount that shall be paid, he will submit his final report and his recommendation for payment. If the Insured does not agree with the recommended figure, he can, of course, approach the Insurers direct.

8.03 WHEN A LOSS TAKES PLACE

Following notification of a loss, the Insurer will instruct the loss adjuster by telephone and a member of the firm will make immediate arrangements to visit the scene of the loss. In this connection, it is of great assistance if, when notification is given, details of the person to contact at the scene are provided. This can save a great deal of time on everyone's part.

On arrival, the loss adjuster will need to see the extent of the damage and learn the cause of the outbreak of fire or whatever was responsible for the loss. It is most beneficial if the same adjuster is also negotiating the material damage loss.

Having satisfied himself that the cause was a peril covered by the policy, the next step is to discuss the remedial measures needed. These may well fall into two stages: immediate steps like salvaging and cleaning up (which would be part of the material damage claim) and arranging for notification of customers that some delay in the delivery of orders may be possible; and the longer term measures like arrangements for overtime working, working elsewhere and alternative supplies.

8.04 INCREASE IN COST OF WORKING

Under the terms of the policy, the Insurers will be prepared to meet "Increase in Cost of Working", if the expenditure is regarded as economic, that is, it will not exceed the amount the Insurers would otherwise have paid. The loss adjuster will discuss with the Insured measures which can be taken to speed up the return to normal production and authorise the necessary expenditure. His experience in such cases is invaluable to the Insured who, frequently, will not have had to face this situation before.

The removal of the debris to enable rebuilding or re-equipping to be carried out is normally part of the material damage loss, but if it is necessary to work overtime to achieve speedy removal, the B/I loss adjuster will include such **additional** cost in the adjustment of the claim.

The loss adjuster will be impressing on the Insured the need to make every effort to resume production. Competition in most markets is intense and measures taken in the first 72 hours could well be crucial to the early return of the business to full production. When the loss adjuster is satisfied that the Insured understands all that is required of him, the loss adjuster will seek a meeting with Insured's accountant.

8.05 THE ROLE OF THE ACCOUNTANT

As will be seen from the demonstration loss settlement which follows, a considerable amount of factual information of the previous year's trading will be required, together with full details of the period during which the business recovers. It will also be necessary to monitor closely expenditure – both on production and on increase in cost of working – after the fire, to follow the level of turnover to decide when the indemnity period is terminated, and to record all the savings which accrue after the fire in consequence of the damage.

8.06 FINAL SETTLEMENT

When it is decided that the firm is now trading at the "would have been" position, steps can be taken to finalise the claim. The accountant will have submitted all the necessary figures on which the claim is based and, at a final conference the figures drawn up will be presented to the Insured for confirmation. The Insured will be invited to sign an Acceptance Note and this will be submitted with the loss adjuster's report for the consideration of the Insurers. The loss adjuster will have kept the insurers informed of the progress of the claim and the cheque in final settlement should not be long delayed.

8.07 "COLLECTIVE" SETTLEMENTS

If the insurance has been placed on a "collective" basis, payment will depend on the size of the loss to be paid. Under £50 000 the whole of the claim will usually be paid by the Leading Office, who will then take steps to recover appropriate proportions from the Co-insurers.

Over £50 000, a date for simultaneous payment will be arranged and all Co-insurers are expected to despatch their cheques for their proportions on the date specified. Occasionally an Insured will mandate his broker to receive the loss money, but the cheques will normally be made payable to the Insured.

8.08 SUMMARY

The appointment of the loss adjuster should be regarded as being of great assistance to the Insured. Most firms seldom experience a fire or other loss and the effect can be devastating. The experience of the loss adjuster can have a steadying influence, particularly in explaining to the Insured the terms of the policy and the way it is designed to provide every assistance for the earliest possible return to full production.

The authorisation by the loss adjuster of the measures needed will greatly assist the decisions necessary at a crucial time and, as will be discussed later, payments on account will enable the Insured to meet bills for the standing charges and provide money for payments to the workforce.

8.09 THE LOSS ASSESSOR

It will quickly become apparent to the Insured that it is impossible to be in two places at once. He will be endeavouring to arrange for the re-establishment of his business – rebuilding, re-equipping and restocking the premises and at the same time he will have to be dealing with the paperwork associated with the claim, both material damage and business interruption.

To whom can he turn for help? The loss adjuster will guide the Insured in the details necessary for the presentation of the claim and the measures necessary to get the business going again, but the actual work required to achieve these objectives must be done by the Insured and his staff at a time when they will be stretched to the limit.

The Insured can turn elsewhere, to another source of assistance, namely a **loss assessor**. It will be recalled that the loss adjuster is appointed by the Insurers, who also pay his fee. The loss adjuster is independent of both parties, his duty being to interpret the contract. The loss assessor, on the other hand, is appointed by the Insured to assist in, for instance, stocktaking after the fire and in the collation of the details required for incorporation in the business interruption claim. The loss assessor will assist the Insured in his dealings with the loss adjuster and be present at the final conference for the settlement of the claim.

An Institute of Public Loss Assessors (current address – 14, Red Lion Street, Chesham, Bucks HP5 1HP (0494 782342)) has been formed and an Insured, if he feels the need, is at liberty to appoint his own loss assessor.

The Insured will, of course, be responsible for the loss assessor's fee, usually based on a percentage of the final amount of the claim. The fee payable does not qualify for inclusion in the loss settlement. The appointment of a loss assessor does not necessarily expedite a settlement and it will still be necessary to deal direct with the loss adjuster.

8.10 THE SPECIFICATION

The way in which a loss under a business interruption policy will be settled is clearly set out on the Specification, a copy of which will be found in the Appendices. There are three stages to the loss settlement where the insurance has been arranged on the "Declaration Linked" basis or four if the original basis (with "average") has been employed.

Following the statement of the stages of the loss settlement are the Definitions of the terms used and at each stage in our study of the loss settlement, reference will be made to the corresponding definition(s).

The wording of the policy incorporates the Specification.
(Note: The wording recommended by ABI under Amendment Issue No. 2: October 1989 will be used in the paragraphs which follow. The wording remains the same as previously, except for the introduction of "Incident", and a definition of this term, to replace the word "damage" used in the earlier specification wordings. The change from "Specified Working Expenses" to "Uninsured Working Expenses" was noted in Chapter 4.)

8.11 DEMONSTRATION LOSS SETTLEMENT

We shall assume it is now some months after the return of the business to the "would have been" position and all the figures necessary to complete the loss settlement have been assembled. For the sake of the Demonstration Loss Settlement, the figures have been assembled on a Data Sheet.

8.12 DATA SHEET

Since we are dealing purely with figures, the £ sign has been omitted.

Sum Insured To demonstrate the importance of the Sum Insured, three alternative amounts will be used.
(1) 1 125 000   (2) 1 000 000   (3) 1 000 000   (Declaration Linked)

Uninsured Working Expenses. In Chapter 4, in which the basis for the Sum Insured was discussed, the Insured in our example agreed to the following Uninsured Working Expenses, in other words, these were the items in his Turnover which he did not wish to insure. They were:
   Raw Materials, Packing, Carriage, Lighting 20%, Heating 20%, Power and Bad Debts.

Maximum Indemnity Period.   12 months.
Date of fire.   1 April.

Turnover

	in year prior to fire	in year including fire
January	131 000	144 100
February	130 000	143 000
March	125 000	137 500
April	120 000	15 000
May	115 000	60 000
June	110 000	85 000
July	114 000	120 000
August	121 000	130 000
September	124 000	136 400
October	130 000	143 000
November	136 000	149 600
December	144 000	158 400
	1 500 000	1 422 000

66 *Business Interruption Insurance: Theory and Practice*

Increase in Cost of Working. Insured spent 35 000 which saved Turnover of 55 000.

Savings	Wages	21 000
	Power	2 000
	Salaries	4 500
	Office Expenses	700
	Advertising	2 000
Accountants' fees		2 000

8.13 LOSS OF GROSS PROFIT

The Specification (Appendix 3) is headed with

Item No.	Sum Insured
1 On Gross Profit	£ _____
Total Sum Insured	£ _____

The reader will recall that Gross Profit *in terms of the Business Interruption policy* refers to the actual amount of the loss the Insured suffers – that is, payments he has to make which are not covered because of shortage of Turnover and the proportion of Net Profit lost.

The sum insured is the amount chosen by the Insured as adequate for his needs and it is, of course, the limit of the Insurer's liability and the basis for the premium calculation.

Then comes the following paragraph –

> The insurance under Item No.1 is limited to loss of Gross Profit due to **(a) Reduction in Turnover and (b) Increase in Cost of Working** and the amount payable as indemnity thereunder shall be:–

There are a number of points to notice in this paragraph.
(1) The loss must be due to Reduction in Turnover – fewer goods to sell and a reduction in the "Sales" item in the Trading Account.

(2) Increase in Cost of Working – the significance of this will be explained later.
(3) The two items together cannot exceed the sum insured.
(4) "Indemnity" in the context of a business interruption policy is putting the Insured in the financial position **they would have occupied** if the Incident had not occurred, as explained in Chapter 3.

3.14 REDUCTION IN TURNOVER

> (a) **in respect of Reduction in Turnover**: the sum produced by applying the Rate of Gross Profit to the amount by which the Turnover during the Indemnity Period shall fall short of the Standard Turnover in consequence of the Incident

This paragraph sets out the way in which the loss of gross profit due to reduction in turnover is to be calculated. We shall take it one step at a time.

"the sum produced by applying the Rate of Gross Profit" . . .

"Rate of Gross Profit" is to be found in the Definitions –

> **Rate of Gross Profit**:– The Rate of Gross Profit earned on the turnover during the financial year immediately before the date of the Incident

One further word requires our attention before we proceed. The amended wording of October 1989 (ABI, Amendment Issue No. 2) has introduced a new word, namely "Incident", defined as

> **Incident**: Loss or destruction of or damage to property used by the Insured at the Premises for the purpose of the Business.

The "Loss or destruction of or damage to" . . . will, of course, be in consequence of any of the perils insured against.

So we are required to go back to the Insured's last set of published accounts and from them to ascertain:

68 Business Interruption Insurance: Theory and Practice

(1) the amount of the Gross Profit, calculated in accordance with the definition of Gross Profit and taking into account the Uninsured Working Expenses (the items the Insured said he did not want to insure); and
(2) the Turnover in that financial year.

We shall use the same accounts (Chapter 2) on which the sum insured was based and for ease of reference, the Uninsured Working Expenses are set out on the Data Sheet.

Following the wording of the definition of Gross Profit, we get

The sum of the
    Turnover   1 500 000
    Closing stock   36 000
    Work-in-progress   9 000   1 545 000

less the sum of the
    Opening stock   40 000
    Work-in-progress   10 000
and the Uninsured Working Expenses
    Raw materials   500 000
    Packing   46 000
    Carriage   30 000
    Lighting (20%)   2 000
    Heating (20%)   4 000
    Power   10 000
    Bad debts   3 000   645,000

                                                                       900 000

So the **Gross Profit** according to the definition, brought out by the accounts for the last financial year is 900 000.

The wording says... "Rate of Gross Profit earned on the turnover...," in other words, the proportion that the Gross Profit bears to the Turnover.

$$\frac{\text{Gross Profit}}{\text{Turnover}} \times \frac{100}{1}$$

(The fraction is multiplied by $\frac{100}{1}$ to provide a percentage.)

Substituting figures for the terms, we get

$$\frac{900\,000}{1\,500\,000} \times \frac{100}{1} = 60\%$$

This "Rate of Gross Profit" is the key to B/I insurance. It tells us that whatever unit of currency we employ, the Insured actually, in this case, loses 60 per cent of every unit in the event of interruption causing loss of turnover.

It follows that if we can calculate how much turnover has been lost because of the fire, and pay the Insured 60 per cent of this amount, he will have the necessary cash to pay his standing charges, pay his workforce and recover the proportion of net profit lost. He will have been indemnified.

Yet the reader may well say, "But those accounts may relate to a period up to 12 months prior to the loss. What if they do not now represent the true rate of gross profit?" The problem was envisaged by the drafters of the Specification and if you read again the definition of Rate of Gross Profit you will see that there is no full stop after "... the date of the Incident". The words after the bracket (see full Specification) therefore form part of the definition. These words are:

> ... to which such adjustment shall be made as may be necessary to provide for the trend of the Business and for variations in or other circumstances affecting the Business either before or after the Incident or which would have affected the Business had the Incident not occurred, so that the figures thus adjusted shall represent as nearly as may be reasonably practicable the results which but for the Incident would have been obtained during the relative period after the Incident.

The words can be summed up in one word – trend – or, as is often done, this section is referred to as the "Other Circumstances Clause".

If, for instance, the cost of the raw materials or the packing had been reduced after the accounts were closed, and the level of turnover was maintained, the rate of gross profit would have been increased. Similarly, if carriage or power cost more, this will reduce the rate of gross profit. This trend can be up or down. For example, if there had been a national strike in the Insured's industry, the trend would have been down, if the Insured had been affected by the strike.

When the loss comes to be settled, a close examination of the changes since the closing of the accounts will be made, to arrive at a rate of gross profit which is as accurate as possible.

For the purpose of this demonstration settlement, we shall assume that no significant changes have occurred and the rate of gross profit of 60 per cent is accepted by the Insured and the loss adjuster.

To continue (following our consideration of Rate of Gross Profit, which we began on page 67):

... to the amount by which the Turnover during the Indemnity Period ... – the Indemnity Period – the period after the Incident during which the business is affected – *shall fall short of the Standard Turnover in consequence of the Incident*

What we have to find is the amount of turnover lost in consequence of the Incident and to do it, we are instructed to compare the turnover after the fire with the **Standard Turnover.**

So we have to refer to the Definitions again to discover the meaning of "Standard Turnover".

> **Standard Turnover:–** The turnover during that period in twelve months immediately before the date of the Incident which corresponds with the Indemnity Period

Here we see that the turnover in the indemnity period is to be compared with the same period in the previous 12 months – in other words, compare like with like.

The difference between these two totals will be the turnover lost. Or will it? What if the unit cost of making an article has gone up with a corresponding increase in the price charged? The level of turnover will increase even if there is no increase in the number of units produced. Or because of better publicity, the number of units sold could have been increased and turnover is correspondingly higher than 12 months ago.

Again, the drafters anticipated this situation and the wording of the qualifying "trend" statement, the "Other Circumstances Clause", applies to Standard Turnover. This means that the Standard Turnover – the total of the turnover in the period in the previous 12 months corresponding with the indemnity period – can be adjusted to represent as nearly as possible the turnover which would have been earned in the indemnity period, had the loss not taken place.

By deducting the turnover actually achieved in the Indemnity Period from the adjusted Standard Turnover, we shall arrive as closely as possible to the actual amount of Turnover lost. This will be the **Shortage in Turnover**. The application of the Rate of Gross Profit to this Shortage in Turnover will produce the figure payable under the heading "Reduction in Turnover".

From the Data Sheet, we know the fire took place on 1 April.

.15 SHORTAGE IN TURNOVER

We must now study the turnover in the year prior to the fire and the turnover in the year in which the fire took place, to see:
(1) what effect the fire had on the business; and
(2) whether there was any "trend".

Comparison between the first and second columns of the monthly trading results set out on the Data Sheet show that for the months of January, February and March, turnover was 10 per cent up in the second year. So the firm was achieving a 10 per cent increase compared with the previous year.

Turnover dropped sharply in April in consequence of the fire and gradually picked up again as the factory returned to full production and customers were won back.

So at what point did the Indemnity Period cease? May, June and July were obviously affected. What about August? 121 000 + 10 per cent = 133 100, so August is still affected. But September was 136 400, up 10 per cent compared with the previous year of 124 000, so the level of turnover was now back on course. The figures for subsequent months confirm this and the Indemnity Period, therefore, will be 1 April to 31 August.

Now that the Indemnity Period has been established, the loss under the category "Reduction in Turnover" becomes a matter of figures, as follows-

To calculate the Shortage in Turnover we refer to the Data Sheet and we take Standard Turnover (the turnover in the months of April to August in the first column + the agreed trend of 10 per cent) less the total of the turnover in the months of April to August after the fire – known as "Achieved Turnover".

Standard Turnover		
April	120 000	
May	115 000	
June	110 000	
July	114 000	
August	121 000	580 000
Trend 10%		58 000
		638 000
Achieved Turnover		
April	15 000	
May	60 000	
June	85 000	
July	120 000	
August	130 000	410 000
Shortage		228 000

Rate of gross profit applied to shortage in turnover =

60% × 228 000 = 136 800.

So the payment by Insurers of 136 800 will provide the money for the balance of the standing charges, payroll and net profit not earned during the Indemnity Period.

8.16 INCREASE IN COST OF WORKING

The loss of turnover after damage has occurred is bad enough, but the thought of incurring heavy additional expenditure to get the business on its feet again is enough to worry very seriously every business person. Insurers appreciate that expenditure which enables the Insured to recover more quickly helps both the Insured and the

Insurer, since the loss under "Reduction in Turnover" will be reduced.

The policy wording therefore continues:

> (b) **in respect of Increase in Cost of Working:** the additional expenditure (subject to the provisions of the Uninsured Standing Charges Clause) necessarily and reasonably incurred for the sole purpose of avoiding or diminishing the reduction in Turnover which but for that expenditure would have taken place during the Indemnity Period in consequence of the Incident, . . .

The wording above has been very carefully drawn up – let's look at it in detail.

the additional expenditure . . .

This means what it says – expenditure over and above the normal expenditure. For instance, if, following a fire in a shop, it is decided to arrange for the builders to work through the weekend to enable the shop to open early the following week, the builders are likely to require an overtime payment. The total cost of the work would be broken down into:
(1) the normal cost which would be met by the material damage Insurers; and
(2) the overtime element which would be met by the business interruption Insurers.

Or suppose an extra shift is worked to catch up on unfulfilled orders. The additional expenditure would be, perhaps, a bonus for working unsocial hours and the cost of lighting and heating which is above the normal cost per shift.

. . . (subject to the . . . Uninsured Standing Charges Clause) . . .

The wording of this clause is as follows:

> **Uninsured Standing Charges Clause:** *If any standing charges of the Business be not insured by this policy (having been deducted in arriving at the Gross Profit as defined herein) then in computing the amount recoverable hereunder as Increase in Cost of Working, that proportion only of any additional expenditure shall be brought into account which the Gross Profit bears to the sum of the Gross Profit and the uninsured standing charges.*

Expenditure on Increase in Cost of Working helps the business as a whole to recover and so earn the money to pay the standing charges. But if a standing charge has not been insured (either deliberately or through a misunderstanding), the Insured will nevertheless receive help with the expenditure on Increase in Cost of Working which has earned the money to pay for the uninsured standing charge.

So the clause makes it clear that in the event of continuing standing charges not being insured, the amount payable under Increase in Cost of Working will be reduced by the proportion

$$\frac{\text{Gross profit}}{\text{Gross profit + uninsured standing charges}}$$

Use of the "Difference" wording means that the clause is only occasionally implemented.

(Note: A footnote in the Specification states that where the Uninsured Working Expenses are recognised variable charges, the Uninsured Standing Charges Clause and the reference to it in paragraph (b) of Item No.1 (above) should be deleted.)

. . . necessarily and reasonably incurred . . .

The Insured may have all sorts of bright ideas for spending money to restart the business. Some will be good, some likely to be unproductive. The loss adjuster will guide the Insured on what is considered necessary and reasonable.

. . . for the sole purpose of avoiding or diminishing the reduction in turnover which but for that expenditure would have taken place during the indemnity period in consequence of the Incident, . . .

The expenditure on Increase in Cost of Working must relate to the matter in hand – the re-establishment of the business and nothing else – and the value of the expenditure must be limited to the Indemnity Period. As we shall see later, expenditure which provides benefit to the Insured after the end of the interruption must be met by the business and not by the Insurers.

8.17 ECONOMIC LIMIT

The promise to pay . . . *additional expenditure necessarily and reasonably incurred* . . . is a very valuable part of the cover, in many cases more valuable even than the cover under the heading "Reduction in Turnover", inasmuch as the additional expenditure can result in the shortage in turnover being reduced to minimal proportions. The business could be maintained virtually unaffected. But the promise to pay is not open ended and Insurers, naturally, are not prepared to pay more as "Increase in Cost of Working" than they otherwise would have done as "Reduction in Turnover".

Control of expenditure on Increase in Cost of Working is exercised through the last part of the paragraph, known as the **Economic Limit**. This completes the paragraph, the first part of which was reproduced near the start of Section 8.16.

> . . . but not exceeding the sum produced by applying the Rate of Gross Profit to the amount of the reduction thereby avoided.

So when the full cost of the increase in cost of working has been ascertained, the loss adjuster will apply the rate of gross profit to the reduction in turnover avoided – in other words, the turnover saved – to check that the expenditure has not exceeded the Economic Limit.

From the Data Sheet, we learn that the Insured spent 35 000, which saved turnover of 55 000. The Economic Limit is thus

$$60\% \times 55\,000 = 33\,000$$

Expenditure, then, has exceeded the Economic Limit by 2 000 and only 33 000 qualifies for inclusion in the loss settlement.

At first glance this may seem harsh on the Insured. He appears to have done his best to get things going and at the end of the day the Insurers deduct 2 000 from his expenditure.

Let us look at this more closely and see the possible circumstances under which this situation might arise.

8.18 CIRCUMSTANCES UNDER WHICH THE ECONOMIC LIMIT MIGHT BE EXCEEDED

1. Unrestrained recovery spending
The Insured may have very strong views on the methods which should be undertaken to maintain his business. Additional advertising, overtime, alternative premises and buying-in are some of the options open to him and he should discuss these options with the loss adjuster before deciding on a course of action.

The loss adjuster might be less than impressed and tries to inject a note of caution into the proposed expenditure on the grounds that the end result will not prove to be as successful as the Insured expects. The Insured, for his part, is determined to go ahead and does so, after being warned by the loss adjuster that, if the expenditure exceeds the Economic Limit, the Insured will have to meet the excess expenditure from his own pocket. This may have happened here.

2. Problems of "residual value"
In order to maintain production, a machine is purchased as a temporary measure and used in alternative premises. In the course of time, the original premises are rendered fit for occupation and a new machine, replacing that destroyed in the fire, is installed and commissioned.

To offset some of the cost of Increase in Cost of Working, the temporary machine should be sold for what can be obtained for it, but the Production Manager says the machine was a godsend in the difficult time and persuades the Managing Director to retain the machine as a standby. The machine will be used beyond the end of the indemnity period and thus has acquired "residual value". An adjustment in the amount payable as Increase in Cost of Working is therefore required.

A similar situation might occur if temporary buildings are acquired to assist in maintaining production. At the end of the indemnity period the buildings should be disposed of. If they are retained for their potential value then an adjustment in the amount allowed for Increase in Cost of Working will have to be negotiated.

3. Inadvertent excess costs
Here the loss adjuster and the Insured agree on a course of action. For a variety of reasons – perhaps a new competitor enters the market

or the temporary arrangements fail to meet the production target – the cost of the Increase in Cost of Working exceeds the stipulated maximum allowance of 33 000 of the Economic Limit by, say, 2000.

When this occurs, the loss adjuster will enter in the loss calculation the amount of the Economic Limit – 33 000 in the settlement we are working on-and at the end of the calculation, the loss adjuster will add "With regard to the 2,000 disallowed as beyond the Economic Limit, this expenditure was incurred with the approval of the loss adjuster and the amount is submitted to Insurers for their consideration".

In these circumstances, it is extremely unlikely that Insurers will object and the additional expenditure will be met.

It is most difficult to forecast with certainty the final result of the expenditure on Increase in Cost of Working. Plans which appear at the time to offer a good solution to the problem occasionally fail, often from circumstances which could not have been envisaged when the expenditure was authorised.

.19 ALTERNATIVE TRADING CLAUSE

Every B/I policy carries either on the policy form or on the Specification, the Alternative Trading Clause, familiarly known to B/I practitioners as "Memo.1" because it was usually the first Memorandum shown.

When a loss occurs, Insurers are prepared to pay "Increase in Cost of Working" if it will assist in maintaining the turnover after a loss. If, for instance, the loss was in respect of a shop or factory where sales or production would be impossible until rebuilding or renovation had taken place, one way of reducing the loss of sales or production would be to move into alternative premises. And subject to the cost of the move etc. being economic, the Insurers will meet the cost.

Readers will recall that emphasis was placed on the fact that the address of the premises had to be stated in the policy and only if the loss occurred at an address stated on the policy document, would the loss be payable. By the same token, the Insured could argue that income (which is obviously reducing the amount of the loss) derived after the loss from an address not stated in the policy should not be included in the loss settlement.

This unsatisfactory situation was resolved by the inclusion of the Alternative Trading Clause, which reads as follows:

> **Alternative Trading Clause**: If during the Indemnity Period goods shall be sold or services shall be rendered elsewhere than at the Premises for the benefit of the Business either by the Insured or by others on his behalf the money paid or payable in respect of such sales or services shall be brought into account in arriving at the Turnover during the Indemnity Period.

Notice that if goods are sold or services rendered elsewhere than at the premises for the benefit of the business *by the Insured or by others on his behalf*, the turnover must be brought into the loss settlement. The policy is one of indemnity and the Insured must not benefit from the incident.

The case which concerned itself with this situation was *City Tailors* v. *Evans* (1921), where City Tailors traded after a fire from an alternative address and, because the Alternative Trading Clause was not inserted in the policy, were able to deny the Insurers the benefit of the turnover generated at the alternative premises. (Details of the case will be found in the Appendices.)

So far, then, our calculations take into account:
(1) Reduction in Turnover (Section 8.15)   136 800
(2) Increase in Cost of Working (maximum allowance)   33 000
                                                      ───────
                                                      169 800

8.20 ADDITIONAL INCREASE IN COST OF WORKING

The possibility that the Economic Limit might be exceeded has prompted at least one Insurer to provide Additional Increase in Cost of Working by adding to the wording of (b), Increase in Cost of Working, the following –

– 5% of the sum insured by the item (but not more than £250 000)

This additional amount is, of course, still subject to the restraint of "necessarily and reasonably incurred . . ." and, bearing in mind that the loss adjuster will normally only authorise expenditure which, in his opinion, will be economically viable, it is felt that this extension will only be required on infrequent occasions.

See also Section 13.02.

9 When Fire Takes Place – Part II

Savings – Proportionate Reduction – Declaration Linked – Professional Accountants Clause – Payments on Account – Alternative Basis of Settlement

9.01 SAVINGS

The last but one paragraph of the previous chapter showed that the Insured is due to receive 136,800 as Loss of Gross Profit – the money to be used to pay the standing charges, pay the workforce and provide a modicum of net profit.

But supposing some of the standing charges are reduced in consequence of the fire – possibly a rent or rates rebate for a building unfit for occupation or some of the workforce decide to quit without waiting for notice or redundancy money.

The Insured will be due to receive the money to meet these costs but will not have had to expend it. The policy is one of indemnity and, as such, the Insured is not permitted to receive more than that to which they are entitled. So steps must be taken to monitor expenditure after a loss to ensure that if there are "Savings", the amount is brought into the loss calculation.

The relevant paragraph (after "(b) in respect of Increase in Cost of Working") in the Specification reads –

> less any sum saved during the Indemnity Period in respect of such of the charges and expenses of the Business payable out of Gross Profit as may cease or be reduced in consequence of the Incident

Notice that:
(1) the "savings" relate to "charges and expenses . . . payable out of Gross Profit . . ." This means that if there is a saving in

respect of an item or items of Uninsured Working Expenses, the Insurer is not entitled to the benefit of this saving.
(2) the "saving" has to be "... *in consequence of the Incident*". Savings do occur, perhaps planned before the fire, and if there is no connection between the fire and the savings, then the amount will be ignored for the purpose of the loss calculation.

The Data Sheet shows the following savings –

Wages	21 000
Power	2 000
Salaries	4 500
Office expenses	700
Advertising	2 000

Before totalling the Savings, a check must be made to ensure that all the savings relate to Gross Profit – a saving of a Uninsured Working Expense is a benefit to the Insured only.

Wages – yes, Power – no, this is a Uninsured Working Expense, Salaries – yes, included in Payroll, Office expenses – yes, Advertising – yes. So the list is

Wages	21 000
Salaries	4 500
Office expenses	700
Advertising	2 000
Total	28 200

The amount of 28 200 will be deducted from the amount arrived at so far, viz.

1. In respect of reduction in turnover	136 800
2. Increase in cost of working	33 000
	169 800
Less savings	28 200
	141 600

9.02 PROPORTIONATE REDUCTION

The premium paid by the Insured will be the result of applying a rate to the sum insured. Rates are quoted on the understanding that the sum insured represents the full extent of the estimated gross profit. A sum insured less than the full amount will mean that the Insured has made a less-than-full contribution to the Common Fund – the pool of premiums from which the claims are paid.

To settle a loss in full, when the Insured has not played his part and made a full contribution, is to allow them to benefit at the expense of the other policyholders who have made a full contribution.

Insurers, therefore, as the last stage in the loss calculation, apply a check to see if the sum insured (which is a factor of the premium) by the policy represents a full amount. The relevant paragraph (following "Savings" above) reads as follows –

> provided that if the sum insured by this item be less than the sum produced by applying the Rate of Gross Profit to the Annual Turnover (or to a proportionately increased multiple thereof where the Maximum Indemnity Period exceeds twelve months) the amount payable shall be proportionately reduced.

In material damage insurance, the comparison between the sum insured and the value at risk at the time of the loss, is known as "average". Some business interruption Insurers use the word "average" in preference to "proportionate reduction", but the effect is the same – a check on the adequacy or otherwise of the sum insured.

Let us examine the paragraph in detail.

> "provided that if the sum insured by this item be less than the sum produced by applying the Rate of Gross Profit [*we know this is 60%*] to the Annual Turnover . . .

"Annual Turnover" is a new expression – we must find out what it means in the Definitions.

> **Annual Turnover.** The Turnover during the twelve months immediately before the date of the incident

In the definition of Rate of Gross Profit, we were referred to the financial year immediately before the date of the Incident. In the definition of Annual Turnover, we are told to use the turnover during the twelve months immediately before the date of the Incident – in other words, the very latest figures which are available.

The proportionate reduction paragraph goes on to instruct that where the indemnity period exceeds twelve months, we are to increase the total of the turnover for the twelve months preceding the loss in proportion – an eighteen months' Maximum Indemnity Period would mean adding 50 per cent to the twelve months' figure.

Looking at the definition of Annual Turnover again, it will be seen that there is no full stop after "Incident" so it is necessary to read on after the bracket. Here we find the "Trend" paragraph and the Annual Turnover must therefore be adjusted by the same percentage for "Trend" as was used to adjust the Standard Turnover.

The Insured demonstrated that his turnover pre-fire was showing a steady increase of 10 per cent and he received the benefit of this when the Standard Turnover was increased by 10 per cent for Trend. The check for the adequacy of the sum insured must therefore be on the same basis and the Annual Turnover pre-fire is increased by 10 per cent to represent the estimated post-fire trading level.

9.03 HOW MUCH WILL BE PAID?

Section 9.02 above explained the importance of the sum insured as a factor in the calculation of the premium. Underpayment of the premium results in the loss settlement being reduced. To show the effect of the sum insured on a loss settlement, we will use three different amounts, two where the standard wording is used and one where the insurance is "Declaration Linked".

	Sum Insured	Wording
1	1 250 000	Standard
2	1 000 000	Standard
3	1 000 000 (Estimated gross profit)	Declaration Linked

Our starting point in checking the adequacy of the sum insured is to calculate the Annual Turnover (the turnover in the twelve months immediately before the date of the Incident). Adding up the monthly turnover figures from March (immediately before the fire) backwards to April of the previous year we obtain the figure for Annual Turnover.

    Annual Turnover   1 538 600

To this figure, we must add the Trend of 10 per cent (Section 8.14)

Annual Turnover	1 538 600
Trend + 10%	153 860
Turnover which would have been earned in the twelve months after the fire	1 692 460

To this adjusted Annual Turnover, we apply the rate of gross profit –

$$60\% \times 1\,692\,460 = 1\,015\,476.$$

1 015 476 is, therefore, the minimum sum insured required to avoid the application of proportionate reduction (average).

9.04 FINAL SETTLEMENT

(1) Sum insured 1 125 000

The sum insured exceeds the minimum required by the "proportionate reduction" clause, so the claim will be paid in full, 141 600.

(2) Sum insured 1 000 000

The sum insured is less than the minimum required amount of 1 015 476 – therefore the loss will be paid in proportion –

$$\frac{1\,000\,000}{1\,015\,476} \times 141\,600 = 139{,}442$$

(3) Estimated gross profit 1 000 000 on Declaration Linked basis.

In Chapter 5 it was explained that, under this scheme, Insurers provide cover for up to 133.3 per cent of the Estimated Gross Profit and undertake not to apply the proportionate reduction requirements to the loss settlement.

The Estimated Gross Profit in this case is 1 000 000, which, plus 33.3 per cent, becomes a "Limit of Liability" of 1 333 000. The effect of this is that all claims up to the limit **are paid in full**. But **nothing** above the limit will be paid.

The Insurers can waive the test of the adequacy of the sum insured, because the Estimated Gross Profit will be subject to adjustment when the Insured"s accounts are published and an additional or return premium will be calculated. Insurers thus receive a full premium for the cover provided.

The loss is below the Limit of Liability and is paid in full, 141 600.

9.05 ASSEMBLING THE FIGURES FOR THE CLAIM

Readers will have observed from the Data Sheet on which the claim settlement was based that considerable information will be required to enable the Insured to submit his claim. When we discussed Claims Condition 1 of the policy (Section 7.14) dealing with claims procedure, we saw that the wording requires the Insured "... *at his own expense* ..." to submit his claim, supported by all the relevant documents and information.

The task of assembling all the information may well be undertaken by the Insured's professional accountants and, when concluded, this work will require certification. Insurers have relented from their time-honoured custom, whereby the cost of submitting a claim has always been regarded as something which concerns the Insured alone, and will add the following Clause to the Specification.

9.06 PROFESSIONAL ACCOUNTANTS CLAUSE

Appendix 9 contains a number of different special clauses, the first being the Professional Accountants Clause, the text of which opens as follows:

> PROFESSIONAL ACCOUNTANTS CLAUSE modifying the Insurer's rights under Claims Conditions 1
>
> Any particulars or details contained in the Insured's books of account or other business books or documents which may be required by the Insurer under Claims Condition 1 of this policy for the purpose of investigating or verifying any claim hereunder may be produced by professional accountants if at the time they are regularly acting as such for the Insured and their report shall be prima facie evidence of the particulars and details to which such report relates.

This first part of the Professional Accountants Clause allows the Insured to use their regular professional accountants to establish the necessary details, rather than bring in strangers. After all, the Insured would probably resent an outsider probing through the books, and a stranger would need time to understand them. The clause refers to "... *their report shall be prima facie evidence*"... The intention of the Insurers is clear – the information will be accepted but is liable to check if, for instance, the Insured's professional accountants have misunderstood the actual details required.

The Clause continues:

> The Insurer will pay to the Insured the reasonable charges payable by the Insured to their professional accountants for producing such particulars or details or any other proofs, information or evidence as may be required by the Insurer under the terms of Claims Condition 1 of this policy and reporting that such particulars and details are in accordance with the Insured's books of account or other business books or documents
>
> provided that the sum of the amount payable under this clause and the amount otherwise payable under the policy shall in no case exceed the liability of the Insurer as stated.

The second part of this Clause is in two paragraphs.

The first paragraph promises the Insured that, notwithstanding the wording of Claims Condition 1 (where "... *the Insured at his own expense*"... must produce the figures needed to support the claim), the Insurers will pay the reasonable charges made by the professional accountants for certifying the figures and reporting to the Insurer that the details submitted are in order.

If, however, the Insured requires the presence of the accountant at the discussion to agree the final loss settlement, for which the accountant will charge, that fee will fall to be met by the Insured.

The second paragraph makes it clear that the total of the accountants' charges and the loss payable must not exceed the liability of the Insurer.

Notice that the Professional Accountants Clause comes **after** the proportionate reduction wording; in consequence, the amount of the accountants' charges will not be reduced in the event of underinsurance. (The wording is reproduced in Appendix 9, page 000).

The Data Sheet shows "Accountants' Fees 2000". If this relates solely to reporting that the necessary information obtained from the Insured's books is in order, the amount will be paid in full in addition to the amount payable as the loss.

9.07 PAYMENTS ON ACCOUNT

After a loss, a major worry for the principals of a firm, faced with the never-ending stream of bills for standing charges and outgoings on wages and salaries, is to find the cash sufficient to keep going.

The burden is eased by the Insurers, who will, on receipt of a request from the loss adjuster, arrange for payments on account to be made. The loss adjuster, when in possession of the preliminary figures required from Insured's accountants, will make the necessary recommendation to the Insurers.

Naturally, because the early payments have to be based on preliminary figures, the payments on account will be kept to the level necessary to maintain the Insured in business and meet the cost of Increase in Cost of Working. Payments on account will be made as required until it is possible to arrive at the final figure and agree the final payment.

9.08 ALTERNATIVE BASIS OF SETTLEMENT

In certain cases it may be simpler and more satisfactory to settle a claim, especially where the stoppage is of short duration, on the basis of a loss of output instead of a loss of turnover, but only where the

Insured was selling everything he produced and could not make up the loss of output.

If the likelihood of this happening is present, Insurers will issue a letter giving the conditions under which they will agree to the alternative basis of settlement, but would not include a clause in the policy, since the alternative basis would not be employed unless the conditions shown above apply.

10 Wider Cover

Special Perils – including Sprinkler Leakage, Limited Engineering Perils and Subsidence, Ground Heave and Landslip – Notifiable Diseases (for Hotels, Schools and Catering Establishments) – Theft – Fines or Damages – Deterioration of Undamaged Stock

10.01 SPECIAL PERILS

The cover provided by the "recommended" wording, as discussed in Chapter 6, is for the financial after-effects of damage to the Insured's premises due to fire, lightning and limited explosion. The cover provided against these perils must be regarded as a minimum and prudence demands that the range of perils insured should be extended to meet the Insured's requirements.

The ABI has provided two wordings –

(a) *Fire and Special Perils policy wording.* This wording carries the complete range of Special Perils and the ones not required can be deleted.

(b) *Special Perils.* The individual perils selected by the Insured are added to the B/I policy by endorsement, either at the time the policy is prepared or at a subsequent stage if the policy is extended to further perils.

Under the previous wording, each of the perils discussed below, unless otherwise stated, had to cause "Damage" to property owned or occupied by the Insured and the business had to be . . . in consequence thereof, interrupted or interfered with . . . , before the policy came into operation.

Appendix 8 reproduces policy wordings for Special Perils and various terms are defined in that Appendix. In current practice the term "CONSEQUENTIAL LOSS" is introduced, defined as follows:

> The words "CONSEQUENTIAL LOSS" in capital letters, shall mean loss resulting from interruption of or interference with the Business carried on by the Insured at the Premises in consequence of loss or destruction of or damage to property used by the Insured at the premises for the purpose of the Business.

It will be seen that each of the perils (see Appendix 8) in the schedule of perils available, commences with the words "CONSEQUENTIAL LOSS".

The Material Damage Proviso will also apply together with the Material Damage Waiver Clause if the Material Damage insurance (normally Storm, Tempest, Flood, Escape of Water, Malicious Damage and Subsidence) is subject to an excess or a deductible. Therefore the corresponding peril must be part of the Material Damage Insurance.

The perils are incorporated into the policy by using the following introduction (see Appendix 8, page 000):

> The insurance by (item(s) ... of) this policy shall be subject to the Exclusions and Conditions of the policy (except in so far as they may be hereby expressly varied) and the Special Conditions set out below extend to include:–

"Exclusions" refers to the exclusion of certain circumstances to be found in a number of the perils.

The "Special Conditions" are:

Number 1 limits the liability of the Insurer under an extension and the policy to the liability stated in the policy. This precludes the Insured claiming up to the total sum insured under both the policy wording and the extension.

Number 2 follows the wording of the General Conditions of the policy by excluding:

(a) CONSEQUENTIAL LOSS occasioned by or happening through –
  (i) riot or civil commotion (unless they have been specifically insured hereby);
  (ii) war invasion etc.
(b) radioactive contamination and explosive nuclear assemblies;
(c) terrorism in Northern Ireland;
(d) pollution or contamination but not excluding –
  (i) pollution or contamination which itself results from a peril hereby insured against;
  (ii) any peril hereby insured against which itself results from pollution or contamination;

Number 3 requires the Insured at his own expense to provide full details within seven days where the loss destruction or damage is due to riot etc. or malicious damage. (See Section 10.4 later.)

Number 4 is the Material Damage Proviso Waiver to deal with the excesses imposed on material damage insurances such as storm and flood etc.

Number 5 and **Number 6** will be referred to when discussing the perils relating to explosion and collapse of steam pipes (See section 10.12).

Number 7 is the Special Condition relating to subsidence, ground heave and landslip.

Before we examine in detail each of the perils provided for, there is one more matter on which comment might be made. Special Condition 5 of the Material Damage Policy States –

> The Insured shall take all reasonable precautions to prevent DAMAGE.

This condition is to be found in "All Risks" policies and is a new feature of the Fire and Special Perils wording. Because of the Material Damage Proviso, the B/I policy would be linked to the Fire policy and if payment of a material damage loss was resisted on the grounds that the Insured had not taken reasonable precautions, it is likely that the B/I claim would also be in jeopardy.

To what extent the Insurer can rely on this condition is open to question. Recently a lady at an airport had her handbag, containing her jewellery, stolen from her luggage trolley. The Insurer declined to meet the claim on the grounds that the Insured had failed to take reasonable precautions to protect her property, but the judge ruled in the lady's favour, saying that insurance was taken out to provide cover for just such an eventuality (*Port-Rose* v. *Phoenix Assurance plc* (1986)).

10.02 EXPLOSION

Explosion is considered in Part C of Sub-Section 1 of the Special Perils wordings (see Appendix 8)

> CONSEQUENTIAL LOSS caused by EXPLOSION excluding
> (a) CONSEQUENTIAL LOSS caused by the bursting of any vessel machine or apparatus (not being a boiler or economiser on the Premises) in which internal pressure is due to steam only and belonging to or under the control of the Insured
> (b) CONSEQUENTIAL LOSS by pressure waves caused by aircraft or other aerial devices travelling at sonic or supersonic speeds

Apart from the CONSEQUENTIAL LOSS caused by the explosion of Insured's own boiler, for which cover is provided on the face of the policy, the extension of the policy to include wider explosion will provide cover in the event of the explosion of
(a) a boiler on neighbouring premises causing damage to Insured's premises
(b) flammable gases and liquids
(c) flue gas
(d) chemicals
(e) dust (In certain risks such as flour mills this will require specific cover)
(f) bombs (except in N. Ireland)

on Insured's premises or anywhere outside the premises causing damage to the Insured's premises

The explosion may be the result of negligence by a third party, but, as was discussed in Chapter 7 (Subrogation), recovery of the *economic* loss may not be possible. It is, therefore, a matter of prudence to effect full explosion cover.

A sonic bang sounds like an explosion. By market agreement, damage caused by sonic bangs is excluded, since compensation, provided the aircraft can be identified, is available elsewhere. It will be seen that the exclusion also appears in the AIRCRAFT extension to make it clear that no payment will be made under either heading.

10.03 AIRCRAFT

The wording for this peril commences:

> CONSEQUENTIAL LOSS (by fire or otherwise) caused by AIRCRAFT or other aerial devices or articles dropped therefrom...

Aircraft crashes have been relatively few, and fewer still have involved business premises. But premises anywhere are at risk, both from falling aircraft and/or articles dropped from them. Parts of planes do fall off and can cause serious damage.

Satellites do not always reach their proper position in orbit and parts of them may return to earth. Fortunately, to date, those that have come down have landed on uninhabited parts of the world.

The ability of Concorde and some military planes to fly at supersonic speed, and the sonic boom which accompanies this speed, has led Insurers to add

> ...excluding CONSEQUENTIAL LOSS by pressure waves caused by aircraft or other aerial devices travelling at sonic and supersonic speeds.

The reader should note that the peril is limited to *"aircraft or other aerial devices..."* and therefore the damage caused by a meteorite for instance, would not be covered under this extension.

10.04 RIOT AND MALICIOUS DAMAGE

The full wording is:

> CONSEQUENTIAL LOSS caused by RIOT CIVIL COMMOTION STRIKERS LOCKED-OUT WORKERS or persons taking part in labour disturbances or MALICIOUS PERSONS excluding CONSEQUENTIAL LOSS
> (a) arising from confiscation or requisition or destruction by order of the government or any public authority

> (b) arising from cessation of work
> (c) caused (other than by fire or explosion) by Malicious Persons (not acting on behalf of or in connection with any political organisation) in respect of any building which is empty or not in use
> (d) arising from deliberate erasure loss distortion or corruption of information on computer systems or other records programs or software

Special Condition No.3 applies to this peril and reads:

> The Insured shall at his own expense deliver to the Insurer within 7 days of its happening full details of loss destruction or damage caused by riot civil commotion locked-out workers persons taking part in labour disturbances or malicious persons.

RIOT: the word "riot" has a legal definition given to it by the Public Order Act 1986. In section 1 of the Act, Riot is defined as:

> Where twelve or more persons who are present together use or threaten unlawful violence for a common purpose and the conduct of them (taken together) is such as would cause a person of reasonable firmness present at the scene to fear for his personal safety, each of the persons using unlawful violence for the common purpose is guilty of riot

The original definition of riot laid down in *Field* v. *Metropolitan Police Receiver* (1907) stated that three people could constitute a riot. That number has now been increased to 12 (as shown above), but the other conditions laid down in the judgement, in the main, remain. Incidentally, where three or more persons are assembled and the same conditions as set out above apply, section 2 of the Act states that the offence is "Violent Disorder".

The Riot (Damages) Act 1886 gives Insurers the right to claim a recovery direct from the police where they have paid a *material damage claim* following riot. Not only must the elements laid down in *Field* v. *Metropolitan Police* be present, but following the case of *J. W. Dwyer Ltd* v. *Receiver of Metropolitan Police District* (1967) the assembly must also be tumultuous. Insurers must submit their claim to the Police Authority within 14 days, the Insured being given seven in which to submit theirs.

The Riot (Damages) Act 1886 does NOT provide for an economic loss and the Act, therefore, provides no relief for B/I Insurers. Nevertheless, claims must be submitted within seven days to ensure that early steps are taken to investigate the matter.

CIVIL COMMOTION: this is regarded as an even more serious event than a riot and represents an insurrection of the people for general purposes. It is not as serious as a rebellion and the element of "tumult" must be present.

STRIKERS LOCKED-OUT WORKERS or persons taking part in labour disturbances; the cover will only come into action provided that CONSEQUENTIAL LOSS has occurred following damage to property owned or occupied by the Insured, that the material damage Insurers have dealt with the claim under this heading and that the business has been interrupted or interfered with by that damage. The occupation of the factory by strikers does not of itself constitute a claim under the policy – only if they cause damage resulting in an interruption of the business will a claim be entertained.

MALICIOUS PERSONS: losses under this heading provide most of the claims under this section of the policy. Damage caused deliberately, for instance the sabotage of a machine, is regarded as malicious damage. Notice that, under Special Condition No. 3, full details of loss destruction or damage must be furnished to the Insurer within seven days of its happening. Obviously a full enquiry into the circumstances of the loss must take place as soon as possible.

Under the material damage insurance, it is a condition precedent to recovery under this heading, that notification must also have been given to the police. The Material Damage Proviso obviates the need for this to appear on the B/I policy.

The material damage wording for this peril also includes the exclusion of *"destruction or damage by theft";* again the Material Damage Proviso will protect the B/I policy.

Under the ABI Recommended Practice issued with Amendment Issue No.2: October 1989, guidance is given in circumstances where there is malicious damage caused in the course of the theft. It reads:

> Malicious Damage cover is regarded as excluding loss or damage to property actually stolen and any incidental damage directly attributable to the theft. It does, however, include any other malicious damage caused by intruders whether or not any element of theft is involved.

This recommendation helps to clear the way to dealing with a claim when extensive malicious damage is involved, as previously the exclusion of "theft" gave room for argument as to whether the loss should be dealt with entirely by the theft Insurer.

The peril of "theft" will be dealt with later in this Chapter (Section 10.15).

The emergence of the computer virus and the potentially enormous economic loss following its attack on a computer installation has led to the exclusion of this form of "malicious" damage. Whether, at a later date when protection against this problem becomes more sophisticated, it will be possible to obtain cover, remains to be seen.

The malicious damage extension may be restricted to malicious persons acting on behalf of or in connection with any political organisation and the premium adjusted accordingly.

An even more restricted wording provides cover for CONSEQUENTIAL LOSS (by fire only) caused by Riot or Civil Commotion.

10.05 EARTHQUAKE

Damage done by earthquake falls under two heads:
(a) fire damage resulting from fire started by the earthquake;
(b) shock damage – fire does not necessarily ensue.
Policyholders have the option of extending the cover under the policy to:

(i) Fire only following earthquake (the exclusion on the face of the policy excludes fire damage following earthquake);
(ii) Shock only;
(iii) Fire and shock, the wording being

CONSEQUENTIAL LOSS caused by EARTHQUAKE

The premium payable depends on the range of cover chosen. While earthquake is not a major problem in the UK, nevertheless tremors do occur and many policyholders extend their cover to include this peril especially as the wider the extensions chosen the better will be the inclusive rate.

10.06 SUBTERRANEAN FIRE

Subterranean fire refers to a fire of volcanic origin, but would include a fire in a coal mine or oil well.

10.07 SPONTANEOUS FERMENTATION

> CONSEQUENTIAL LOSS (by fire only) resulting from any property's own SPONTANEOUS FERMENTATION OR HEATING

This peril is frequently added without charge if it relates solely to coal and coke.

10.08 STORM AND FLOOD

This peril was previously termed "Storm, tempest and flood". The wording reads:

> CONSEQUENTIAL LOSS caused by STORM or FLOOD excluding CONSEQUENTIAL LOSS
> (a) attributable solely to change in the water table level
> (b) caused by frost subsidence ground heave or landslip
> (c) in respect of movable property in the open, fences and gates

Insurers envisage "Storm" as unusual weather conditions – very high winds, heavy rain, thick snow, damaging hail. "Flood" is water from an overflowing river or canal, or inundation from the sea. Because rivers tend to overflow their banks following heavy rain, making it difficult to decide between "storm" and "flood", some Insurers insist that the perils are insured together, unless there are particular underwriting difficulties with regard to either of the perils. Dispute as to the peril involved is thus avoided.

The exclusions (a), (b) and (c) above follow the material damage insurance exclusions.

Exclusion (a) is a recent development. Anxiety is beginning to be shown in many circles at the rate at which the water table is rising in the London area. Both before and after the Second World War, many firms had an artesian well on the premises and drew their own water.

(A charge, based on the volume of water withdrawn, was payable.) So many, in fact, were withdrawing water that the table fell and wells had to be dug deeper. With the dispersal of factories and offices from London, the volume of water being withdrawn has decreased to such an extent that the water table is now rising. Insurers are concerned that damage done to foundations and basements may be the subject of a claim on the grounds that the damage is due to water from storm and the exclusion is to anticipate this situation.

If the Insured decides to limit the cover to STORM, the peril of FLOOD will be specifically excluded.

10.09 ESCAPE OF WATER

> CONSEQUENTIAL LOSS caused by ESCAPE OF WATER FROM ANY TANK APPARATUS OR PIPE excluding CONSEQUENTIAL LOSS
> (a) caused by water discharged or leaking from any automatic sprinkler installation
> (b) in respect of any building which is empty or not in use

This peril was previously known as "Bursting or overflowing of water tanks, apparatus or pipes". It will be seen that the new wording is slightly wider than the previous wording, inasmuch as water which escapes from a hole in the bottom of a rusty tank, causing damage below, is hardly "bursting or overflowing". Nevertheless, Insurers have dealt with these claims in the past, payment being based on the damage and the interruption which results. The cost of replacement of the rusty tank was, of course, the responsibility of the Insured.

The escape of water from a sprinkler system is treated as a separate peril – Sprinkler Leakage – and is the subject of a separate section of this Chapter.

The water installation in a building which is left empty would be at risk from freezing and is therefore excluded.

10.10 IMPACT (THIRD PARTY)

The wording reads:

> CONSEQUENTIAL LOSS caused by IMPACT by any road vehicle or animal not belonging to or under the control of the Insured or any occupier of the premises or their respective employees

Road vehicles should carry Third Party insurance and if the vehicle causing damage can be traced, recovery of the cost of the material damage should be possible. But, as we discussed under the policy condition dealing with subrogation, recovery of the *effect* of the material damage – the economic loss – is not so straightforward. In addition, "Third Party" means what it says – one cannot be one's own Third Party – so firms with their own vehicles can arrange for the words "... not belonging to or under the control etc ..." to be deleted at an additional premium. Then, if one of their own vehicles or one belonging to an occupier collides with the building or damages the contents, causing an interruption of the business, the cover will operate. This is often referred to as "own impact", the full title being "Impact (Third Party and Own Vehicles)".

Fork lift trucks are not necessarily licensed for the road and therefore would fall outside the category of "road vehicles". But careless handling of a fork lift truck could result in serious damage to a machine with the consequent interruption of the business. Most Insurers are prepared to extend the "own impact" to include fork lift trucks provided, of course, that the material damage policy is also suitably endorsed.

Own impact under the material damage insurance is normally subject to an excess and the Material Damage Proviso Waiver under Special Condition No. 4 would apply.

0.11 SPRINKLER LEAKAGE

> CONSEQUENTIAL LOSS caused by ACCIDENTAL ESCAPE OF WATER FROM ANY AUTOMATIC SPRINKLER INSTALLATION in the Premises not caused by
> (a) freezing whilst the building in so far as it is in the Insured's ownership or tenancy is empty or not in use
> (b) explosion earthquake subterranean fire or heat caused by fire

The presence of water under pressure in the system of automatic sprinklers poses a distinct threat to the premises. Fracture of a pipe, the accidental discharge from a sprinkler head when no heat is involved, or accidental damage when workmen are on the premises can cause substantial material damage losses. In addition, production is inevitably affected, perhaps seriously if a key machine is put out of commission by the leakage. Subject to there being a material damage insurance against this hazard, the B/I policy can be extended to provide the required cover in accordance with the wording above.

The severe weather during the past few years has resulted in the freezing of pipes in the roof space, particularly if the extreme weather arrives at the weekend when the level of heating has been reduced, with the consequent deluge when the pipes unfreeze.

It follows that the risk of the pipes freezing in an empty building is unacceptable – hence exclusion (a).

If the perils in (b) lead to the escape of water from the installation and damage ensues leading to CONSEQUENTIAL LOSS, the loss would fall to be dealt with as a claim under that peril.

Where the premises are protected by an automatic sprinkler installation, sprinkler leakage insurance is normally effected. The addition of this cover to the business interruption policy should follow as a matter of prudence; the cost is not prohibitive.

10.12 EXPLOSION AND COLLAPSE AND OVERHEATING

The policy can be extended to cover CONSEQUENTIAL LOSS caused by explosion and collapse of steam pipes, vessels and boilers. A further extension provides cover for CONSEQUENTIAL LOSS caused by the overheating of tubes, boilers and economisers.

The interpretation of the words "EXPLOSION", "COLLAPSE" and "OVERHEATING" is set out in Special Condition No. 5. Special Condition No. 6 makes it clear that payment for CONSEQUENTIAL LOSS following explosion and collapse of steam pipes is not dependent on there being any material damage insurance.

The wording will be found in Appendix 8, page 000.

10.13 SUBSIDENCE, GROUND HEAVE, LANDSLIP

Until the recent series of dry summers, subsidence cover was not generally required and, when asked for, a special policy would be prepared. Because of the infrequent demand, applications for subsidence cover would have been treated with great care, the feeling being that possibly an element of selection against the Insurer was involved. The considerable damage which followed the dry summer of 1976 and repeated in subsequent years, has resulted in a much increased demand for this cover and a recommended wording (see

Appendix 8) is now provided. The need remains for a survey of premises where subsidence is required.

After the summer of 1976 it was found that frequently, where subsidence had occurred, it did not follow that the ground returned to its former state when moisture returned. Instead, the ground would rise nearby, adding to the damage caused by the subsidence. Consequently, ground heave and landslip have been added to the original peril of subsidence.

Special Condition No. 7 applies to this range of perils.

0.14 NOTIFIABLE DISEASE, VERMIN, DEFECTIVE SANITARY ARRANGEMENTS, MURDER AND SUICIDE

Businesses providing food, drink and accommodation to members of the public are particularly susceptible to the perils in the heading, including disease attributable to food or drink supplied from the premises.

Cover against these perils has been available to hotels for many years, but the advent of numerous restaurants, fast food outlets and the many other establishments catering for the public has led to the cover being available on a wide scale. (The recommended wordings are to be found in Appendix 8.)

Because there is no physical damage caused by the above perils, a special wording is required to incorporate the perils in the policy.

> The insurance ... shall ... extend to include loss resulting from interruption of or interference with the Business carried on by the Insured at the Premises in consequence of:–

The following wording is used for hotels, restaurants and public houses. Similar wordings, slightly modified, are available for schools, private hospitals, food processors and distributors.

> 1 (a) any occurrence of a Notifiable Disease (as defined below) at the Premises or attributable to food or drink supplied from the Premises
> (b) any discovery of an organism at the premises likely to result in the occurrence of a Notifiable Disease
> (c) any occurrence of a Notifiable Disease (in the town/borough of ...) (within a radius of 25 miles of the Premises)

> 2 the discovery of vermin or pests at the Premises which causes restrictions on the use of the Premises on the order or advice of the competent local authority
> 3 any accident causing defects in the drains or other sanitary arrangements at the Premises which causes restrictions on the use of the Premises on the order of a competent local authority
> 4 any occurrence of murder or suicide at the Premises.

Special Condition 1 of the extension states –

> 1 Notifiable Disease shall mean illness sustained by any person resulting from –
> (a) food or drink poisoning, or
> (b) any human infectious or human contagious disease, an outbreak of which the competent local authority has stipulated shall be notified to them.

Food and drink are obviously of vital importance to hotels, both for guests and for meals served to non-residents. For many hotels, catering for functions is a valuable part of the income. Contamination of food or drink will affect turnover at the time and could have a damaging effect on subsequent turnover, until the source of the contamination is traced and confidence in the hotel is re-established.

It may be impossible to accommodate guests, or guests may refuse to come if there is an outbreak of disease. Cover can apply to the hotel only, or to a defined area near the hotel, or to a geographical location (say the Isle of Wight). An incident of this sort can affect bookings seriously both at the time of the outbreak and subsequently, and a seasonal business is especially vulnerable. If cover wider than notifiable human infectious or contagious diseases is required, negotiations with the underwriter will be necessary. The outbreak of Legionnaires Disease, and the time taken to trace the cause, come to mind in this connection. Cover for items such as AIDS (which is not at present a notifiable disease) is very difficult to obtain.

Most of the considerations in the previous paragraph will also apply to schools, private hospitals, food processors and distributors.

The discovery of vermin or pests at the premises or an accident causing defects in the drains may result in the premises being closed until the local authority is satisfied that there is no danger to the public. Apart from the immediate loss of revenue, there may be, due to adverse publicity, some delay before the level of trading is resumed.

It is not difficult to imagine the disruption caused to a hotel when a murder or suicide takes place on the premises. A section or sections of the hotel may be cordoned off while the police pursue their enquiries, guests may have to be accommodated elsewhere and in-coming guests switched to other parts of the hotel or to neighbouring hotels. All of this may involve extra cost and, in addition, prospective guests may be put off by the publicity, and custom is lost.

Similarly, the other types of business may be affected to some degree by a murder or suicide on the premises.

The full wording will be found in the Appendices. Attention is drawn to the amended wording for the Indemnity Period, depending on the type of business being covered.

As no material loss is involved, the requirement of material damage insurance will not apply to this extension of cover.

0.15 THEFT

The wording of the extension for cover for malicious damage under the material damage insurance excludes DAMAGE by theft.

Subject to there being material damage theft cover, the B/I policy can be extended to include this peril. The theft of valuable tools or valuable items of stock and the damage done whilst the intruders are on the premises could interfere with production, and the cover is well worth considering.

Whilst the Recommended Practice for the Conduct of Business now gives guidance on the differentiation between theft and malicious damage, it is an advantage if the malicious damage insurance and the theft cover are placed with the same Insurer or the same panel of Insurers, to avoid the argument as to whether the loss is to be treated as malicious damage or theft.

0.16 FINES OR DAMAGES

Many contracts carry a requirement that completion must be effected within a specified time, otherwise a fine or damages may be levied. Due to a peril insured against, production may be disrupted and the firm unable to complete the contract in time, leaving themselves open to the penalties provided for in the contract.

To protect themselves against this eventuality, firms may add an item to the policy, the sum insured being the maximum penalty that they could suffer.

The usual wording is:

> Item No.........   Sum insured..............
> On fines or damages for breach of contract £.............
> The insurance under Item...... is limited to fines or damages for breach of contract and the amount payable as indemnity thereunder shall be such sums as the Insured shall be legally liable to pay and shall pay in discharge of fines or damages, incurred solely in consequence of the damage, for non-completion or late completion of orders.

The rating (rate %) charged for this item will be considerably above that charged for the gross profit item, due to the possibility that the total amount insured may be payable in respect of a loss.

10.17 DETERIORATION OF UNDAMAGED STOCK

Stock, particularly raw materials, can suffer deterioration or loss of value if it is not used at the appropriate time. Examples could be foodstuffs, or materials used in the fashion trade. The loss of value is not the direct consequence of the fire or other peril responsible, but the interruption or interference of the business causes the delay in putting the stock into use. The material damage policy will not entertain the loss as no damage as such has occurred and the deterioration may have no effect on the turnover, so no claim can be made under the B/I insurance.

An item can be added to the policy to cover loss due to deterioration of undamaged stock and the sum to be insured is the maximum loss that the Insured feels is likely to happen. The rating for this item will depend on the Insurer's judgement of the factors which could lead to a claim.

11 Miscellaneous

Various clauses: Departmental – Salvage Sale – New Business – Accumulated Stocks – Damage Occurring to Office Premises – Insurance of Rent – Rating

1.01 DEPARTMENTAL CLAUSE

Many big firms today operate a number of different sections or divisions under the "umbrella" of the main organisation. The products may or may not be related and the profitability of each section will vary. To enable control to be exercised, separate accounting systems will be installed.

In the event of an Incident, it would not be possible to provide true indemnity if the overall results of the business were used as the basis for the claims settlement, since the Gross Profit will vary from one section to another. In fact, the loss adjuster would find great difficulty in completing the claim settlement without the assistance of the individual sets of accounts.

Where separate accounting systems are employed, the following Departmental Clause may be added to the policy:

> If the Business be conducted by departments the independent trading results of which are ascertainable, the provisions of clauses (a) and (b) of the item on Gross Profit shall apply separately to each department affected by the Incident [except that if the sum assured by the said item be less than the aggregate of the sums produced by applying the Rate of Gross Profit for each department of the Business (whether affected by the Incident or not) to its relative Annual Turnover (or to a proportionately increased multiple thereof where the Maximum Indemnity Period exceeds twelve months) the amount payable shall be proportionately reduced]

> **Note:** For insurances on the declaration-linked basis the words in square brackets should be omitted.

11.02 SALVAGE SALE CLAUSE

An almost inevitable result of an Incident to a shop or departmental store is to produce the problem of disposing of stock partially damaged by heat, smoke and water. One method employed is to hold a "Salvage Sale", when the goods are priced to be attractive to bargain hunters (the **proceeds** of the Salvage Sale reduce the claim under the material damage insurance). But the lower prices mean less profit for the shopkeeper and, in fairness, a method of meeting the problem must be sought.

Readers will recall that the claim for loss of Gross Profit is based on "Shortage of Turnover", to which figure the Rate of Gross Profit is applied. If the Insured holds a salvage sale, the Turnover will be increased and the Shortage correspondingly decreased, meaning that the Insured will receive less in compensation than true indemnity.

By incorporating the following Salvage Sale Clause when the policy is prepared, argument and worry when a loss occurs is prevented.

> If, following any Incident giving rise to a claim under this policy, the Insured shall hold a salvage sale during the Indemnity Period, clause (a) of the item on Gross Profit shall, for the purpose of such claim, read as follows:–
> (a) **In respect of Reduction in Turnover**: the sum produced by applying the Rate of Gross Profit to the amount by which the Turnover during the Indemnity Period (less the turnover for the period of the salvage sale) shall, in consequence of the Incident, fall short of the Standard Turnover, from which sum shall be deducted the Gross Profit actually earned during the period of the salvage sale.

It will be seen that the Insurers are prepared to disregard the Turnover generated by the salvage sale – the Turnover is thus artificially low and the Shortage in Turnover correspondingly high – provided the Gross Profit earned by the salvage sale is deducted from the loss payable under the heading "Loss of Gross Profit". True indemnity is thus achieved.

1.03 NEW BUSINESS CLAUSE

In Chapters 8 and 9, the method of settling a claim was set out, following the pattern laid down in the Specification. This called for the use of historical information, that is, basing the loss payable on figures obtained from the Insured's books for the previous year's trading. The Rate of Gross Profit, the Standard Turnover and the Annual Turnover all look back and are then adjusted for current circumstances.

But a business which has only just been set up has no historic background of figures on which to base the claim and therefore some adjustment of the wording is required to meet the situation.

The method adopted is to take the figures from the commencement of the business to the date of the Incident and to use them as the basis, with the "Other circumstances" clause (trend) applied to provide as nearly as possible a replica of the "would have been" position.

The wording used is:

MEMO. For the purpose of any claim arising from an Incident occurring before the completion of the first year's trading of the Business at the Premises the terms Rate of Gross Profit, Annual Turnover and Standard Turnover shall bear the following meanings and not as within stated.

Rate of Gross Profit:– The Rate of Gross Profit earned on the turnover during the period between the date of the commencement of the Business and the date of the Incident

Annual Turnover:– The proportional equivalent, for a period of twelve months, of the Turnover realised during the period between the commencement of the Business and the date of the Incident

Standard Turnover:– The proportional equivalent, for a period equal to the Indemnity Period, of the Turnover realised during the period between the commencement of the Business and the date of the Incident

to which such adjustments shall be made as may be necessary to provide for the trend of the Business and for variations in or other circumstances affecting the Business either before or after the Incident which would have been affecting the Business had the Incident not occurred, so that the figures thus adjusted shall represent as nearly as may be reasonably practicable the results which but for the Incident would have been obtained during the relative period after the Incident

Let us suppose the Business has been trading for three months when the loss occurs. Thus:
(a) the Rate of Gross Profit is based on the three months' trading:
(b) the Annual Turnover will be the three months' trading multiplied by 4 to provide the equivalent of a year:
(c) the Standard Turnover will be the equivalent proportion of the three months' trading as the Indemnity Period bears to the time the Business has been trading. So if the Indemnity Period is six and one-half weeks the Standard Turnover would be half the Turnover of the Business from commencement to the date of the Incident.

All the figures obtained would be adjusted to reflect the probable course of trading had the loss not occurred.

11.04 ACCUMULATED STOCKS CLAUSE

Most manufacturing concerns carry a fair amount of finished stock, perhaps enough for three months. A fire or other incident interfering with production would not necessarily affect immediate turnover, inasmuch as customers could be accommodated from the warehouse. But the "buffer" stock would be depleted and it is only fair to the Insured to take this factor into consideration when settling a claim.

The Accumulated Stocks Clause (see Appendix 9) can be added to a policy where the Indemnity Period is not less than 12 months and the usual wording is:

> In adjusting any loss account shall be taken and an equitable allowance made if any reduction in Turnover due to the Incident is postponed by reason of the Turnover being temporarily maintained from accumulated stocks of finished goods in warehouses or depots.

The clause could be of value if there is a long interruption, involving most of the Maximum Indemnity Period, during which time the "buffer" stocks would become exhausted. Time would be needed beyond the Maximum Indemnity Period, during which stocks could be rebuilt and the clause provides for this. (The introduction of the system of 'just in time' means that it is less likely that large stocks of finished goods will be held).

1.05 DAMAGE OCCURRING TO OFFICE PREMISES

Damage occurring to the office of a manufacturing concern would probably have a limited or no effect on the level of turnover, since there is no interference with production. Nevertheless the Insured would want to have the office back in use as soon as possible and Increase in Cost of Working would be expended to achieve this aim. The wording of (b) Increase in Cost of Working on the Specification makes it clear that I.C.W. can only be incurred if it is "for the sole purpose of avoiding or diminishing the reduction in turnover...".

Insurers are usually prepared to issue a letter confirming that I.C.W. incurred for this purpose will be favourably regarded, notwithstanding the absence of any reduction of turnover. (This is often referred to as a "Blundell Spence" letter.)

1.06 INSURANCE OF RENT

The insurance of rent falls to be considered under four heads.
1. Property owners.
2. Property developers.
3. A person running a business, who has an empty building available.
4. Tenants.

1.07 PROPERTY OWNERS

The owner of a building which is let out will normally arrange for the building to be insured against fire and special perils, and this material damage insurance will be paid by the tenant, either by inclusion in the total rent charge or by a separate payment.

Loss of rent due to an Incident needs to be insured, since in the event of a severe fire or explosion, it is likely that the tenant will seek alternative accommodation.

Depending on the lease, the obligation to pay rent may cease immediately or, more frequently, the tenant may have relief under a cessor of rent clause, whereby the tenant is released from the payment of rent, say, three months after the date of the Incident. Either way, the landlord will lose the rent income and can arrange to include the insurance of rent on the same policy as protects the building, by an item –

On twelve months' rent £x.

Under a material damage policy, the payment for loss of rent terminates when the repair/rebuilding is completed, irrespective of the absence or presence of a tenant willing to take over the lease, or whether the previous tenant is ready to return. The landlord could thus be faced with a sizable loss if a tenant is hard to find.

If, however, the insurance of the rent is provided by a B/I policy with a suitable Indemnity Period, the loss of rent will be payable by the Insurer (less any Savings) until a tenant is found or the Maximum Indemnity Period expires, whichever is first. In addition, Increase in Cost of Working is available to help find another tenant quickly.

The Insured's business would be described in the schedule and would include the description "Property Owner".

The one difficulty may be that if the insurance of rent is the only item on the B/I policy the premium may be less than the minimum premium charged by the Insurer and the Insured may feel that the additional expense is not warranted.

11.08 PROPERTY DEVELOPERS

Insurers are sometimes approached to cover under a B/I policy loss of rent following an Incident to a building which is approaching completion or is being refurbished. Obviously, an Incident occurring during the months prior to completion of the work will set back the date on which income can be expected.

Insurers are, however, wary of providing cover where the project is of a speculative nature, since it is very difficult to establish whether or not a tenant would have been found to take over the premises on completion.

Where firm commitments have been entered into with prospective tenants, no difficulty arises and a loss of rent policy can be provided. The description of the business will be "Property Owners". The Indemnity Period will not start until the due date of completion or refurbishment as with an Advance Profits policy. (See 13.03)

11.09 WHERE THE LETTING IS NOT THE MAIN BUSINESS

For various reasons a firm may find itself with an empty building on its hands and, naturally, seeks to obtain an income in the shape of rent from it.

No difficulty will be experienced in adding an item to the B/I policy on the rent of this building, or to including this in the Gross Profit item, the words "Property Owners" being added to the description of the business. It is not even necessary to employ the same Maximum Indemnity Period as the main insurance, if it is felt that a longer or shorter time than the Maximum Indemnity Period stated in the policy would be more suitable for the Rent item.

As was mentioned in Section 11.07, the advantage of covering rent as an item on the B/I policy is that payment commences when the tenant ceases to be bound by the lease and continues until the payment of rent by a tenant recommences (subject to the Maximum Indemnity Period). Any Savings in consequence of the building being empty – for example the local council may not levy rates on empty property – must be deducted in the loss settlement.

11.10 TENANTS

If the Insured occupies a building or buildings not owned by them, rent will be one of the Standing Charges and included automatically in the Gross Profit item if the insurance is arranged on the "Difference" basis. Any relief from the rent payable, due to the terms of the lease, will be treated as Savings in the loss settlement.

11.11 RATING

The demise of the Fire Offices' Committee (the FOC, which controlled the Tariff) provided an opportunity for the Insurers to devise their own system of rating but, in many cases, the old pattern has been maintained, with, perhaps, modifications to suit individual circumstances.

The main factors involved in rating are:
(1) the fire basis rate based on the contents rate of the premises;
(2) Consequential Loss List of Rating Adjustments (CLORA), or similar adjustments;
(3) the Maximum Indemnity Period;
(4) Payroll;
(5) the range of perils;
(6) extensions;
(7) the underwriter's judgement as to the likely extent of any interruption.

11.12 THE FIRE BASIS RATE

Traditionally the fire rate (including any discounts such as the discount for Fire Extinguishing Appliances) has been the basis of rating for B/I. Some will argue that a small fire can cause a disproportionate B/I loss, if, for instance, a key machine or the boiler house is put out of action. But it is true to say that the fire rate also reflects the level of hazard involved.

If the Insured is operating from more than one premises, it will be necessary to calculate an "average" rate, which will become the fire basis rate. The average rate is obtained by multiplying the total of the sum insured on Machinery/Plant plus 75 per cent of the Stock sum insured at each address by the contents fire rate applicable to that address. If premises are sprinklered, Insurers allow a further third off the premium in the calculation after allowing the discounts given in the Material Damage rating for sprinklers. The premiums applicable to the addresses are totalled and divided by the total of the sums insured which produced that premium. The result is the average fire rate.

11.13 CONSEQUENTIAL LOSS LIST OF RATING ADJUSTMENTS (CLORA)

Under the aegis of the Consequential Loss Committee of the FOC, statistics of the premiums and losses of the various classes of business were collected from the Tariff offices. The results were published in the form of percentage adjustments which were a loading to or a discount off the premium calculated in accordance with the preceding paragraphs. By general agreement, the list of adjustments to the premium was adopted by the whole market.

With the ending of the Tariff, offices were free to make their own assessment of the loading. Some offices created their own rating guides, incorporating the loading, others continue to use the CLORA adjustments for existing business, and their own rating guide for new business. The statistics of premiums and losses for various classes of business are now collected by the Association of British Insurers (ABI) but no recommendations are made as to adjustment of premiums.

11.14 THE MAXIMUM INDEMNITY PERIOD

The Insured, when discussing his insurance arrangements with the broker or consultant, must come to a decision as to the Maximum Indemnity Period required. The decision will be based on the assessment of the time necessary to rebuild and re-equip the premises in the event of a major loss, and the time required to return to the level of turnover at which he would have been trading, had the Incident not occurred.

It is customary to select a period, expressed in months, and for this period to be stated in the policy. The underwriter then takes the fire basis rate and adjusts this rate according to the following table. (Only a small number of examples are shown.)

Table 11.1: Sum Insured   Annual Figure 100 000 Basis Rate 0.20%

Indemnity Period	Proportional Increase	100,000	Basis Rate	Percentage Multiplier	Effective Rate	Payroll Percentage
5 months	100%	100 000	0.20%	100%	0.20%	–
12 months	100%	100 000	0.20%	150%	0.30%	112
18 months	150%	150,000	0.20%	140%	0.28%	98
24 months	200%	200,000	0.20%	125%	0.25%	81

It must be emphasised that the table above is the traditional "tariff" method of adjusting the rate according to the maximum indemnity period. Now that insurers are no longer bound by a tariff, they are free to make their own judgement as to the appropriate rate. But having said that, there is plenty of evidence that the table above continues to be used as a guide by the underwriters. A better than normal interruption position will, however, lead to a reduction in the Percentage Multiplier, especially with longer Indemnity Periods, as discussed in Section 11.19.

While the table above refers to an Indemnity Period of five months, it would be unusual for Insurers to agree to such a short period. Experience has shown that the insuring public tends to be over-optimistic when it comes to estimating the time it could take a business to recover.

The policy is concerned not only with the time taken for buildings to be repaired or rebuilt, or machines to be able to resume production, but with the additional time during which **the results of the Business shall be affected in consequence of the Incident.** It is this last aspect which is so difficult, if not impossible, to estimate with any accuracy. A check on the lead time for delivery of a specialised machine may well provide grounds for a longer Indemnity Period.

11.15 THE SUM INSURED

This will have been agreed at the meeting between the Insured and the broker or consultant and must be reviewed each year in the light of the level of trading and the expectation for the coming year.

Readers are reminded that:
(a) if the insurance is not on the Declaration Linked basis, then provision must be made for a sum insured which will be sufficient to avoid proportionate reduction (average), even if the loss occurs on the last day of the policy year and the Maximum Indemnity Period is required.
(b) if the insurance is on the Declaration Linked basis, the sum insured is the estimated Gross Profit for the forthcoming year of insurance. No extra amount is necessary as Insurers provide additional cover of up to 133.3 per cent of the sum insured. The Insured agrees to provide a certificate of the actual earned Gross Profit when the accounts are published, to enable the final premium to be calculated, and an Additional Premium will be charged or a Return Premium will be allowed as appropriate.

If the Maximum Indemnity Period is longer than 12 months, the sum insured must be increased in both cases in proportion (see Table 11.1 – Section 11.14).

11.16 PAYROLL

The insurance of Wages on Dual Basis (see Chapter 14) provides only partial cover, inasmuch as the Insured selects 100 per cent cover for the Initial Period of, say, 13 weeks and then a limited percentage of the Wage Roll for the Remainder of the Indemnity Period. In consequence, failure to choose a long enough Initial Period or a high enough percentage for the Remainder Period will result in the Insured having to meet from his own pocket the difference between what the labour cost and what he obtains from his Insurer.

Legislation has also brought about changes. The statutory burden on an employer when it becomes necessary to discharge an employee is laid down in the Employment Protection (Consolidation) Act 1978. The period of notice will depend on the length of service and the redundancy money on length of service, wage/salary, and age, and agreements with specific trade unions, which are often more than that required by law.

No distinction is made between wage-earning and salaried employees and if it is not economical to retain either category after an Incident has disrupted production, notice and redundancy money will have to be found.

This burden on an employer, together with the need to retain skilled staff, who represent an increasing proportion of the work force, has led Insurers to provide cover for "Payroll" – the combined total of Wages and Salaries.

The Insured is invited to include Payroll in the Gross Profit sum insured, thereby providing 100 per cent cover for the whole of the Indemnity Period. But the likelihood of a 100 per cent loss on Payroll is virtually impossible, as, in the event of a total shutdown of the factory for the whole of the Indemnity Period, notice will have to be given and redundancy payments made to most employees and in consequence, there will be a massive saving, since the employees will not be there to collect their wages/salaries for a substantial part of the time. During the Indemnity Period there will be some employees who reach retirement age and others who would have left anyway.

It would be manifestly unfair to the Insured to charge a full premium on the Payroll element of the Gross Profit item, when it is known in advance that a total loss is most unlikely. Accordingly, Insurers charge a reduced premium on the Payroll element of the Gross Profit item. Reference to the Table 11.1 in Section 11.14 will show that where the basis rate for 12 months' Indemnity Period is loaded 150 per cent, the Payroll loading is reduced to 112 per cent and the other Indemnity Periods are reduced similarly.

To give effect to all this requires a calculation. The Accounts in Chapter 2 show Wages as 420 000, Salaries as 80 000 and in Chapter 4 we arrived at 900 000 as the Gross Profit.

The calculation of the reduced multiplier is as follows:

Gross Profit		900 000
Payroll –	420 000	
Wages		
Salaries	80 000	500 000
Gross Profit ex. Payroll		400 000

Gross profit ex Payroll is 400 000 out of 900 000 = 44.5%
Payroll is 500 000 out of 900 000 = 55.5%

Each percentage is applied to the appropriate multiplier viz.:

12 months' Maximum Indemnity Period.

Gross Profit ex Payroll is 44.5% of 150% = 66.75%
Payroll is 55.5% of 112% = 62.16%

Total = 128.91%

The multiplier is thus 128 per cent instead of 150 per cent. (The amount after the decimal point is always ignored.)

The application of the revised multiplier will be shown in the rating example at the end of this Chapter.

11.17 THE RANGE OF PERILS

In addition to the perils of fire, lightning and limited explosion, the Insured will require a range of Special Perils, limited perhaps, to Aircraft and Explosion, or any stage up to the full range, as discussed in Chapter 10.

Depending on the perils chosen and the size of the sum insured, a combined rate for the perils is available, which is cheaper than taking each peril individually. Consideration must also be given to including sprinkler leakage and theft cover (the Material Damage Proviso will apply), and, for a hotel, the "Notifiable Diseases etc" cover.

11.18 EXTENSIONS

The extensions (see Chapter 12) are individually rated. The rating for Suppliers' and Customers' extension is based on the fire rate, actual or assumed, of the premises to which the extension applies, adjusted for the dependency percentage. The higher the percentage, the higher the rate. Insurers will have their own rates for extensions pertaining to Public Utilities and to Prevention of Access.

11.19 THE UNDERWRITER'S JUDGEMENT

The foregoing paragraphs are really rule-of-thumb rules for the rating of a risk, which take no account of any special features of the premises or the business to be underwritten.

Having studied the plan and report and discussed the case with the Insured or the broker, the underwriter may feel that there are some specially good features about the risk, such that he would want to charge less than the normal rate.

An example of a good feature could be that the insurance is to apply to two similar manufacturing facilities on separate sites, each with the capacity to absorb some increased output if required. A lengthy interruption of Turnover is not envisaged. A way to achieve a reduction in rate if, for instance, the Indemnity period is 12 months, is to reduce the loading of the rate from 150 per cent to 125 per cent. Perhaps the business is run by a highly motivated Board, keen on Risk Management and with a very good loss record. The underwriter will be keen to retain the business and will adjust the Indemnity Period loading to remain competitive.

If the fire rate does not, in the underwriter's opinion, reflect the full hazard involved, there is nothing to stop him increasing the fire rate, except the possibility that another underwriter may not view the hazard so critically and underquote to obtain the business.

11.20 DISCOUNTS

Long Term Agreements. Most Insurers will be prepared to offer a discount of 5 per cent in return for an agreement by the Insured to continue to offer the business to them for a period of three years. Both the discount and the period of three years may differ with some insurers.

Deductibles. For major insurances, most Insurers will be prepared to offer a discount in return for the agreement of the Insured to bear the first amount of any claim. This amount is known as a 'Deductible' and will vary considerably from a small amount of say £5000 up to a six figure amount and very occasionally, as high as £1m. The amount of discount will depend on the Deductible agreed upon. In certain very hazardous activities, Insurers may insist on a Deductible but without any discount being given. It is understood that a Deductible must not be covered by any other insurance.

11.21 SPECIMEN PREMIUM CALCULATION

Note: this is a specimen premium calculation and all the rates etc. shown are for demonstration purposes only.

Fire basis rate				0.15%
CLORA	50%	(see Section 11.13)		0.075%
				0.225%
Special perils –				
Aircraft		0.004%		
Explosion		0.012%		0.016%
				0.241%
Multiplier	128%	(Section 11.16)	+ 28%	0.067%
				0.308%
S/T, F, Escape of water, Impact				
(say) 0.20% × 50% × $\frac{12}{12}$ §				0.100%
				0.408%
Extensions *				0.15%
Business Interruption rate				0.558%

(say) £1 000 000 @ 0.558%   =   £5 580
            less 5% L.T.A.‡   279
                                              ———
                                         £5,301
                                         ══════

§ Insurers feel that the maximum interruption which could be expected following Storm/Tempest etc is less than 12 months. Hence the 50 per cent. 12/12 is for 12 months' Indemnity Period. If the Indemnity Period is 18 months, the fraction would be 12/18, and 24 months, 12/24. The sum insured for these Indemnity Periods has been multiplied by 1½ and 2 respectively – using these fractions brings them back to the equivalent of 12 months. (Individual Underwriters' methods of charging for these perils will often differ.)

* For example, Suppliers, Customers, Public Utilities etc.
‡ Long Term Agreement.

12 Damage away from Insured's premises

The Effect on the Business of Incidents occuring other than on the premises of the Insured:
Specified Suppliers – Unspecified Suppliers and Storage Sites – Motor Vehicle Manufacturers – Property Stored – Patterns etc – Transit – Motor Vehicles – Contract Sites – Prevention of Access – Public Utilities and Accidental Failure of the Public Supply – Professional Insured – Documents – Specified Customers – Unspecified Customers – Bomb Scares

(Reminder. To save repetition, the word "Incident" will be used to represent the result of the operation of an insured peril.)

12.01 EXTENDING THE COVER

The wording of the policy specifically limits the cover to the consequences of an Incident to property owned or occupied by the Insured. But virtually all businesses are dependent, in some form, on someone else, be it the supplier of raw materials, the customer to whom goods are supplied, the public utilities or the well-being of the surrounding property.

It follows then, that an Incident at premises not in the control of the Insured, but with which he could have a special connection, could have a marked effect on the level of Turnover and hence the net profit of the business.

Insurers are prepared to extend the B/I insurance to these premises *for the same perils as are shown on the policy.* In the case of several of the extensions a percentage of the sum insured limit or a limit of amount will be applied and, naturally, the larger the percentage or the limit, the more it will cost the Insured.

To extend the policy, Insurers can use the following recommended wording (see Appendix 10):

> Any loss as insured by this policy resulting from interruption of or interference with the Business in consequence of loss destruction or damage at the undernoted situations or to property as undernoted shall be deemed to be an Incident provided that after the application of all other terms conditions and provisions of the policy the liability under this memorandum in respect of any occurrence shall not exceed
> (a) the percentage of the total sums insured (or 133.3% of the Estimated Gross Profit) by the policy
> or
> (b) the amount
> shown below against such situations or property as the limit

The appropriate wording, shown in each heading following, including the limit applying, then follows

12.02 SUPPLIERS

Every manufacturer finds it necessary to buy in raw materials from which to manufacture the product he sells. The raw materials may be basic – sheet or bar metal, baulk timber or granules for plastic goods manufacture, through to semi-finished or finished components, where the "manufacture" consists mainly of assembly. Whatever the situation, interruption of supplies could lead to interruption of production with the consequent shortage in turnover and possibly the increased cost of buying elsewhere to maintain production.

One of the major sources of interruption is fire or explosion on the supplier's premises and Insurers will extend an insurance to specified suppliers *for the same perils* as apply to the Insured's premises, although sometimes they will restrict the perils for underwriting reasons.

The insurance extension to the supplier's premises will be subject to a percentage limit of the sum insured (or 133.3 per cent of the Estimated Gross Profit) or a maximum amount which the Insured considers adequate. This "dependency", as it is called, must be calculated carefully, bearing in mind the two important factors:
(1) that the limit must be fixed high enough to provide adequate cover; and
(2) the higher the limit, the higher the cost to the Insured.

The "dependency" percentage will have to take into account –
(1) The extent to which the Insured is dependent on each supplier expressed as a percentage.
(2) The extent to which a supplier's flow of goods could be interrupted by damage by fire or other insured peril. If the supplier has a number of similar premises, the dependency may well be reduced.
(3) The period for which the supply could be interrupted.
(4) The maximum period for which the Insured's business could be interrupted.
(5) Alternative supplies –
are these available?
is the capacity available?
is production to Insured's specification available?
how long to set up alternative arrangements?
what is the additional cost involved?
(6) What stocks of materials or finished goods are kept on own premises (i.e. number of days/weeks for which the lowest stockholding would support normal production)?
(7) Is there an alternative way of maintaining sales and, if so, at what extra cost?

As an example, let us take the case where 60 per cent of the manufacturer's gross profit is derived from one product and his normal supply arrangements are met by Supplier A to the extent of 70 per cent and by Supplier B to the extent of 30 per cent. Each of the suppliers could increase output to some extent, the figures being 80 per cent and 50 per cent respectively. The manufacturer carries one month's stock of his requirements and the Indemnity Period is 12 months.

Position 1. Supplier A has a serious fire.

Supplier B can supply 50 per cent (say) of the requirements, so there is a shortfall of 50 per cent. The Insured will therefore receive half his supplies from Supplier B and draw the other half from stocks he holds. The one month's stock will therefore last two months (half is used each month) and thereafter the manufacturer will be dependent on the 50 per cent supplied by Supplier B for the remaining 10 months of the Indemnity Period.

Bringing this all together, we get –

$$\frac{50}{100} \times \frac{60}{100} \times \frac{10}{12} = 25\% \text{ dependency.}$$

Position 2. Supplier B has a serious fire.

Supplier A can supply 80 per cent – the shortfall is therefore 20 per cent.
The one month's stock held will last 5 months.
The possible loss is 20 per cent of 60 per cent for the 7 months (balance of the Indemnity Period):

$$\frac{20}{100} \times \frac{60}{100} \times \frac{7}{12} = 7\% \text{ dependency.}$$

While it is certainly worth extending the insurance to Supplier A, doubt might be expressed as to the need to include Supplier B, where the dependency is less than 10 per cent, but it is possible, in most cases, to have cover for an unspecified amount of 5 per cent or 10 per cent as an addition to specified extensions, as shown in Section 12.04. It is worth noting that if the Insured is satisfied that he can obtain alternative supplies in a short time, these dependencies would be reduced.

12.03 SUPPLIERS' SUPPLIERS

Because some suppliers rely on another supplier for a vital part of their product, it is possible for a "Suppliers' suppliers" extension to be added to the policy, as protection should there be an interruption in the production of the vital part.

The wording for the Suppliers and Suppliers' suppliers extension is:

> The premises (situate in Great Britain or Northern Ireland) of the following supplier(s) (situate):

The percentage of the sum insured or the limit is then added against each supplier.

Note. Although Great Britain or Northern Ireland has been shown in the wording, it is possible to obtain cover for Overseas Suppliers, although the perils may be restricted.

12.04 UNSPECIFIED SUPPLIERS AND STORAGE SITES

Because of uncertainty during the insurance year and the fact that they have a large number of alternative suppliers at any one time, many manufacturers like to include an extension of their insurance to "Unspecified Suppliers and Storage Sites". This can be done provided the insurance has already been extended to a specified supplier. Because the insurer is taking on an unknown situation, the premium charged is much higher than that for a specified supplier. The extension will also be subject both to a percentage limit and to a limit on the amount of the loss. The wording used is:

> The premises of any (other) of the Insured's suppliers manufacturers or processors of components, goods or materials but excluding the premises of any supply undertaking from which the Insured obtains electricity gas or water or telecommunications systems
>
> and
>
> premises not in the occupation of the Insured, where property of the Insured is stored
>
> all in Great Britain and Northern Ireland

A limit applies.

12.05 MOTOR VEHICLE MANUFACTURERS

The manufacture of motor vehicles involves the assembly of numerous components, many of which will be bought in from various specialist firms. It follows that an Incident on the premises of a supplier could seriously interfere with the production of the vehicle. These suppliers, in turn, may be dependent on other suppliers and it is possible to include these suppliers' suppliers in the extension.

The wording is as follows:

> The premises of ....
> (and any manufacturer supplying them with components or materials) all in Great Britain or Northern Ireland.

> Note: This extension applies to the insurance of motor garage proprietors and motor traders.

A limit applies.

Motor garage proprietors and motor traders are totally dependent on the motor cars and spares reaching them without delay. An Incident on the premises of the motor car manufacturer could deprive the garage or motor trader of vital material for his trade and this extension of the insurance of the garage proprietor and motor trader to the motor car manufacturer is a prudent precaution.

12.06 PROPERTY STORED

It will be noted that the extension of the insurance to Unspecified Suppliers and Storage Sites relates to an Incident affecting the *premises*.

Many businesses arrange for bulk storage of stock away from the manufacturing premises to enable them to supply a local market economically. Loss, destruction of or damage to this stock could adversely affect the business by making it difficult to supply orders from the storage site. Temporary storage arrangements and additional expense are likely to be involved in a bid to maintain the goodwill of customers.

Protection for this situation can be arranged by adding the following extension wording:

> Property of the Insured whilst stored anywhere in Great Britain or Northern Ireland elsewhere than at the premises in the occupation of the Insured.

A limit applies.

12.07 PATTERNS ETC.

Many firms deposit their patterns with machine makers and founders on a fairly permanent basis, so that supplies can be readily ordered and obtained. An Incident at these premises, involving the loss, destruction of or damage to the patterns, could have a serious effect on the output of the owner of the patterns, until new patterns can be prepared and supplied.

Cover is available, the wording of the extension being as follows:

> Patterns, jigs, models, templets, moulds, dies, tools, plans, drawings and designs, the property of the Insured or held by them in trust for which they are responsible, whilst at the premises of any machine makers, engineers, founders or other metal workers (excluding any premises wholly or partly occupied by the Insured) and whilst in transit, all in Great Britain or Northern Ireland.

A limit applies.

12.08 TRANSIT

Cover is available for the physical loss or destruction of goods in transit, but while this will pay for the replacement of the goods, it could be that the loss of the goods could cause a serious holdup in production, for which no compensation is provided under Goods-in-Transit insurance. This is particularly so in respect of clothing manufacturers sending their new model garments to an exhibition, where they would be unable to exhibit as a result of the loss of their garments in transit.

Insurers will extend an insurance to include the effect on the business of an Incident involving Insured's goods-in-transit by the following wording:

> Property of the Insured whilst in transit in Great Britain or Northern Ireland.

A limit applies.

Note that the Incident refers to loss, destruction of or damage to Insured's property due to a peril insured against under the policy. It would be prudent, therefore, to extend the B/I insurance to include the peril of theft whilst the goods are in transit, remembering always that there must be material damage insurance which includes this peril.

12.09 MOTOR VEHICLES

The Insured's fleet of motor vehicles plays a crucial part in the running of the business, particularly if specialist vehicles are involved. Loss of a vehicle or the fleet due to an Incident in a vehicle park would seriously disrupt deliveries to customers. The Insured's own specialist vehicles may be involved in the delivery of raw materials to the factory and their loss could affect production, resulting in loss of Gross Profit. Cover against these contingencies is available by adding the following extension wording to the policy;

> Motor vehicles of the Insured in Great Britain or Northern Ireland elsewhere than at the premises in the occupation of the Insured.

A limit applies.

> **Note:** The Insurer may not wish to include cover against the risk of impact or accidental damage to vehicles.

12.10 CONTRACT SITES

A contractor or sub-contractor working on someone else's site would be unable to carry out his contract if the site or building(s) are affected by an Incident. He could also face delay in completing his work if he is unable to resume until the repairs have been carried out. Meanwhile, his standing charges and payroll have to be met.

An extension of the B/I policy covering his office and workshops can be made to contract sites with the following wording:

128 *Business Interruption Insurance: Theory and Practice*

> Any situation in Great Britain or Northern Ireland not in the occupation of the Insured where the Insured is carrying out a contract.

A limit applies.

Note: The cause of the damage to the site or building(s) must be a peril covered by Insured's policy.

12.11 PREVENTION OF ACCESS

In certain circumstances, an Incident involving neighbouring property may be such that the Insured, his staff and his customers are unable to reach the premises. For instance, a shopping mall or precinct containing various and, perhaps, numerous shops. A serious fire occurring on the premises of a shop at the entrance to the mall, rendering the building unsafe, might cause the local authorities to bar the public from access to the other shops. The shopkeeper's premises are not physically affected but he has no or, at best, a reduced number of customers.

Cover against this eventuality is provided by the Prevention of Access extension wording as follows:

> Property in the vicinity of the Premises, loss or destruction of or damage to which shall prevent or hinder the use of the Premises or access thereto, whether the Premises or property of the Insured therein shall be damaged or not but excluding loss or destruction of or damage to property of any supply undertaking from which the Insured obtains electricity, gas or water, or telecommunications services which prevents or hinders the supply of such services, to the Premises.

No limit applies.

Note: The cause of the damage to the property must be a peril covered by Insured's policy.

LOSS OF ATTRACTION. In a shopping mall, it is quite usual to find a large supermarket or store, which is the focal point of the area.

Shoppers go regularly to the supermarket and the other shops rely on the passing trade.

A serious fire in the supermarket, which might close the supermarket but not affect access to the mall, could result in shoppers going elsewhere for their groceries, to the detriment of the other shopkeepers. It may be possible to extend the Prevention of Access wording to include "Loss of Attraction" – the supermarket is named in the extension.

Notes: The cause of the damage to the supermarket must be peril covered by Insured's policy.

The term "Prevention of Access" is interchangeable with "Denial of Access".

12.12 PUBLIC UTILITIES

Every factory is dependent to some extent on electricity, and/or gas and/or water and/or telecommunications services and failure of supply may well halt production, albeit for 24/48 hours. If the damage at the power station or transformer sub-station, or the gas depot or the pumping station or the telephone exchange is due to *a peril insured against under the policy* and this interruption of supply results in a loss of production, there would be a claim under the policy, provided the extension had been added to the policy.

Perhaps the lost production can be made up by overtime or weekend working and the additional cost may well be regarded as Increase in Cost of Working. Some factories operate round the clock and it becomes impossible to make good the lost production – the Insurer will pay loss of gross profit on the shortage in turnover involved.

The wording used is:

Property at any	Limit
[generating station or sub-station of the public electricity supply undertaking]	....
[land based premises of the public gas supply undertaking or of any natural gas producer linked directly therewith]	....

> [water works or pumping station of the public water supply undertaking]   ....
>
> [land based premises of the public telecommunications undertaking]   .... but in no case exceeding £..........................
>
> from which the Insured obtains (electricity)(gas)(water) or (telecommunications services) all in Great Britain or Northern Ireland.

This extension is subject to a limit of the percentage of the sum insured (or 133.3 per cent of the Estimated Gross Profit) and to an all-over limit.

If the Insured receives his power, gas or water from other than public sources, for example on an industrial estate which has its own power station or gas other than the public supply, it will be necessary to show this separately.

Cover set out in the extension above is linked to the same perils as are covered by the Insured's own policy. Until recently, the wider cover of "Failure of supply" was only available as part of an Engineering B/I policy, making it difficult for an Insured to have protection against "Accidental Failure", which might be the result of many things apart from the perils specified under the policy.

It is now possible to extend the B/I policy to include "Accidental Failure of the Public Supply of Electricity Gas Water or Telecommunications Services", the wording being as follows:

> Any loss as insured by (item nos of) this policy resulting from interruption of or interference with the Business in consequence of the Contingencies specified below shall be deemed to be an Incident provided that after the application of all other terms, conditions and provisions of the policy the liability under this memorandum in respect of any one occurrence shall not exceed –
> (a) the percentage of the total of the sums insured (or 133.3% of the Estimated Gross Profit) by (item nos of) the policy
>   or
> (b) the amount shown below against such Contingencies as the limit
>   shown below against such Contingencies as the limit

The Contingencies	Limit
The accidental failure of –	
[the public supply of electricity at the terminal ends of the supply undertaking's service feeders at the Premises]	....
[the public supply of gas at the supply undertaking's meters at the Premises]	....
[the public supply of water at the supply undertaking's main stop cock serving the Premises]	....
[the public supply of telecommunications services at the incoming line terminals or receivers at the Premises resulting from –	....
i) failure of satellites	.... but in no case exceeding
ii) failure from any other cause]	£..........................

in Great Britain or Northern Ireland

but excluding any failure -

i) which does not involve a cessation of supply for at least .... consecutive minutes/hours
ii) due to an Excluded Clause

Excluded Causes

(1) Loss resulting from –

a) failure caused by –
   i) the deliberate act of any supply undertaking or by the exercise by any such undertaking of its power to withhold or restrict supply or services
   ii) strikes or any labour or trade dispute
   iii) drought
   iv) other atmospheric or weather conditions, but this shall not exclude failure due to damage to equipment caused by such conditions
b) failure of any satellite prior to its attaining its full operating function or whilst in or beyond the final year of its design life.
c) temporary interference with transmissions to and from satellites due to atmospheric, weather solar or lunar conditions
d) failure due to the transfer of the Insured's satellite facility to another party.

Excluded Causes Nos. 2, 3 and 4 are the Standard Exclusions of War and kindred risks, Radioactive Contamination and Explosive Nuclear Assemblies and Terrorism in Northern Ireland respectively, slightly amended.

12.13 PROFESSIONAL INSURED – DOCUMENTS

Documents, be they projects, accounts, plans, specifications or any similar material are valuable, not for their intrinsic value, but for what they represent and their loss or damage or destruction could entail severe dislocation. Protection against the eventuality that an Incident involving documents belonging to the Insured when they are away from Insured's Premises – for instance account books collected regularly by an outside firm of accountants for making up – is available and the policy can be endorsed with the following extension wording:

> Documents belonging to or held in trust by the Insured whilst temporarily at premises not in the occupation of the Insured or whilst in transit, all in Great Britain or Northern Ireland.

No limit applies.

12.14 SPECIFIED CUSTOMERS

A manufacturer may find that a customer is unable to accept delivery of a product due to an Incident at the customer's premises. If the manufacturer has little or no other outlet for his products, suspension of delivery to the customer could be a disastrous situation. Payment of the loss based on shortage in Turnover will meet the cost of the standing charges and the payroll, but, perhaps of equal importance, is the availability of "Increase in Cost of Working" to help meet the cost of seeking and supplying an alternative market, which is much more difficult to find than obtaining alternative suppliers.

The wording used is:

> The premises (situate in Great Britain or Northern Ireland) of the following customers(s) (situate):–

A limit applies.

2.15 UNSPECIFIED CUSTOMERS

An Insured may well feel that the naming of his customers is insufficient to deal with a potential loss and therefore wishes to have unrestricted cover by extending the insurance to Unspecified Customers. The wording recommended is:

> The premises of any (other) of the Insured's   Limit ....
> customers situate in Great Britain   but in no case
> or Northern Ireland   exceeding £.........
>
> Provided that for the purposes of this extension the term 'customers' means those companies, organisations or individuals with whom, at the time of the Incident, the Insured has contracts or trading relationships to supply goods or services.

2.16 BOMB SCARES

The reader will be aware from all that has gone before that, in most cases, before a business interruption policy can come into operation there must be an "Incident", either to the property owned or occupied by the Insured or by his supplier/customer etc.

In recent years, the growing tendency to violence and the threat of the use of explosive devices has become more prevalent. Department stores, in particular, have been the target of real threat and also of the telephoned warning, which in most cases proved to be a hoax. Loss of trade in these circumstances is inevitable as shoppers are prevented from reaching or entering the premises.

Naturally, cover has been sought in the market, though this type of insurance is only undertaken to a limited extent. Insurers normally look for a time excess, say 12 hours, from the time of the occurrence. A specimen wording is as follows:

> The premises or any part thereof, or any other premises in the vicinity including rights of way being:
> (a) occupied by terrorists;
> (b) unlawfully occupied by third parties EXCEPT in the course of a trade dispute;
> (c) closed down or sealed off in accordance with instructions issued (1) by the Police or (2) by any statutory body except where the cause of such

closing or sealing off is the condition of the business carried on within the property or any other premises owned or occupied by the Insured;
- (d) thought to contain or actually containing an explosive or incendiary or toxic gas device;
- (e) Sealed off by the appropriate authority due to gas leaks.

12.17 REMINDER

These are useful and, on occasion, vital extensions of the cover, but it must be remembered that the cover away from Insured's premises is no wider than that which applies to the main insurance (except for the special cases outlined above). The Material Damage Proviso does not, of course, apply.

13 Special covers

Increase in Cost of Working Only – Additional Increase in Cost of Working – Advance Profits – Book Debts – Research Establishments – Engineering Business Interruption Insurance – Computers – Exhibitions – Gross Revenue.

3.01 INCREASE IN COST OF WORKING ONLY

Professional people, such as architects and solicitors, are not necessarily restricted to operating from any particular premises. In the event of an Incident occurring to the premises to the extent that it was necessary to move elsewhere, there could be little effect on the income of the firm, but there might be a heavy drain on the capital available to pay for the cost of transfer to alternative accommodation and the expenses connected with the move, such as postage to advise clients their new address, urgent installation of telephones, overtime working to catch up after the move and other expenses such as moving or installing new computer equipment.

Cover is available in the shape of "Increase in Cost of Working Only", designed to provide the money needed in these circumstances. The sum insured is the amount estimated to be required in the event of having to move in consequence of an Incident and some Insurers place a limit on the amount, say 50 per cent of the sum insured, which will be paid in the first three months, the balance of the amount being spread over the ensuing months of a Maximum Indemnity Period, as necessary. This is done to ensure that an adequate sum insured is obtained, as average cannot apply.

It must, however, be emphasised that today most service industries – and this includes tour operators, theatre ticket agencies, the provision of home shopping services and taxi cab services – rely heavily on computer services for the maintenance of their business.

Many have powerful computers on site or rely on a database for their operation and loss of this equipment and/or the database is likely to lead to a significant loss of income.

The office revolution has led to the extensive use of and reliance on electric and electronic equipment, including facsimile machines, access to networks and electronic mail, and high speed accountancy.

While some professional Insured might be able to catch up on lost work, many of the other businesses engaged in the service industries would be quite unable to operate until re-equipped and will suffer a loss which cannot be made good, except by insurance.

Consideration should therefore be given to covering loss of income (or fees) under a "Revenue" policy in the same way as loss of Gross Profit is normally covered. (For wording, see Appendix 13.)

A further expense which may be incurred is the cost of replacing deeds and documents destroyed in the course of the Incident and an item to cover this expense can be added to the policy. The item on legal and other costs and fees would also include cover for up to 10 per cent on deeds and documents while temporarily on premises not in the Insured's occupation – in other words, cover for deeds and documents which might get damaged or destroyed whilst in the care of someone else.

Note: When this type of cover is arranged, it is necessary to amend suitably the cover under the material damage insurance to avoid a possible overlap of cover on "Documents, Manuscripts and Business Books" included in the "All Other Contents" Memorandum on the material damage insurance. The material value of such records as stationery will normally continue to be covered under the material damage insurance.

In some cases a policy will be issued on:

Item 1. Loss of income (which will include the usual Increase in Cost of Working).
Item 2. Additional Increase in Cost of Working beyond that recoverable under Item 1.
Item 3. Cost of replacing deeds and documents.

Doctors and dentists at one time customarily worked from the front room of their (or someone else's) house. But the increased sophistication employed by the doctor or dentist has led to the creation of purpose-built surgeries with expensive equipment, such that in the event of a fire or any other catastrophe, there might be difficulty in finding alternative accommodation and, when found, considerable expense would be incurred in setting it up. In these circumstances, it might be felt that an Increase in Cost of Working Only policy will provide insufficient cover and a Revenue policy should be effected.

3.02 ADDITIONAL INCREASE IN COST OF WORKING

For some trades, the deadline is paramount. In magazine and newspaper publishing, for instance, the material must be available to the public at the right time. Failure to achieve this will result in loss of sales and the wrath, if nothing more, of the advertisers. Firms providing a regular service of groceries, ice cream etc., printers and drycleaners all wish to deliver on time even if it means paying a heavy additional cost or purchasing alternatives from "friendly" competitors.

Cover to meet this situation is available in the shape of "Additional Increase in Cost of Working". This is a sum over and above the amount available as part of the normal Increase in Cost of Working cover of the policy and can only come into use when the normal Increase in Cost of Working cover has been exhausted. This will usually be charged at the same rate as the Gross Profit item.

The Increase in Cost of Working cover provided by the policy is normally sufficient for most situations and only if there is a genuine need for this additional amount, should the cover be arranged. (See also section 8.20.)

3.03 ADVANCE PROFITS

The enlargement of existing premises, the installation of more up-to-date machinery or the creation of a new factory involves heavy capital expenditure, the main aim of which is to increase/improve production and, consequently, earn a greater Net Profit.

The Insured's Directors will have satisfied themselves that the capital is available, either from their own resources or from the finance market. If the latter, the Insured will have a contractual obligation to pay interest on the amount of money lent to them. Obviously the Insured would not have embarked on the scheme without being convinced that it made economic sense.

Plans are prepared, planning permission obtained and the work of construction or installation is put in hand. New machinery is ordered for delivery at the appropriate time and everyone confidently looks forward to the time when the expenditure of that capital starts to show results.

But all the effort put into the development could be negated if, following an Incident, the extension or the new machinery or the new factory is damaged or destroyed before the expected commencement date of production and the anticipated profit will, in consequence be lost.

It is always possible to obtain Advance Profits insurance, which would cover the loss of anticipated profit and the payment of the standing charges/payroll if, following the Incident, the repair or rebuilding could not be completed by the due date, resulting in the delay of the commencement of production. Increase in Cost of Working is also included, enabling reconstruction to be carried out as expeditiously as possible. The premium will depend on the length of time before the expected date of commencement of the new production that cover is requested for. It is preferable that the request for the cover is made as soon as the starting date of the alterations or the new construction is known.

Note an important difference between normal B/I insurance and Advanced Profits insurance. Under the latter, "Reduction in Turnover" applies from the planned date of the commencement of production, but the "Increase in Cost of Working" applies immediately after the occurrence of the Incident.

At the same time as the Advance Profits insurance is arranged, the Insurer should be approached to include in the cover both the Insured's machinery whilst under construction and the supplier's premises, in case an Incident causes delay in despatch and installation. Cover should also be sought for delay following breakdown of the Supplier's machinery.

To this cover should be added Transit insurance for the new machinery, to cover the journey from the machine manufacturer's premises to installation on Insured's premises. Most claims managers can tell horrendous stories of the effect on the turnover of a business of a new machine being involved in a collision on the road or of the machine being dropped whilst being installed on the Insured's premises. To allow for such contingencies, it may be necessary to have All Risks insurance.

One further important point is that arrangements must be made for the sum insured of the existing business interruption policy to be increased to cover the extra gross profit expected to be generated by the new premises. The Advance Profits policy "dies" immediately construction/installation is completed and the increase in the sum insured on the main policy must date from this point in time.

3.04 BOOK DEBTS

The business interruption policy covers the effect on the business of an Incident occurring to the premises – in other words, only the effect of a fire etc. on the turnover *after* the date of the Incident is envisaged by the policy.

If the Insured's books of account are destroyed or the computer disks are corrupted by the heat of the fire, it will be impossible for the Insured to prepare the monthly statements for the customers for work already done or goods supplied. Many customers will keep a low profile and just wait for the statement to appear! The outstanding amounts may be considerable. The firm cannot afford to forego them and will be faced with the expense of tracing the major debts and writing off those too small to warrant time being spent on them.

Protection for both the expense of tracing as many debts as possible and the untraceable amounts necessarily written off is available under Book Debts insurance, the wording for which will be found in Appendix 11.

Things to note are:
(1) The sum insured is the estimate of the outstanding Debit Balances.
(2) The initial premium is a provisional premium.
(3) The Insured must declare each month the amount outstanding. If the Insured fails to declare the full sum insured is assumed.
(4) When the 12 declarations for the year are received, a monthly average is calculated and the final premium agreed. If there has been an overpayment, the Insured will receive a refund not exceeding one half of the First or Annual Premium. In some special cases, a lower number of declarations (for example, quarterly) may be agreed.
(Since the initial premium is provisional, it is worth pitching the sum insured on the high side to ensure that in the event of loss, average will not apply.)
(5) There is usually a warranty in the policy that, when not in use, the records, disks etc. are stored in fireproof safes or cabinets.

(6) Once the debt has been established, the Insured is responsible for collecting the debt.
(7) The policy pays the amount of the untraced debts, based on the shortfall between the last declaration and amounts traced, adjusted to allow for special circumstances.
(8) Even though the Insured claims that he has duplicate books or good backup arrangements, the Incident will occur at the most inopportune time and, as the premium is not high, serious consideration must be given to effecting this insurance.

13.05 RESEARCH ESTABLISHMENTS

A Research and Development Establishment is fairly frequently found as an adjunct to a manufacturing concern. The R & D may be a straightforward research establishment engaged in pure research or in applied research with the object of producing a new product sometime in the future. The staff will, in the main, consist of highly trained scientists and technicians with very expensive equipment as their tools.

In a number of cases, the establishment will also be checking the quality of the incoming raw materials, coal and water, and exercising quality control of the manufacturing process.

The cost of maintaining an establishment for checking and quality control is bound up with the production of the goods sold and a fire or explosion or other insured peril which causes damage to the establishment could have an effect on production and turnover, giving rise to a claim under the business interruption policy.

But a fire in a pure research or applied research establishment will have little or no bearing on current production. It simply delays future production and profit, which is in any case problematic, as only a proportion of research will eventually end in production.

Although the research effort is curtailed or abruptly stopped, the standing charges in the shape of rent, rates, etc., and salaries to staff must continue, and a special policy for research establishments has been developed.

The policy will pay a weekly amount of one-fiftieth part of the Annual Research Establishment Expenditure to meet the cost of maintaining the R & D establishment and, in addition, provide cover for Increase in Cost of Working as a result of the Incident. It may well be necessary to seek alternative accommodation, if only on a temporary basis, and for staff to work overtime to make good the time lost in having to set up again and rework experiments where records have been lost.

The policy will also have an item in respect of the cost of renewing the records and, as mentioned in Section 13.01 under Increase in Cost of Working Only, some adjustment of the material damage insurance may be required.

Partial interruption is recognised by a proportionate payment of the weekly amount and any savings in consequence of the Incident are deducted from the payment.

The policy follows the standard method of incorporating the Other circumstances (trend) clause, proportionate reduction (average), an indemnity period and the adjustment of premium clause. A wording will be found in the Appendix 12.

13.06 ENGINEERING BUSINESS INTERRUPTION INSURANCE

While fire, explosion and kindred perils are a source of interruption of the productive capacity of a factory, a further potent source is the breakdown of a key machine or failure of supply of the Public Utilities, due to causes other than those which could be covered under Section 12.12.

The Engineering Business Interruption insurance policy is on similar lines to the normal business interruption policy, inasmuch as the same wording is used for loss of Gross Profit and Increase in Cost of Working.

The peril covered – ACCIDENT – is defined as:

---

1. Sudden and unforeseen damage from an accidental cause to a machine whilst at the situation shown against the machine in the schedule.
2. Failure of the supply of an Insured Public Utility at the terminal point of the supply undertaking's feed to any situation which is not caused by a deliberate act of the supply undertaking unless performed for the sole purpose of safeguarding life or protecting part of the supply undertaking's system or not caused by a scheme of rationing unless necessitated solely by physical damage to a part of the supply undertaking's system.

There are important exclusions:

Under 1 above: the "Period of Excess". This will be the period for which the Insurer will not be responsible. For instance – 72 hours' Period of Excess. If the breakdown causes the machine to be silent for up to 72 hours, nothing is payable. If the machine takes 90 hours to be rendered fit to resume, Insurers will pay 90 – 72 = 18 hours' stoppage. The Period of Excess starts as soon as the machine breaks down. If this occurred on Friday afternoon and the machine would in any case have been silent for the weekend, the Period of Excess still starts as soon as the breakdown occurs, unless an adjustment has been made to the policy wording.

Under 2 above: the Period of Franchise. This is slightly different from Period of Excess. Assume 72 hours Franchise. If the breakdown lasts up to 72 hours nothing is payable. If however the failure of supply exceeds the agreed franchise of 72 hours, then the *total* number of hours that there is a failure of supply will be eligible for the claim. It will be apparent that the Insured has no control of the length of time which it takes for the supply undertaking to resume supplies.

The object of the Excess and the Franchise is to avoid petty losses and make the Insured a "partner" in the insurance, by arranging for him to carry the first period. Obviously, good maintenance will prevent minor breakdowns and the insurance will not be involved in what is probably maintenance cost. The length of the Excess will also affect the premium charged.

The insurance differs from Fire B/I insurance inasmuch as:

(1) usually, only the key machines will be insured and they will be nominated in the policy:
(2) the Maximum Indemnity Period is much shorter – up to perhaps 3 months only for many businesses.

The rating will take into account:
(1) the extent to which the machines are key machines;
(2) the origin of the machines to be insured;
(3) the history of breakdown of the machines;
(4) the level of spares carried and the repair or standby facilities available;
(5) the probable replacement time; and
(6) the quality of any maintenance staff employed by the Insured.

Apart from "key" machines, the insurance can apply to a wide range of other equipment including boilers, gas/oil engines, electric motors, lifts and cranes.

The reader will be surprised to note that there is no Material Damage Proviso, but no doubt the importance of material damage insurance will be stressed when the insurance is arranged.

The wider cover under "Failure of Supply" will mean that there is no necessity to include the extension to Public Utilities (electricity, gas and water and telecommunications systems), but this must be discussed with the Broker or Insurer, as differences do exist between Insurers. (See also Section 12.12.)

The initial premium is provisional. After the annual accounts are published, the Insured will be required to provide a certificate of the details needed to establish the actual Gross Profit earned during the year of insurance. It is prudent to establish a sum insured at the outset of the insurance which will be in excess of possible requirements, as, under the Rebate Clause, up to 50 per cent of the premium paid can be returned. The policy may be subject to "Average", as with some Fire/B/I policies.

13.07 COMPUTERS

Computers can be insured under a "package" policy, which covers both material damage loss – "Material Damage" – and the effect of the loss of use of the computer – termed "Consequences of Damage".

The material damage insurance will include:
(1) Accidental Damage, excluding the cost of reinstatement of data; and
(2) Breakdown, excluding damage caused by fire or any other cause external to the item of Property (i.e. the Computer, excluding the tapes, disks etc.) and the cost of reinstatement of data.

The terms "Accidental Damage" and "Breakdown" are defined in the policy.

Under Consequences of Damage, the perils of Accident and Breakdown include Accidental Damage, or Breakdown, or Failure of Electricity or Prevention of Access.

Insured can choose to insure:
(1) increase in cost of working only; or
(2) loss of Revenue; or
(3) loss of Gross Profit.

The wording follows the B/I policy wording and includes automatic reinstatement of the sum insured following a loss, the Insured agreeing to pay the appropriate additional premium.

Cover may also be required and obtained for loss following breakdown of the associated software and hardware, and the air conditioning equipment.

There is no generally accepted wording for this type of cover, so it may be that smaller details of the cover will vary from Insurer to Insurer.

13.08 EXHIBITIONS

Exhibitions provide an interesting example of the various types of B/I cover required. A number of different interests are involved, the main ones being:
(1) the proprietor of the exhibition building(s) and/or grounds;
(2) the organiser of exhibitions;
(3) the exhibitors;
(4) the caterers;
(5) the car park lessees, if the running of the car park has been leased to a separate organisation.

13.09 EXHIBITION PROPRIETORS

The proprietors of the exhibition building(s) and/or grounds may be:
(1) merely concerned with letting the premises to exhibition organisers, in which case a Revenue policy would be appropriate. Damage to the property could involve loss of revenue, which would form the basis of the claim, with Increase in Cost of Working available to speed up repairs, if economically viable;
(2) exhibitors in their own right, for example, safari parks and leisure centres. A normal B/I policy would be suitable, special consideration being given to ensure that a long enough Maximum Indemnity Period is chosen.

13.10 EXHIBITION ORGANISERS

The organisers lease the exhibition premises from the exhibition proprietors and sub-lease space to the exhibitors. An Incident affecting the Premises could involve them in loss of rent and a revenue policy would be appropriate.

Additional cover should be arranged to cover the general expenses involved in the advertising etc. of the exhibition, which would be lost as a result of the exhibition being cancelled due to an Incident affecting the premises.

13.11 EXHIBITORS

Exhibitors caught up in the cancellation of the exhibition due to an Incident affecting the premises, face losses under two heads.
There will be:
(1) loss of the costs incurred in mounting the exhibition stand. For this, a short period policy should be arranged;
(2) loss of gross profit due to the cancellation of the exhibition. It is possible to extend the normal B/I policy to cover the exhibition but underwriters would wish to be certain that turnover would be lost in consequence of the cancellation and that evidence would be available afterwards to support the claim.

13.12 STAND FITTERS

These firms would normally have an office and a workshop as a base and their B/I policy can be extended to cover sites on which they are working under contract. (See Section 12.10.)

13.13 CATERERS ON EXHIBITION PREMISES

The caterers will face a loss of revenue as a result of the cancellation of the exhibition and their B/I policy should be extended to include premises on which they operate.

13.14 CAR PARK LESSEES

The official car park for the exhibition may well be on separate premises, adjoining or near to the exhibition premises. Cancellation of the exhibition will involve loss of car park fees and the B/I insurance should include "Prevention of Access" and "Loss of Attraction". (See Section 12.11.)

13.15 GROSS REVENUE

Professional people, such as solicitors, architects and surveyors, receive their income as fees. There is very little in the way of uninsured working expenses and the income is virtually all "Gross Profit". To define more clearly the amount insured, the term "Gross Revenue" is adopted.

The cover can be either on a Sum Insured or Declaration Linked basis; a specimen of the latter will be found as Appendix 13.

14 Insurance of Wages using "Dual Basis"; and "All Risks" Insurance

14.01 BACKGROUND TO DUAL BASIS WAGES

As discussed earlier in Chapter 11, social changes and legislation which does not distinguish between the wage earning and salaried employee when it comes to layoff or dismissal have combined to change the basis of the insurance of wages and salaries. The reader will recall that the combined total was labelled "Payroll" and included in the Gross Profit item.

But in a number of countries outside the UK there is not the same pressure on the employer to provide substantial sums by way of notice and redundancy for those whose services have to be dispensed with, and the need to retain a sizable body of skilled staff on the books during the rebuilding of the business is not so pressing.

So the 100 per cent cover provided by Payroll is frequently found to be unduly expensive for the cover really needed and "Dual Basis" for the insurance of Wages payable to the factory employees is regarded as adequate, but the Dual Basis cover can also be used for Payroll, i.e. Wages and Salaries.

The theory behind Dual Basis is that the employer needs cover for the time immediately after the date of the Damage, during which he will be faced with paying up to 100 per cent of the wage roll for some weeks. This period is necessary to assess the extent of the damage and to estimate the time needed before production can be resumed.

When plans for recovery are completed, consideration has to be given to the level of the workforce which will be retained and to those for whom there is no prospect of work until the premises and machinery have been reinstated.

148   *Business Interruption Insurance: Theory and Practice*

The skilled staff will be retained to make sure they are available when the new machinery is installed. The advancement of technology means that it is likely that a more sophisticated machine will replace the damaged equipment and some retraining, even of skilled employees, may be necessary. Equally, no employer would wish to see his skilled staff, in whom he has invested time and money, transferring their allegiance to a competitor.

Those for whom no work will be available in the foreseeable future will need to be paid notice and severance pay, if that is the custom or the law.

14.02 ARRANGEMENT OF COVER

The liability of the employer for the payment of wages can, therefore, be expressed as 100 per cent for x number of weeks (say 13), as in Fig. 8.

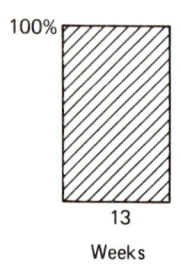

Fig. 8   Employer's wages liability, 100 per cent of wages for 13 weeks.

Following the departure of those whose services have been terminated, the employer will continue to pay the wage earners retained and it will be necessary for him to estimate what *percentage of his wage roll* (not how many heads) will need to be protected. Shall we say 25 per cent bearing in mind that it is the expensive wage earners who will be retained.

So now the diagram of cover required looks like Fig. 9:

The Insured will ask his Insurers to arrange cover for 100 per cent of his wage roll for 13 weeks and for 25 per cent of the wage roll for the remainder of the Indemnity Period of (say) 12 months. It means, of course, that an underestimation of the Initial Period (the first 13

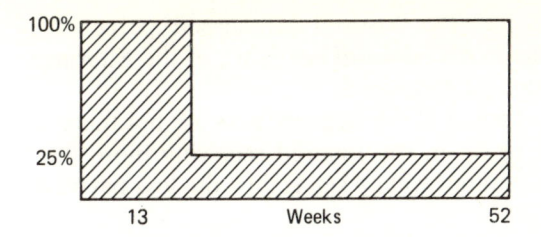

Fig. 9 Employer liable for 100 per cent of wage roll for 13 weeks and 25 per cent for the rest of the year.

weeks) or the level (in this case 25 per cent) of the wage roll for the Remainder Period will result in the employer paying the shortfall himself.

As will be seen from the diagrams, the Insured has bought two areas of cover – the Initial Period and the Remainder Period. Insurers appreciate that when the insurance is arranged it is only possible to estimate the likely extent of any Damage to the factory and, consequently, some flexibility of the cover is required. Who knows, really, how many of the work force will be there to receive their wages – some may feel that the prospect of the firm restarting may be slim – competition is fierce and the firm may lose their share of the market. So they leave, preferring to obtain other employment and their wages will not be paid – hence "Savings".

4.03 DEFINITION OF WAGES

Wages are defined in the Dual Basis Specification as:

> The remuneration (including national insurance, bonuses, holiday pay and other payments pertaining to wages) of all employees (other than those whose remuneration is treated as salaries in the Insured's books of account)...

Note: If using Dual Basis Payroll, salaries would not be excluded.

4.04 OPERATION OF DUAL BASIS

Wages represent an identifiable proportion of the turnover and, consequently, as we saw with the payment of a loss under Gross

150 *Business Interruption Insurance: Theory and Practice*

Profit, it is possible to pay the Insured an agreed percentage (ascertainable from the Insured's books of account), of the Shortage in Turnover, as Indemnity.

Payment of full wages, if some of the wage earners are not there to receive their money, will result in the Insured receiving more than indemnity and this excess amount will be set against the loss payment and labelled "Savings".

The desired flexibility is achieved by promising the Insured that if the cover in the Remainder Period is insufficient, "Savings" in the Initial Period can be transferred to the Remainder Period for his benefit. This is known as "carry over proviso".

If the insured found himself able to effect savings in the initial period these would be carried over to the remainder period

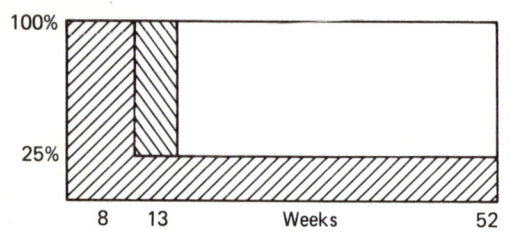

This would enable him to employ additional staff in the remainder period

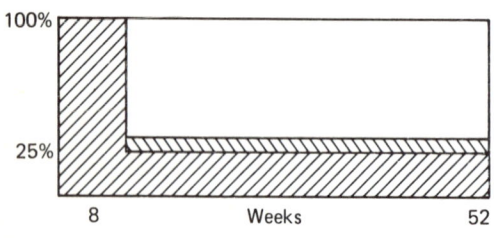

Fig. 10 Savings can help achieve flexibility between the initial period and the remainder period.

14.05 CONSOLIDATION

Can this flexibility operate in the other direction? Can the Initial Period when 100 per cent cover is needed, be extended? The answer

Insurance of Wages: "Dual Basis" and "All Risks" 151

is "Yes it can", the method being to consolidate the cover into 100 per cent for a longer Initial Period, at the same time, sacrificing or reducing the limited cover of the Remainder Period. And in many cases, where the length of the interruption exceeds the Initial Period selected by just a few weeks, the Consolidation will provide the better indemnity. This extended Initial Period is known as the Alternative Period and the number of weeks of cover will be stated in the policy. Tables showing the conversion of Initial/Remainder Period into the Alternative Period are available in most offices, where Dual Basis cover is provided.

This policy states the consolidation period, in this case 19 weeks:

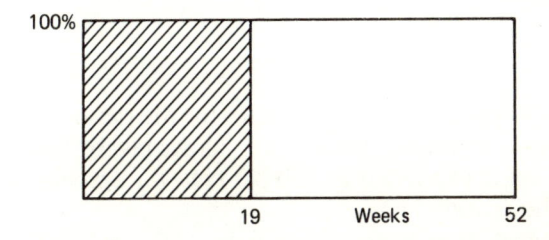

Fig. 11 An alternative method: consolidation provides cover for 19 weeks.

One last point on the flexibility of the cover. If there are Savings in the Alternative Period (100 per cent for 19 weeks) and the Insured is still suffering some loss after 19 weeks, these Savings can be utilised as far as they will go to assist the Insured during the period after the end of the Alternative Period, the equivalent of the Remainder Period.

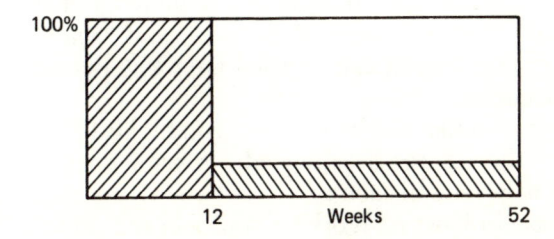

Fig. 12 Yet more flexibility. Savings from the alternative period may be used as far as they will go.

14.06 INCREASE IN COST OF WORKING

Wages are an integral part of Turnover. It follows that, if Wages are taken out of Gross Profit and insured as a separate item, the Wages item must bear its share of Increase in Cost of Working.

In a loss settlement, Increase in Cost of Working is initially paid up to the Economic Limit of the Gross Profit item, any amount disallowed falling to be considered under the Wages item.

The operation of this aspect of Dual Basis Wages is set out in the Loss Settlement in the Appendices.

14.07 SUMMARY

To sum up -
(1) The Insured buys 100 per cent cover for wages for the period of weeks, representing his estimated liability for full wages for this period, the liability being expressed as 100 per cent for x weeks. This is known as the *Initial Period*.
(2) The Insured estimates what proportion of the wage roll will need to be paid after the end of the Initial Period for the balance of the Indemnity Period. This is expressed as a percentage of the wage roll and the period is known as the *Remainder Period*.
(3) The Insurers agree that Savings in the Initial Period can be made available in the Remainder Period. It is usually found, in fact, that the Savings provide benefit towards the end of the Indemnity Period, when a virtually full staff is not achieving a 100 per cent output.
(4) The Insurers agree that if the result is more favourable to the Insured they will consolidate the cover to give a longer Initial Period – now known as the *Alternative Period* – and, again, Savings in the Alternative Period can be used after this Period by the Insured, if needed.
(5) It must never be forgotten that the Insured is buying PARTIAL cover and, however the figures are juggled, an inadequately arranged insurance is never satisfactory.
(6) If part of the Increase in Cost of Working is disallowed under the Gross Profit item, it will fall to be considered under the Wages item.

14.08 PAYROLL ON DUAL BASIS

It should be noted that occasionally it is decided to place the Payroll (Wages and Salaries) on Dual Basis. It is sometimes felt that in the event of Damage causing an interruption in production, it would be possible to discharge not only wage earners, but salaried staff as well, without impairing the productive capacity of the firm.

Obviously, since Dual Basis provides partial cover only, the cost is usually less than the full insurance with Payroll and it becomes even more important that the greatest care is exercised in selecting the appropriate basis for the Initial and Remainder Periods.

14.09 LOSS SETTLEMENT

A worked example of loss settlement under Dual Basis will be found in Appendix 6.

14.10 "ALL RISKS" INSURANCE

Whilst the wide cover provided by the policy with the whole range of special perils added was regarded as adequate for most purposes, competition dictated that even wider cover should be offered.

This wider cover is provided by the "All Risks" policy, a specimen wording of which will be found in Appendix 2. The operative wording is:

> The Insurer agrees ... that if ... any building or other property used by the Insured at the Premises for the purpose of the Business be accidently lost destroyed or damaged ... and in consequence the business carried on by the Insured at the Premises be interrupted or interfered with ...

The words "*accidently lost destroyed or damaged*" provide very wide cover, only restricted by the exclusions, which will be examined below.

The material damage proviso follows the usual lines, provision being made for the situation where the material damage insurance is subject to an excess or a deductible. (See Section 6.09 et seq.)

The exclusions fall under three main heads.

(1) The usual exclusions under an "All Risks" insurance: corrosion, rot, vermin, electrical or mechanical breakdown etc.
(2) The usual exclusions found in the recommended wording of the B/I policy: property undergoing any heating process or any process involving the application of heat, war, invasion etc., radioactive contamination, pollution or contamination
(3) The specific exclusions of:
   (i) theft or attempted theft;
   (ii) acts of fraud or dishonesty;
   (iii) cover found under an engineering policy (boilers etc);
   (iv) subsidence;
   (v) damage to fixed glass;
   (vi) damage to computers and data processing equipment.

The policy can be extended to include (i) theft, (iv) subsidence and (v) damage to fixed glass on payment of an additional premium. The remainder are dealt with by means of separate policies.

This new "All Risks" policy wording has been the subject of an interesting innovation – the proximate cause overrider.

Under an "All Risks" insurance, the Doctrine of Proximate Cause means that all losses must be met by the Insurer unless the Proximate Cause is stated to be an Exclusion.

Because an "All Risks" insurance provides the widest possible cover, there must be Exclusions if the Insurer is not to be faced with a multitude of claims which would normally be regarded as outside the scope of insurance.

But, if the loss due to a peril normally regarded as insurable is followed by an excluded peril, then, technically, the liability of the Insurer ceases when the second peril operates.

This may not be the Insurer's real intention and, to overcome the problem, two definitions have been introduced.

---

1   The words "CONSEQUENTIAL LOSS", in capital letters, shall mean loss resulting from interruption of or interference with the Business carried on by the Insured at the Premises in consequence of accidental loss or destruction of or damage to property used by the Insured at the Premises for the purpose of the Business.

> 2 The words "Defined Peril" shall mean fire, lightning, explosion, aircraft... *the familiar special perils*

Three of the groups of EXCLUSIONS are followed by a proximate cause overrider and the reader is referred to the full wording in the Appendices. To take one example – corrosion. Under EXCLUSIONS the wording states:

> This policy does not cover...
>
> 2 CONSEQUENTIAL LOSS
> 2.1 caused by or consisting of corrosion, rust, wet or dry rot, shrinkage, evaporation, loss of weight, dampness, dryness, marring, scratching, vermin or insects...
> but this shall not exclude
> (a) such CONSEQUENTIAL LOSS not otherwise excluded which itself results from a Defined Peril or from any other accidental loss destruction or damage

Where corrosion (which is itself excluded) results from exposure to acid which escapes from accidently punctured containers, the exclusion would be overridden. Where, however, the acid escapes from pipework which fractures through normal wear and tear, then because this is a separate, excluded cause, the overrider would not operate and payment of a claim would be refused.

As shown in Appendix 2, the wording provides for the situation where there is a Deductible under the Material Damage insurance and caters for an Insured who wishes to have a Deductible under the B/I policy.

The policy conditions follow the normal B/I wording, being grouped into General Conditions and Claims Conditions.

15 Employing a Broker

Interview between Client and Broker – Completion of proposal form

15.01 BROKERS AND THEIR DUTIES

In previous chapters, we have sometimes referred to "your broker or consultant", and we feel that at this point we should expand upon this subject.

The more usual practice for an insurance of consequence is to employ the services of a firm of Insurance Brokers (this term will also be used to describe Principals within the firm).

A firm of Insurance Brokers must be able to provide professional advice on arranging insurances, to obtain the most appropriate cover and to place the business in the most suitable market. It should provide details of the fullest cover and such options and alternatives as may be available. It is for you, the Insured, to decide if you wish to accept the full cover or restrict the cover to obtain a lower premium.

Before either a firm, or a person within the firm, can use the term, or trade as an Insurance Broker, they must be registered by the Insurance Brokers Registration Council, a body set up to administer the provisions of the Insurance Brokers (Registration) Act 1977.

The Act sets out certain standards and requirements both as regards financial and other standards with which the firm and its Principals must comply, the object of which is to ensure policyholders' interests are adequately safeguarded and that they are represented by appropriately qualified persons.

Brokers may be members of one or more of the trade associations, the principal one being the British Insurance and Investment Brokers' Association (BIIBA), whose main offices are BIIBA House, 14 Bevis Marks, London EC3A 7NT.

Some brokers have joined a smaller, but growing, organisation called the Institute of Insurance Brokers. Their offices are at Higham Business Centre, Midland Road, Higham Ferrars NN9 8DW.

Many brokers are also Lloyd's Brokers.

Lloyd's is an important sector of the insurance market but, by its Constitution, syndicates can only underwrite business through the intermediary of a Lloyd's Broker.

Lloyd's have their own operational rules and standards and these include the regulation of Lloyd's Brokers. Other brokers wishing to place business at Lloyd's must first find a Lloyd's Broker willing to represent them, since it is the Lloyd's Broker who is responsible to the Underwriters, and to Lloyd's, for business placed by them.

In the context of insurance, an agent is a firm or person, other than a broker, with whom an Insurer is prepared to deal as an intermediary. It can be anyone who has the opportunity to influence the Insured as to with whom the insurance is placed. The agent receives a commission from the insurance company for directing the business to them. The number of such agents is diminishing with the increasing legislation requiring professional qualifications and standards of all legal, financial and other representatives.

The benefits of using an Insurance Broker can easily be seen.

(1) They are not tied to obtaining cover from one source, but can use the full market.
(2) They must have experience and knowledge of all classes of insurance from which to advise on the cover needed to give the best degree of protection following any contingency, and can obtain alternative quotations to ensure the most economical cost commensurate with a satisfactory market.
(3) They will check all documents received from Insurers to see that they correctly express the cover negotiated.
(4) In some cases they will have their own Fire Surveyors, not only to provide information for underwriters but also to advise on fire protection, to discuss the Interruption position following a fire and to help decide the length of the Maximum Indemnity Period.
(5) They will be responsible for discussions before each renewal date to consider whether the cover then current is still correct and arranging alternatives, especially watching for the necessary increase in the sum insured.

(6) Should a claim arise, they will also assist in the compilation, submission and negotiation with the adjuster, who will be appointed by the Insurers.

Although the Broker receives his income by way of commission from the Insurers, he is *the client's* agent and not that of the Insurers.

15.02 INITIAL DISCUSSION OF THE B/I INSURANCE WITH A BROKER

It will be apparent to you from previous chapters the type of question which will be asked by a broker to enable him to place the cover and to obtain competitive quotations. However, for ease of reference, we are listing the major points which will enable him to prepare a single document (known as a slip) to place before underwriters.

(1) It is possible that you will be discussing material damage insurance with the same broker who will already be in possession of full details giving the construction, occupation, etc., of the premises and may already have a fire surveyor's report. If not, it will be necessary to obtain details from the material damage insurers or for him to complete his own fire surveyor's report.

(2) Information will be required as to the present insurance arrangements and confirmation that no insurance business has been declined or renewal refused. If there are any such declinatures, full details will be required and failure to give such information may invalidate this insurance. Information will also be required of any claims which have been made against Insurers for risks similar to those which are at present being proposed.

(3) What are the perils insured by the material damage insurance? Is it desired to include all the same perils under the B/I policy? The answer should be "Yes"

(4) Is there cover against Engineering Breakdown or is there an Inspection Contract? Is it desired to have a quotation for B/I following a breakdown or failure of public utilities? (This cover can now be added to the Fire B/I policy.)

(5) The Broker will, after discussion, guide the client as to the definition of Gross Profit and whether the standard definition requires amendment for specific circumstances.

(6) The Broker will consider the length of time that it would take to get the client back to the full level of activity after the worst possible fire. This period would normally be adopted as the Maximum Indemnity Period under the policy.
(7) What was the Gross Profit figure, as it will be defined in the policy, in the last financial year?
What is the figure estimated for the coming financial year?
Is the business expected to expand in the next two years and what is the estimate of that expansion?
(8) Are all the premises to be included in the insurance? If not, why not?
(9) Are all of the activities to be included in the insurance?
(10) Are there any other items of income, such as Rents Receivable, to be included in the cover under the policy? You will recall that it is recommended that such items should be insured separately from the Gross Profit.
(11) Are any extensions of cover required, for example to Suppliers and/or Customers?
(12) Are any special covers required, for example, Book Debts?

It is obvious that these headings are not exhaustive and each Broker (or Company) will have their own methods of approaching the discussion and, in fact, may send a pro-forma to complete in advance of the discussions. The Aide Memoire which we have included after Chapter 17 goes into greater details of the points which may be raised either by the client or the Broker and where you may require fuller information.

15.03 COMPLETION OF THE PROPOSAL FORM

The completion of a proposal form is not usually required for most major Insureds. The information which is needed to place the business with insurers is obtained in discussion and then should be confirmed to the Insured and to Insurers in correspondence.

If it is a new insurance and the Insurers have not had any previous connection with the Insured, some Insurers might require completion of a proposal form to enable them to have on record the signature of the Insured to the statement that they have not had any declinatures and for information as to any previous losses.

If a Broker has placed the business, it is usually accepted that he is responsible for having satisfied himself on this matter. He would presumably have this on record in correspondence.

For smaller insurances which are often included in an overall package, for example, hotels, retail risks and small industrial risks, the completion of a combined proposal form is usual, but the B/I section would be only one small part of the proposal form. It provides a useful method of ensuring that all information is available and that the cover is as complete as possible.

16 Brief Thoughts on Risk Management

16.01 INTRODUCTION

Business Interruption insurance is concerned with the after-effects of a fire, explosion or other Incident causing damage to the premises and their contents, and with the steps taken to get the business on its feet again.

Risk management seeks to protect the assets and profitability of the business as economically as possible. The two concepts of insurance and risk management go hand-in-hand, since measures taken to reduce the loss and the level of interruption or interference should a loss happen, have a marked effect on the size of the claims sustained.

Profits depend on uninterrupted production, so it is not out of place to consider briefly some of the steps which can be taken to reduce the hazards, and measures which will speed the return to normality should a loss occur.

The conventional risk management process is depicted in Fig. 13.

16.02 RISK IDENTIFICATION

Risk management starts when the Risk Manager identifies the various risks involved in a creative business. Loss by fire, explosion and theft come quickly to mind, followed by the after-effects of these perils. Other hazards such as the malfunctioning of the computer, machinery breakdown and the loss of supplies of raw materials from a variety of causes will also become apparent.

16.03 RISK ANALYSIS

The next stage is to take each risk in turn and decide:
(1)   the probability of occurrence;

The risk management process

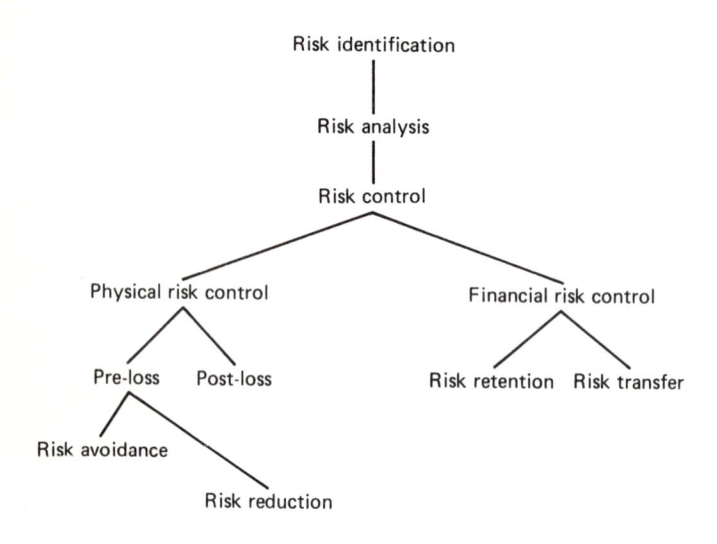

```
                    Risk identification
                            |
                      Risk analysis
                            |
                      Risk control
                     /            \
          Physical risk control    Financial risk control
           /         \              /            \
      Pre-loss    Post-loss    Risk retention  Risk transfer
       /     \
  Risk avoidance
            \
         Risk reduction
```

Fig. 13   Stages in the risk management process.

(2) the anticipated probable severity of the loss;
(3) the maximum probable severity of the loss.

Records of past claims give a guide to this analysis, as does a realistic appraisal of the likely extent of the damage.

16.04 PHYSICAL RISK CONTROL

The measures taken to control the physical risk can be divided between Pre-loss and Post-loss, with Pre-loss being further divided into Risk avoidance and Risk reduction

16.05 PRE-LOSS – RISK AVOIDANCE

This is the first of the "tools" of the Risk Manager. Can the risk be avoided? Is it possible, for instance, to eliminate the use of adhesives with a flammable base, substituting a safe adhesive? Can a hazardous process be removed from the main works and housed separately? Is it possible to substitute payment by cheque for payment in cash to reduce the theft risk and the possibility of a hold-up?

16.06 PRE-LOSS – RISK REDUCTION

Here the Risk Manager is aware of a risk but manufacture cannot be maintained without it. But it may be possible to reduce the hazard by, for instance, segregating the hazardous process.

The fire surveyor, during the inspection, will be on the lookout for possible measures of risk reduction and the surveyor's suggestions may well be linked to premium reduction.

Electricity is high in the table of causes of fire and arrangements for the regular check of all wiring will greatly reduce the possibility of fire due to overloading of cables, poor insulation, faulty connections and earthing.

The Fire Protection Association recommends that every employee should be made responsible for their own area and charged with the duty of shutting off the power to their own machines when work ceases. This responsibility can be backed up by a security patrol carried out when the premises are empty to ensure that potential hazards are eliminated.

Study of the Journal of the Fire Protection Association – *Fire Prevention* – shows that most of the causes of loss lie with failure to maintain a high standard of housekeeping. Fires break out after the premises have been vacated and, in consequence, have obtained a firm hold by the time the alarm is given, due to the presence of uncleared rubbish.

Steps should also be taken to check the perimeter protection. Gaps in fences, unsecured gates in walls and unsecured windows invite intruders. Arson is now one of the major causes of fires and however good the internal housekeeping, all will be lost if the arsonist can effect an entry.

Still in the field of risk reduction, are steps taken to safeguard supplies of raw materials and packing? On-site storage should be divided if possible, so that fire will not wipe out the entire stockholding at one time. Checking the source of supplies can reveal that key items are supplied by one firm only. Should steps be taken to arrange an alternative source, so that a fire at a supplier's premises will not starve the factory of raw materials? (Should a supplier's extension be added to the policy?)

Planned maintenance is another area of risk reduction, particularly of key machines. The possibility of breakdown and injury to employees is reduced; trouble free runs are a major contribution to profitability.

16.07 POST-LOSS RISK CONTROL

Steps can be taken to reduce the amount of the loss, if it occurs, by installing fire alarms, sprinklers and other firefighting equipment. Other measures are the fitting of fireproof doors to openings and roof vents to the roofs.

Finally, Disaster Planning, almost a subject in its own right. Everyone on the premises must be aware of their responsibility if fire breaks out, or when the fire bell is sounded. Summoning the fire brigade, evacuation of the premises, shutting down and the protection of the records should be a matter of routine. The protection of the computer and the software should be carefully investigated.

In the aftermath of the fire, the Disaster Plan should be put into action. Protection of the premises from intruders and from the weather needs prompt action. Measures to restart production will have been discussed with the loss adjuster. It is to be hoped that the records have been saved and customers can be notified by a carefully worded letter that some delay in fulfilling their orders may be expected but that urgent steps to resume production are being taken.

Where a computer forms the basis of the business, thought must be given to alternative computer facilities, possibly joining a syndicate which maintains a "warm" computer.

Included in the Disaster Plan, which should be constantly updated, should be arrangements for the delegation of authority if senior management are not immediately available as well as the appointment of a press officer.

16.08 FINANCIAL RISK CONTROL

Financial risk control is divided into Risk Retention and Risk Transfer.

16.09 RISK RETENTION

The catastrophe potential of fire or explosion is such that it is likely that very few firms can afford carry the whole of the risk themselves.

A number will study the statistics of premiums and claims over the past (say) five years and decide to ask for a "Deductible", that is, they are willing to bear the first (say) £20 000 of each and every loss, with an annual aggregate of (say) £100 000. The "Deductible" may apply to the Material Damage insurance only or to both the Material Damage and the B/I.

In return, Insurers grant a discount off the premium.

6.07 RISK TRANSFER

It follows that even with a programme of risk reduction, the remaining risk is normally still too large to be acceptable to the firm concerned and transferring the risk is the only solution. Hence insurance.

6.08 SUMMARY

Active risk management can have positive results. Not only do clean and tidy premises present a lower fire hazard, thereby affecting the material damage fire rate and consequently the B/I premium, but, also, the good conditions have the effect of lifting the morale of the workforce. Potential hazards will be reported and pride taken in maintaining the standard.

Too many claims may well affect the attitude of the Insurers to the insurance.

17 Insurance concepts as applied to Business Interruption insurance

17.01 INTRODUCTION

Many people buy insurance without knowing very much about their purchase. The law says you must have Third Party insurance before you can take a car onto the road, the bank requires insurance of the security before it will grant a loan and the building society requires the house to be insured as part of the mortgage arrangements.

So what is insurance and why do people willingly, or unwillingly, buy it? In its simplest form it is transfer of risk. Payment of a regular premium will buy the promise that a loss from an insured cause up to an agreed amount will be paid within the terms of the policy.

For most people, that is the end of the matter. Having paid the premium, the subject crops up again only when the policy is due for renewal or if a loss takes place. It is to be hoped that, with good advice, the loss will be fully covered. Unfortunately, due to lack of knowledge or lack of cash or both, an unsatisfactory contract may be set up and the result, at best, is an unhappy policy holder, at worst, a business in disarray.

So what are the ground rules for this important aspect of running a business? We can consider them in the context of:
(1) the law of contract;
(2) a fair and equitable premium;
(3) insurable interest;
(4) utmost good faith;
(5) indemnity;
(6) proximate cause.

7.02 THE LAW OF CONTRACT

Insurance is a simple contract, an agreement between two parties, which each party regards as being legally binding.

The proposer will *offer* his proposal, either direct or through a broker or consultant, to the Insurer, who will quote a premium.

If the premium is quoted with no preconditions, this constitutes the *acceptance* and payment of the premium the *consideration*. If the premium is quoted with the requirement that, for instance, "all rubbish be removed from the yard at rear", this would be considered a *counter-offer* and it would be up to the Proposer to decide if the offer is to be accepted. Acceptance of the offer would be signified by payment of the premium.

The contract must be within the law and the parties must have the capacity to contract.

7.03 FAIR AND EQUITABLE PREMIUM

All the premiums received by Insurers are placed in "pools" or "funds" in respect of the different classes of insurance business. Claims are paid from the pools. In that way, Insurers can monitor the premiums received and the losses incurred to ensure that, as far as possible, each class pays its way and is not subsidised by other classes. The law requires Insurers to keep each type of business underwritten as a separate fund.

The statistics produced for each class of risk serve only to ensure that the pool remains solvent – it does not tell the underwriter what premium to charge for an individual risk. The premium charged is made up of two factors – a combination of

the amount at risk – measured by the sum insured and
the hazard involved – measured by the rate charged.

The term "rate" means the amount of premium to be paid for each £100 of sum insured. For example, a rate of 0.15 per cent means that the Insurer is charging 15 pence for each £100 of sum insured. Hence:

Sum insured × Rate = Premium.

The underwriter is assisted in his decision as to what level of rating to employ by a guide list of rates. These are based on a normal rate for that particular class of risk, that is for a risk with no particularly good or bad features, and to that normal rate will be added additional rates for features which increase the hazard. For instance, the premises may be occupied as an engineering workshop, which also does spray painting. The normal rate for the engineering workshop would be increased by the underwriter's judgement as to the additional hazard brought about by the spray painting.

Features which improve the risk will also be recognised by applying a discount to the premium, for instance, the installation of a sprinkler system would attract a very big discount.

The combination of penalties for features which increase the risk and discounts for features which reduce the hazard ensures that each Insured contributes a fair and equitable premium to the pool of premiums, from which the losses are paid.

It will be seen from the foregoing that where the sum insured is inadequate, the contribution to the pool or "common fund" is inequitable. The application of proportionate reduction (average) is the Insurer's way of securing fairness between all the policyholders.

17.04 INSURABLE INTEREST

A person or Company effecting an insurance contract must have a legal relationship to the subject matter of the insurance, such that they benefit from its safety, are prejudiced by its loss or can incur a liability from it.

Thus the owner of a business can insure against loss following damage or destruction of the premises. A limited liability company is an entity in its own right and shareholders, as such, cannot insure the premises or business interruption following loss. The responsibility for insurance would rest with the Directors.

17.05 UTMOST GOOD FAITH

Normal business relationships require that both sides deal fairly with one another. Unless asked, there is no duty to disclose defects, but any questions must be answered truthfully. And there should be no question of fraud or fraudulent intent.

Insurance on the other hand, has for centuries been governed by the doctrine of Utmost Good Faith. The proposer is presumed to know all the facts about the risk, the underwriter only knows what he is told. The doctrine requires the proposer to disclose all material particulars, a material particular being anything which would influence a prudent (now interpreted as 'reasonable') underwriter as to whether or not he would accept the risk and, if he did, what rate he would charge and what conditions should be imposed.

For business interruption insurance, this duty of utmost good faith may be slightly modified as premises of any size are usually surveyed. Nevertheless, the proposer must not mislead the surveyor.

The duty of utmost good faith commences with the proposal and ends when the contact is formed, that is, when the offer receives unqualified acceptance. The duty is revived at renewal and alterations or changes affecting the insurance, if not already advised, must be disclosed now. During the currency of the policy, Common Law merely requires Good Faith (not Utmost good Faith), but General Condition 2 reminds the Insured that "this policy shall be avoided if after commencement of this insurance any alteration be made either in the Business or in the Premises or property therein whereby the risk of loss destruction or damage is increased unless admitted by the Insurer in writing." It will be seen that Insurers regard notification of changes as having the utmost importance and therefore the duty of disclosure is made a continuing requirement.

7.06 INDEMNITY

Indemnity has been defined as putting the Insured, so far as is possible, in the same financial position after the loss as he was in immediately before the loss.

For business interruption insurance, this is amended to "the same financial position as would have been occupied had the Incident not occurred." This is to take into account the period after the loss until the effect of the interruption has ceased.

The Insured may receive less than indemnity if the insurance is not Declaration Linked and the sum insured is inadequate. The loss will be paid in proportion to the adequacy of the sum insured. (See "Fair and equitable premium" earlier in this Chapter, 17.03.)

The two corollaries of Indemnity are Contribution and Subrogation: neither of them is greatly involved in Business Interruption insurance.

Contribution requires that if there is more than one policy covering the same interest for the same peril, then the Insurers must each contribute to the loss, the contribution being based on the "independent liability" of each policy, that is, the liability of each policy as if it had been the only one covering the loss sustained. (See Section 7.17.)

Subrogation, as was explained in Section 7.18, is the Common Law right of an Insurer having paid a claim, "to stand in the shoes of the Insured to exercise all the rights and remedies available to the Insured, to recover the payment".

While this concept does not provide many problems for the material damage Insurer, readers will recall that the Courts are reluctant to extend subrogation to the economic results of negligence and the recovery aspect, so far as business interruption insurance is concerned, is, at the moment, minimal.

17.07 PROXIMATE CAUSE

Proximate Cause has been defined as "the active, efficient cause which sets in motion a train of events, which brings about a result, without the intervention of any force started and working actively from a new and independent source." (*Pawsey* v. *Scottish Union & National* (1907)).

The loss must be the direct result of a peril insured against – for instance, damage done by water from a fireman's hose is treated as fire damage.

By the same token, loss stemming directly from a peril, stated in the policy to be excluded, will fall outside the scope of the policy. Policies exclude war, and fire damage to a house caused by a bomb being dropped on it during the war was treated as war damage.

Uninsured perils, for instance theft under a fire policy, would also be outside the scope of the policy.

The position becomes more complicated when there are concurrent perils, or a sequence of perils, some of which are insured, some excluded. The reader is referred to an insurance textbook for further details of this subject, as these complications seldom have a bearing on business interruption insurance.

Aide Memoire

Reference should be made to this Aide Memoire when considering:
A. the content of a B/I policy;
B. action to be taken following an Incident which is likely to lead to a claim under the policy.

A.01 GROSS PROFIT AND REVENUE COVER

Is the insurance to be "with average" or "without average"?

If "with average", the Sum Insured will need to be projected forward for a minimum of 12 months following the expiry of the current period of insurance.

If "without average", the Sum Insured will be the Estimated Gross Profit for the financial year most nearly concurrent with the period of insurance.

These figures will be for any Indemnity Period up to 12 months. If the Indemnity Period is greater than 12 months, the Sum Insured must be increased proportionately.

A.02 INDEMNITY PERIOD

The maximum Indemnity Period should be sufficient to allow for:
(1) clearance of the site;
(2) preparation of plans and drawings;
(3) obtaining local authority permits and obtaining tenders;
(4) erection;
(5) obtaining raw materials and installing machinery and equipment (check leadtime for special machines);
(6) recruiting and training new staff, if necessary;
(7) regaining lost customers after full production is restored.

A.03 GROSS PROFIT SUM INSURED

This is calculated on the following basis:

> Turnover plus
> Closing Stock & Work in progress
> LESS the total of
> Opening Stock & Work in progress plus
> Purchases of materials less discounts received,
> Packing, Carriage and Freight (other than by own vehicles) and Bad Debts.*
> (*Note. Bad Debts will not be excluded if you have a Reserve for Bad Debts to which an amount is transferred each year.)

These deductions (from the total of Turnover plus Closing Stock and Work in progress), known as Specified or Uninsured Working expenses, are the standard ones and any addition to these deductions should be avoided unless there are special reasons.

A.04 PAYROLL

The calculation in A.03 above assumes that **all** remuneration (i.e. Salaries and Wages) is included in full in the Sum Insured. If it should be decided to cover remuneration on a reduced basis as a separate item, Payroll would then be shown as a Uninsured Working Expense and deducted from the Turnover.

In this case you will need to watch the cover carefully each year and change to 100 per cent Payroll cover as soon as practicable.

The amount of Payroll will need to be advised to the Insurer.

A.05 PERILS TO BE INCLUDED IN THE COVER

(1) Fire, Aircraft, Explosion, Riot and Civil Commotion.
(2) Malicious Damage (only given as an extension of Riot and Civil Commotion).
(3) Earthquake.
(4) Storm, Flood, Escape of Water, Impact.
(5) Engineering Perils (whether a separate policy or item such as Collapse or Overheating, which can be added to a B/I policy).
(6) "All Risks" (including Theft).

(7) Subsidence (not included in (6)).
(8) Any specialised perils such as Notifiable Disease and Sprinkler Leakage where applicable.

Reminder. Cover can be given only for Perils which are included under the Material Damage Contents policy, except where no Material Damage cover is applicable, as, for example, Notifiable Disease.

A.06 EXTENSIONS TO BE CONSIDERED

(1) Specified Suppliers.
(2) Suppliers' Suppliers.
(3) Unspecified Suppliers and Storage Sites.
(4) Patterns etc.
(5) Transit.
(6) Contract sites
(7) Prevention of Access/Loss of Attraction.
(8) Public Utilities – Electricity, Gas, Water and Telecommunications Systems.
(9) Specified Customers.
(10) Unspecified Customers.
(11) Failure of Supply (wider than (8)).

A.07 DEPOSIT PREMIUM

Has a 75 per cent Deposit Premium been negotiated?

A.08 CLAUSES TO BE CONSIDERED WITH THE INSURER OR BROKER

(1) Payments on account. (Section 9.07).
(2) Alternative basis of settlement (i.e. Output instead of Turnover (Section 9.08).
(3) Departmental (Section 11.01).
(4) Salvage Sale (Section 11.02).
(5) New Business (Section 11.03).
(6) Accumulated Stocks (Section 11.04).
(7) Professional Accountants' Fees for producing and certifying figures following a loss (Section 9.06).

A.09 PREMISES AND BUSINESS

Ensure that these two items are correctly defined in the policy to show only those premises which are to be included in the Gross Profit cover and that the definition of the Business shows all those items which are to be included in the Gross Profit cover.

A.10 OTHER COVERS

Have the following covers been considered?
(1) Rent Receivable;
(2) Research Expenditure;
(3) Advance Profits;
(4) Loss of Book Debts;
(5) Engineering B/I;
(6) "All Risks" material damage and B/I on computer installation.

A.11 DEDUCTIBLES AND LONG TERM AGREEMENTS

Have these been considered?

B.01 ACTION TO BE TAKEN FOLLOWING AN INCIDENT

(1) Immediate advice must be given to the Brokers and Insurers unless prior arrangements have been made for advice to be given to a particular Loss Adjuster in case of an Incident.
(2) Make sure that full details are given of the premises involved, the extent of the damage, and the name and location of the individual whom the Loss Adjuster should contact.
(3) Set up a separate account to record all Increase in Cost of Working above that normally incurred.
(4) Record any savings in expenditure.
(5) Ensure that records of Turnover after the Incident are kept separately from those of before the Incident.
(7) Make sure that all members of staff who are likely to be of assistance to the Loss Adjuster are available as soon as an appointment with him is arranged.

Appendices

RECOMMENDED POLICY WORDINGS
1 Standard Fire Policy (Business Interruption)
2 Standard "All Risks" Policy (Business Interruption)

BUSINESS INTERRUPTION SPECIFICATION WORDINGS
3 "Gross Profit" Wording – Sum Insured Basis
4 "Gross Profit" Wording – Declaration-Linked Basis
5 Wages: "Dual Basis" Wording – Sum Insured Basis
6 "Dual Basis": Example of Loss Settlement
7 Fines or Damages; and Premium Adjustment Clauses
8 Special Perils
9 Special Clauses
10 Business Interruption Extension Wordings
11 Book Debts Insurance Wording
12 Research Expenditure Wording
13 Gross Revenue Wording – Declaration-Linked Basis
14 Collective Policies
15 City Tailors Ltd v. Evans (1921)
16 Overseas Wording: Model Five and Special Perils Policy
17 Standard Policy (Pre-October 1989)

Note: Within the documents contained in these appendices there are various cross-references. These are generally to other items/documents in the standard reference work, the ABI's publication *Recommended Practices, Wordings and Procedures relating to Material Damage and Business Interruption, Commercial and Industrial Insurance.*

APPENDIX 1

Standard Fire Policy (Business Interruption)

The Insurer agrees (subject to the terms, definition, exclusions and conditions of this policy) that if after payment of the first premium any building or other property used by the insured at the Premises for the purpose of the Business be lost destroyed or damaged by

1 FIRE but excluding loss destruction or damage caused by
    (a) explosion resulting from fire
    (b) earthquake or subterranean fire
    (c) (i) its own spontaneous fermentation or heating, or
        (ii) its undergoing any heating process or any process involving the application of heat

2 LIGHTNING

3 EXPLOSION
    (a) of boilers used for domestic purposes only
    (b) of any other boilers or economisers on the Premises
    (c) of gas used for domestic purposes only

    but excluding loss destruction or damage caused by earthquake or subterranean fire

during the period of insurance (or any subsequent period for which the Insurer accepts a renewal premium) and in consequence the business carried on by the Insured at the Premises be interrupted or interfered with then the Insurer will pay to the Insured in respect of each item in the Schedule the amount of loss resulting from such interruption of interference provided that

1 at the time of the happening of the loss destruction or damage there shall be in force an insurance covering the interest of the Insured in the property at the Premises against such loss destruction or damage and that

   (i) payment shall have been made or liability admitted therefor, or
   (ii) payment would have been made or liability admitted therefor but for the operation of a proviso in such insurance excluding liability for losses below a specified amount

2 the liability of the Insurer under this policy shall not exceed

   (i) in the whole the total sum insured or in respect of any item its sum insured at the time of the loss destruction or damage
   (ii) the sum insured remaining after deduction for any other interruption or interference consequent upon loss destruction or damage occurring during the same period of insurance, unless the Insurer shall have agreed to reinstate any such sum insured

This policy incorporates the Schedule, Specification and Endorsements which shall be read together as one contract. Words and expressions to which specific meaning is given in any part of this policy shall have the same meaning wherever they appear.

Signed on behalf of the Insurer

DEFINITION

The words "CONSEQUENTIAL LOSS", in capital letters, shall mean loss resulting from interruption of or interference with the Business carried on by the Insured at the Premises in consequence of loss or destruction of or damage to property used by the Insured at the Premises for the purpose of the Business

GENERAL EXCLUSIONS

This policy does not cover

1 CONSEQUENTIAL LOSS occasioned by riot civil commotion war invasion act of foreign enemy hostilities (whether war be declared or not) civil war rebellion revolution insurrection or military or usurped power

2 loss destruction or damage occasioned by or happening through or occasioning loss or destruction of or damage to any property whatsoever or any loss or expense whatsoever resulting or arising therefore or any consequential loss directly or indirectly caused by or contributed to by or arising from
   (a) ionising radiations or contamination by radioactivity from any nuclear fuel or from any nuclear waste from the combustion of nuclear fuel
   (b) the radioactive toxic explosive or other hazardous properties of any explosive nuclear asembly or nuclear component thereof

3 CONSEQUENTIAL LOSS in Northern Ireland occasioned by or happening through
   (a) civil commotion
   (b) any unlawful wanton or malicious act committed maliciously by a person or persons acting on behalf of or in connection with any unlawful association

   For the purpose of this exclusion

   "unlawful association" means any organisation which is engaged in terrorism and includes an organisation which at any relevant time is a proscribed organisation within the meaning of the Northern Ireland (Emergency Provisions) Act 1973

   "terrorism" means the use of violence for political ends and includes any use of violence for the purpose of putting the public or any section of the public in fear

   In any action suit or other proceedings where the Insurer alleges that by reason of the provisions of this exclusion any CONSEQUENTIAL LOSS is not covered by this policy the burden of proving that such CONSEQUENTIAL LOSS is covered shall be upon the Insured

4 loss resulting from pollution or contamination but this shall not exclude loss resulting from destruction of or damage to property used by the Insured at the Premises for the purpose of the Business, not otherwise excluded, caused by

(a) pollution or contamination at the Premises which itself results from a peril hereby insured against
(b) any peril hereby insured against which itself results from pollution or contamination

GENERAL CONDITIONS

1 Policy Voidable
This policy shall be voidable in the event of misrepresentation or non-disclosure in any material particular.

2 Alteration
This policy shall be avoided if after commencement of this insurance
(a) the Business be wound up or carried on by a liquidator or receiver or permanently discontinued or
(b) the interest of the Insured ceases other than by death or
(c) any alteration be made either in the Business or in the Premises or property therein whereby the risks of loss destruction or damage is increased

unless admitted by the Insurer in writing.

CLAIMS CONDITIONS

1 Action by the Insured
(a) In the event of any loss destruction or damage in consequence of which a claim is or may be made under this policy the Insured shall
 - notify the Insurer immediately
 - with due diligence carry out and permit to be taken any action which may reasonably be practicable to minimise or check any interruption of or interference with the Business or to avoid or diminish the loss.
(b) In the event of a claim being made under this policy the Insured at his own expense shall
 - not later than 30 days after the expiry of the Indemnity Period or within such further time as the Insurer may allow, deliver to the Insurer in writing particulars of his claim together with details of all other insurances covering property used by the Insured at the Premises for the purpose of the Business or any part of it or any resulting consequential loss
 - deliver to the Insurer such books of account and other business books vouchers invoices balance sheets and other documents proofs information explanation and other evidence as may reasonably be required by the Insurer for the purpose of investigating or verifying the claim together with, if demanded, a statutory declaration of the truth of the claim and of any matters connected with it.
(c) If the terms of this condition have not been complied with
 - no claim under this policy shall be payable and
 - any payment on account of the claim already made shall be repaid to the Insurer forthwith.

2 Fraud
If a claim is fraudulent in any respect or if fraudulent means are used by the Insured or by anyone acting on his behalf to obtain any benefit under this policy or if any loss destruction or damage to property used by the Insured at the Premises for the purpose of the Business is caused by the wilful act or with the connivance of the Insured all benefit under this policy shall be forfeited.

Appendices 179

3 **Contribution**
If at the time of any loss destruction or damage resulting in a loss under this policy there be any other insurance effected by or on behalf of the Insured covering such loss or any part of it the liability of the Insurer hereunder shall be limited to its rateable proportion of such loss.

4 **Subrogation**
Any claimant under this policy shall at the request and expense of the Insurer take and permit to be taken all necessary steps for enforcing rights against any other party in the name of the Insured before or after any payment is made by the Insurer.

5 **Arbitration**
If any difference arises as to the amount to be paid under this policy (liability being otherwise admitted) such difference shall be referred to an arbitrator to be appointed by the parties in accordance with statutory provisions. Where any difference is by this condition to be referred to arbitration the making of an award shall be a condition precedent to any right of action against the Insurer.

Note: For an insurance relating solely to premises not in the occupation of the Insured the following should be omitted:–

the words "used by the Insured" in line 2 (front page), the Definition, General Exclusions 4, Claims Conditions 1(b) and 2 (line 2 only)

the words "for the purpose of the Business" in line 2(front page), the Definition, General Exclusion 4, Claims Conditions 1(b) and 2

the words "at the Premises" in line 16 (front page)

General Condition 2(c)

180 *Business Interruption Insurance: Theory and Practice*

Policy No

THE SCHEDULE

THE INSURER	
THE INSURED	
THE BUSINESS	
THE PREMISES	
ITEMS	As detailed in the attached Specification
TOTAL SPECIFICATION ESTIMATED GROSS PROFIT/SUM INSURED	£
THE ESTIMATED GROSS PROFIT/ SUM INSURED BY THIS POLICY	£ being % of the total Specification sum insured
INSURER'S LIABILITY	The Insurer's liability under this policy is limited to % of the amount otherwise payable under the provisions of the Specification
PERIOD OF INSURANCE	From to
RENEWAL DATE	
FIRST PREMIUM	£
ANNUAL PREMIUM	£
AGENCY	

Note: For insurances solely on a Sum Insured basis references to Estimated Gross Profit should be deleted.

APPENDIX 2

Standard "All Risks" Policy (Business Interruption)

The Insurer agrees (subject to the terms, definitions, exclusions and conditions of this policy) that if after payment of the first premium any building or other property used by the Insured at the Premises for the purpose of the Business be accidentally lost destroyed or damaged during the period of insurance (or any subsequent period for which the Insurer accepts a renewal premium) and in consequence the business carried on by the Insured at the Premises be interrupted or interfered with then the Insurer will pay to the Insured in respect of each item in the Schedule the amount of loss resulting from such interruption or interference provided that

1 at the time of the happening of the loss destruction or damage there shall be in force an insurance covering the interest of the Insured in the property at the Premises against such loss destruction or damage and that
   (i) payment shall have been made or liability admitted therefor, or
   (ii) payment would have been made or liability admitted therefor but for the operation of a proviso in such insurance excluding liability for losses below a specified amount

2 the liability of the Insurer under this policy shall not exceed
   (i) in the whole the total sum insured or in respect of any item its sum insured or any other limit of liability stated in the Schedule at the time of the loss destruction or damage
   (ii) the sum insured (or limit) remaining after deduction for any other interruption or interference consequent upon loss destruction or damage occurring during the same period of insurance, unless the Insurer shall have agreed to reinstate any such sum insured (or limit).

This policy incorporates the Schedule, Specification and Endorsements which shall be read together as one contract. Words and expressions to which specific meaning is given in any part of this policy shall have the same meaning wherever they appear.

Signed on behalf of the Insurer

DEFINITIONS

2 The words "CONSEQUENTIAL LOSS", in capital letters, shall mean loss resulting from interruption of or interference with the Business carried on by the Insured at the Premises in consequence of accidental loss or destruction of or damage to property used by the Insured at the Premises for the purpose of the Business.

3 The words "Defined Peril" shall mean fire, lightning, explosion, aircraft or other aerial devices or articles dropped therefrom, riot, civil commotion, strikers, locked-out workers,

persons taking part in labour disturbances, malicious persons, earthquake, storm, flood, escape of water from any tank apparatus or pipe or impact by any road vehicle or animal.

EXCLUSIONS

This policy does not cover

1 CONSEQUENTIAL LOSS caused by or consisting of
   1.1 inherent vice, latent defect, gradual deterioration, wear and tear, frost, change in water table level, its own faulty or defective design or materials
   1.2 faulty or defective workmanship, operational error or omission, on the part of the Insured or any of his employees
   1.3 the bursting of any vessel machine or apparatus (not being a boiler or economiser on the Premises or a boiler used for domestic purposes only) in which internal pressure is due to steam only and belonging to or under the control of the Insured
   1.4 pressure waves caused by aircraft or other aerial devices travelling at sonic or supersonic speeds

   but this shall not exclude subsequent CONSEQUENTIAL LOSS which itself results from a cause not otherwise excluded

2 CONSEQUENTIAL LOSS
   2.1 caused by or consisting of corrosion, rust, wet or dry rot, shrinkage, evaporation, loss of weight, dampness, dryness, marring, scratching, vermin or insects
   2.2 caused by or consisting of change in temperature colour flavour texture or finish
   2.3 arising directly from theft or attempted theft
   2.4 consisting of joint leakage, failure of welds, cracking, fracturing, collapse or overheating of boilers, economisers, superheaters, pressure vessels or any range of steam and feed piping in connection therewith
   2.5 consisting of mechanical or electrical breakdown or derangement in respect of the particular machine apparatus or equipment in which such breakdown or derangement originates
   2.6 caused by the deliberate act of a supply undertaking in withholding the supply of water, gas, electricity, fuel or telecommunications services

   but this shall not exclude
   (a) such CONSEQUENTIAL LOSS not otherwise excluded which itself results from a Defined Peril or from any other accidental loss destruction or damage
   (b) subsequent CONSEQUENTIAL LOSS which itself results from a cause not otherwise excluded

3 loss resulting from pollution or contamination but this shall not exclude loss resulting from destruction of or damage to property used by the Insured at the Premises for the purpose of the Business, not otherwise excluded, caused by
   (a) pollution or contamination at the Premises which itself results from a Defined Peril
   (b) a Defined Peril which itself results from pollution or contamination

4 CONSEQUENTIAL LOSS caused by or consisting of
   4.1 subsidence ground heave or landslip unless resulting from fire explosion earthquake or the escape of water from any tank apparatus or pipe
   4.2 normal settlement or bedding down of new structures
   4.3 acts of fraud or dishonesty

CONSEQUENTIAL LOSS arising directly or indirectly from
4.4 disappearance, unexplained or inventory shortage, misfiling or misplacing of information
4.5 (a) erasure loss distortion or corruption of information on computer systems or other records programs or software caused deliberately by rioters strikers locked-out workers persons taking part in labour disturbances or civil commotions or malicious persons
     (b) other erasure loss distortion or corruption of information on computer systems or other records programs or software unless resulting from a Defined Peril in so far as it is not otherwise excluded

5 loss resulting from destruction of or damage to a building or structure used by the Insured at the Premises caused by its own collapse or cracking unless resulting from a Defined Peril in so far as it is not otherwise excluded

6 CONSEQUENTIAL LOSS in respect of movable property in the open, fences and gates caused by wind rain hail sleet snow flood or dust

7 CONSEQUENTIAL LOSS
7.1 caused by fire resulting from its undergoing any heating process or any process involving the application of heat
7.2 (other than by fire or explosion) resulting from its undergoing any process of production packing treatment testing commissioning servicing or repair

8 CONSEQUENTIAL LOSS
8.1 caused by freezing
8.2 caused by escape of water from any tank apparatus or pipe
8.3 caused (other than by fire or explosion) by malicious persons not acting on behalf of or in connection with any political organisation

in respect of any building which is empty or not in use

9 CONSEQUENTIAL LOSS in respect of
9.1 fixed glass
9.2 glass (other than fixed glass) china earthenware marble or other fragile or brittle objects
9.3 computers or data processing equipment
9.4 vehicles licensed for road use (including accessories thereon) caravans trailers railway locomotives rolling stock watercraft or aircraft
9.5 property or structures in course of construction or erection and materials or supplies in connection with all such property in course of construction or erection
9.6 land roads pavements piers jetties bridges culverts or excavations
9.7 livestock growing crops or trees

other than in respect of such CONSEQUENTIAL LOSS caused by a Defined Peril in so far as it is not otherwise excluded

10 CONSEQUENTIAL LOSS occasioned by war invasion act of foreign enemy hostilities (whether war be declared or not) civil war rebellion revolution insurrection military or usurped power nationalisation confiscation requisition seizure or destruction by the government or any public authority

184 Business Interruption Insurance: Theory and Practice

11 loss destruction or damage occasioned by or happening through or occasioning loss or destruction of or damage to any property whatsoever or any loss or expense whatsoever resulting or arising therefrom or any consequential loss directly or indirectly caused by or contributed to by or arising from

   (a) ionising radiations or contamination by radioactivity from any nuclear fuel or from any nuclear waste from the combustion of nuclear fuel
   (b) the radioactive toxic explosive or other hazardous properties of any explosive nuclear assembly or nuclear component thereof

12 CONSEQUENTIAL LOSS in Northern Ireland occasioned by or happening through
   (a) riot civil commotion and (except in respect of CONSEQUENTIAL LOSS by fire or explosion) strikers locked-out workers or persons taking part in labour disturbances or malicious persons
   (b) any unlawful wanton or malicious act committed maliciously by a person or persons acting on behalf of or in connection with any unlawful association

For the purpose of this exclusion

"unlawful association" means any organisation which is engaged in terrorism and includes an organisation which at any relevant time is a proscribed organisation within the meaning of the Northern Ireland (Emergency Provisions) Act 1973

"terrorism" means the use of violence for political ends and includes any use of violence for the purpose of putting the public or any section of the public in fear

In any action suit or other proceedings where the Insurer alleges that by reason of the provisions of this exclusion any CONSEQUENTIAL LOSS is not covered by the policy the burden of proving that such CONSEQUENTIAL LOSS is covered shall be upon the Insured.

DEDUCTIBLES

This policy does not cover the amounts of the deductibles stated in the Schedule in respect of each and every loss as ascertained after the application of all other terms and conditions of the policy.

GENERAL CONDITIONS

1 **Policy Voidable**
   This policy shall be voidable in the event of misrepresentation misdescription or non-disclosure in any material particular.

2 **Alteration**
   This policy shall be avoided if after the commencement of this insurance
   (a) the Business be wound up or carried on by a liquidator or receiver or permanently discontinued or
   (b) the interest of the Insured ceases other than by death or
   (c) any alteration be made either in the Business or in the Premises or property therein whereby the risk of loss destruction or damage is increased

   unless admitted by the Insurer in writing.

CLAIMS CONDITIONS

1 **Action by the Insured**
   (a) In the event of any loss destruction or damage in consequence of which a claim is or may be made under this policy the Insured shall
   - notify the Insurer immediately
   - deliver to the Insurer at the Insured's expense within 7 days of its happening full details of loss destruction or damage caused by riot civil commotion strikers locked-out workers persons taking part in labour disturbances or malicious persons
   - with due diligence carry out and permit to be taken any action which may reasonably be practicable to minimise or check any interruption of or interference with the Business or to avoid or diminish the loss.
   (b) In the event of a claim being made under this policy the Insured at his own expense shall
   - not later than 30 days after the expiry of the Indemnity Period or within such further time as the Insurer may allow, deliver to the Insurer in writing particulars of his claim together with details of all other insurances covering property used by the Insured at the Premises for the purpose of the Business or any part of it or any resulting consequential loss
   - deliver to the Insurer such books of account and other business books vouchers invoices balance sheets and other documents proofs information explanation and other evidence as may reasonably be required by the Insurer for the purpose of investigating or verifying the claim together with, if demanded, a statutory declaration of the truth of the claim and of any matters connected with it.
   (c) If the terms of this condition have not been complied with
   - no claim under this policy shall be payable and
   - any payment on account of the claim already made shall be repaid to the Insurer forthwith.

2 **Fraud**
If a claim is fraudulent in any respect or if fraudulent means are used by the Insured or by anyone acting on his behalf to obtain any benefit under this policy or if any loss destruction or damage to property used by the Insured at the Premises for the purpose of the Business is caused by the wilful act or with the connivance of the Insured all benefit under this policy shall be forfeited.

3 **Contribution**
If at the time of any loss destruction or damage resulting in a loss under this policy there be any other insurance effected by or on behalf of the Insured covering such loss or any part of it the liability of the Insurer hereunder shall be limited to its rateable proportion of such loss.

4 **Subrogation**
Any claimant under this policy shall at the request and expense of the Insurer take and permit to be taken all necessary steps for enforcing rights against any other party in the name of the Insured before or after any payment is made by the Insurer.

5 **Arbitration**
If any difference arises as to the amount to be paid under this policy (liability being otherwise admitted) such difference shall be referred to an arbitrator to be appointed by the parties in accordance with statutory provisions. Where any difference is by this condition to be referred to arbitration the making of an award shall be a condition precedent to any right of action against the Insurer.

Notes: 1. For an insurance relating solely to premises not in the occupation of the Insured the following should be omitted:–
the words "used by the Insured" in line 2(front page), Definition 1, Exclusions 3, 4.5 and 5, Claims Conditions 1(b) and 2 (line 2 only)
the words "for the purpose of the Business" in line 2 (front page), Definition 1, Exclusions 3 and 4.5, Claims Conditions 1(b) and 2
the words "at the Premises" in line 4 (front page) and in Exclusions 4.5 and 5 General Condition 2(c)
2. The deductible wording should be suitably amended if variations apply.
3. It is recommended that where CONSEQUENTIAL LOSS by Subsidence Ground Heave and Landslip is included the wording provided in Appendix 8 para. 21 be used amended by the addition of the introductory phrase "Notwithstanding exclusions 4.1 and 4.2 of this policy this insurance is extended to include CONSEQUENTIAL LOSS caused by . . ."

Policy No

THE SCHEDULE

THE INSURER	
THE INSURED	
THE BUSINESS	
THE PREMISES	
ITEMS	As detailed in the attached Specification
TOTAL SPECIFICATION ESTIMATED GROSS PROFIT/SUM INSURED	£
LIMIT OF LIABILITY AND DEDUCTIBLE	LIMIT OF LIABILITY DEDUCTIBLE

In respect of:

(i) CONSEQUENTIAL LOSS by fire lightning explosion aircraft or other aerial devices or articles dropped therefrom riot civil commotion strikers locked-out workers persons taking part in labour disturbances malicious persons or earthquakes

the sum insured or as detailed in the Specification   the first £

(ii) CONSEQUENTIAL LOSS by storm flood escape of water from any tank apparatus or pipe or impact by any road vehicle or animal

£   )
)
)
) the first £
)
)

(iii) Other insured CONSEQUENTIAL LOSS

£   )

THE ESTIMATED GROSS PROFIT/ SUM INSURED BY THIS POLICY

£ being   % of the total Specification estimated gross profit/sum insured

INSURER'S LIABILITY

The Insurer's liability under this policy is limited to   % of the amount otherwise payable under the provisions of the Specification and this Schedule

PERIOD OF INSURANCE

From
to

RENEWAL DATE

FIRST PREMIUM   £

ANNUAL PREMIUM   £

AGENCY

Note: For insurances solely on a Sum Insured basis references to Estimated Gross Profit should be deleted.

APPENDIX 3

"Gross Profit" Wording – Sum Insured Basis

BUSINESS INTERRUPTION SPECIFICATION WORDINGS

NOTE APPLICABLE TO ALL WORDINGS IN THIS APPENDIX:

When used with earlier policy forms substitute "Damage" for "Incident" wherever it appears and delete the definition of "Incident".

"GROSS PROFIT" WORDING – SUM INSURED BASIS

Item No.		Sum Insured
1	On Gross Profit	£
	Total Sum Insured	£

The insurance under Item No. 1 is limited to loss of Gross Profit due to (a) **Reduction in Turnover** and (b) **Increase in Cost of Working** and the amount payable as indemnity thereunder shall be:–

(a) **in respect of Reduction in Turnover:** the sum produced by applying the Rate of Gross Profit to the amount by which the Turnover during the Indemnity Period shall fall short of the Standard Turnover in consequence of the Incident

(b) **in respect of Increase in Cost of Working:** the additional expenditure (subject to the provisions of the Uninsured Standing Charges Clause) necessarily and reasonably incurred for the sole purpose of avoiding or diminishing the reduction in Turnover which but for that expenditure would have taken place during the Indemnity Period in consequence of the Incident, but not exceeding the sum produced by applying the Rate of Gross Profit to the amount of the reduction thereby avoided

less any sum saved during the Indemnity Period in respect of such of the charges and expenses of the Business payable out of Gross Profit as may cease or be reduced in consequence of the Incident

provided that if the sum insured by this item be less than the sum produced by applying the Rate of Gross Profit to the Annual Turnover (or to a proportionately increased multiple thereof where the Maximum Indemnity Period exceeds twelve months) the amount payable shall be proportionately reduced.

DEFINITIONS

Notes: 1 To the extent that the Insured is accountable to the tax authorities for Value Added Tax, all terms in this policy shall be exclusive of such tax.
2 For the purpose of these definitions, any adjustment implemented in current cost accounting shall be disregarded.

Incident: Loss or destruction of or damage to property used by the Insured at the Premises for the purpose of the Business.

Indemnity Period: The period beginning with the occurrence of the Incident and ending not later than the Maximum Indemnity Period thereafter during which the results of the Business shall be affected in consequence thereof.

Maximum Indemnity Period: months.

Turnover: The money paid or payable to the Insured for goods sold and delivered and for services rendered in course of the Business at The Premises.

Gross Profit: The amount by which –
(i) the sum of the amount of the Turnover and the amounts of the closing stock and work in progress shall exceed
(ii) the sum of the amounts of the opening stock and work in progress and the amount of the Uninsured Working Expenses.

Note: The amounts of the opening and closing stocks and work in progress shall be arrived at in accordance with the Insured's normal accountancy methods, due provision being made for depreciation.

Uninsured Working Expenses:

Note: The words and expressions used in this definition (other than wages) shall have the meaning usually attached to them in the books and accounts of the Insured.

Rate of Gross Profit:- The Rate of Gross Profit earned on the Turnover during the financial year immediately before the date of the Incident

Annual Turnover:- The Turnover during the twelve months immediately before the date of the Incident

Standard Turnover:- The Turnover during that period in twelve months immediately before the date of the Incident which corresponds with the Indemnity Period

) to which such adjustments shall be made
) as may be necessary to provide for the
) trend of the Business and for variations in
) or other circumstances affecting the Busi-
) ness either before or after the Incident
) which would have affected the Business
) had the Incident not occurred, so that the
) figures thus adjusted shall represent as
) nearly as may be reasonably practicable
) the results which but for the Incident
) would have been obtained during the
) relative period after the Incident
)
)

Alternative Trading Clause: If during the Indemnity Period goods shall be sold or services shall be rendered elsewhere than at the Premises for the benefit of the Business either by the Insured or by others on his behalf the money paid or payable in respect of such sales or services shall be brought into account in arriving at the Turnover during the Indemnity Period.

Uninsured Standing Charges Clause: If any standing charges of the Business be not insured by this policy (having been deducted in arriving at the Gross Profit as defined herein) then in computing the amount recoverable hereunder as Increase in Cost of Working, that proportion only of any additional expenditure shall be brought into account which the Gross Profit bears to the sum of the Gross Profit and the uninsured standing charges.

Premium Adjustment Clause: (See Appendix 7)

Note: Where the Uninsured Expenses are recognised variable charges, the Uninsured Standing Charges Clause and the reference thereto under paragraph (b) of Item No. 1 should be deleted.

APPENDIX 4

"Gross Profit" Wording – Declaration-Linked Basis

"GROSS PROFIT" WORDING – DECLARATION-LINKED BASIS

Item No.		Estimated Gross Profit
1	On Gross Profit	£ _____
		–

The insurance under Item No. 1 is limited to loss of Gross Profit due to (a) Reduction in Turnover and (b) Increase in Cost of Working and the amount payable as indemnity thereunder shall be:–
(a) **in respect of Reduction in Turnover:** the sum produced by applying the Rate of Gross Profit to the amount by which the Turnover during the Indemnity Period shall fall short of the Standard Turnover in consequence of the Incident
(b) **in respect of Increase in Cost of Working:** the additional expenditure (subject to the provisions of the Uninsured Standing Charges Clause) necessarily and reasonably incurred for the sole purpose of avoiding or diminishing the reduction in Turnover which but for that expenditure would have taken place during the Indemnity Period in consequence of the Incident, but not exceeding the sum produced by applying the Rate of Gross Profit to the amount of the reduction thereby avoided

less any sum saved during the Indemnity Period in respect of such of the charges and expenses of the Business payable out of Gross Profit as may cease or be reduced in consequence of the Incident

Notwithstanding proviso 2 on the face of this policy

(i) the liability of the Insurer shall in no case exceed, in respect of Gross Profit 133.3% of the Estimated Gross Profit stated herein, in respect of each other item 100% of the sum insured stated herein, nor in the whole the sum of 133.3% of the Estimated Gross Profit and 100% of the sums insured by other items, or such other amounts as may be substituted therefor by memorandum signed by or on behalf of the Insurer
(ii) in the absence of written notice by the Insured or the Insurer to the contrary the Insurer's liability shall not stand reduced by the amount of any loss, the Insured undertaking to pay the appropriate additional premium for such automatic reinstatement of cover.

DEFINITIONS

Notes: 1 To the extent that the Insured is accountable to the tax authorities for Value Added Tax, all terms in this policy shall be exclusive of such tax.
2 For the purpose of these definitions, any adjustment implemented in current cost accounting shall be disregarded.

192 *Business Interruption Insurance: Theory and Practice*

Incident: Loss or destruction of or damage to property used by the Insured at the Premises for the purpose of the Business.

Indemnity Period: The period beginning with the occurrence of the Incident and ending not later than the Maximum Indemnity Period thereafter during which the results of the Business shall be affected in consequence thereof.

Maximum Indemnity Period: months.

Turnover: The money paid or payable to the Insured for goods sold and delivered and for services rendered in course of the Business at the Premises.

Gross Profit: The amount by which –
(i) the sum of the amount of the Turnover and the amounts of the closing stock and work in progress shall exceed
(ii) the sum of the amounts of the opening stock and work in progress and the amount of the Uninsured Working Expenses.

Note: The amounts of the opening and closing stocks and work in progress shall be arrived at in accordance with the Insured's normal accountancy methods, due provision being made for depreciation.

Uninsured Working Expenses:

Note: The words and expressions used in this definition (other than wages) shall have the meaning usually attached to them in the books and accounts of the Insured.

Estimated Gross Profit: The amount declared by the Insured to the Insurer as representing not less than the Gross Profit which it is anticipated will be earned by the Business during the financial year most nearly concurrent with the period of insurance (or a proportionately increased multiple thereof where the Maximum Indemnity Period exceeds twelve months).

Rate of Gross Profit:- The Rate of Gross Profit earned on the Turnover during the financial year immediately before the date of the Incident

Standard Turnover:- The Turnover during that period in twelve months immediately before the date of the Incident which corresponds with the Indemnity Period

) to which such adjustments shall be made
) as may be necessary to provide for the
) trend of the Business and for variations in
) or other circumstances affecting the Business either before or after the Incident
) which would have affected the Business
) had the Incident not occurred, so that the
) figures thus adjusted shall represent as
) nearly as may be reasonably practicable
) the results which but for the Incident
) would have been obtained during the
) relative period after the Incident
)

Alternative Trading Clause: If during the Indemnity Period goods shall be sold or services shall be rendered elsewhere than at the Premises for the benefit of the Business either by the Insured or by others on his behalf the money paid or payable in respect of such sales or services shall be brought into account in arriving at the Turnover during the Indemnity Period.

Uninsured Standing Charges Clause: If any standing charges of the Business be not insured by this policy (having been deducted in arriving at the Gross Profit as defined herein) then in computing the amount recoverable hereunder as Increase in Cost of Working, that proportion only of any additional expenditure shall be brought into account which the Gross Profit bears to the sum of the Gross Profit and the uninsured standing charges.

Renewal Clause: The insured shall prior to each renewal provide the Insurer with the Estimated Gross Profit for the financial year most nearly concurrent with the ensuing year of insurance.

Premium Adjustment Clause: The first and annual premiums (in respect of Item 1) are provisional and are based on the Estimated Gross Profit.
The Insured shall provide to the Insurer not later than six months after the expiry of each period of insurance a declaration confirmed by the Insured's auditors of the Gross Profit earned during the financial year most nearly concurrent with the period of insurance.
If any Incident shall have occurred giving rise to a claim for loss of Gross Profit the above mentioned declaration shall be increased by the Insurer for the purpose of premium adjustment by the amount by which the Gross Profit was reduced during the financial year solely in consequence of the Incident.
If the declaration (adjusted as provided above and proportionately increased where the Maximum Indemnity Period exceeds 12 months).
(a) is less than the Estimated Gross Profit for the relative period of insurance the Insurer will allow a pro rata return of premium paid on the Estimated Gross Profit (but not exceeding 50% of such premium)
(b) is greater than the Estimated Gross Profit for the relative period of insurance the Insured shall pay a pro rata addition to the premium paid on the Estimated Gross Profit

Note: 1 Where the Uninsured Expenses are recognised variable charges, the Uninsured Standing Charges Clause and the reference thereto under paragraph (b) of Item No. 1 should be deleted.
2 When the combined Material Damage and Business Interruption policy forms are used substitute "B" for "2" in line 1 of second paragraph.

APPENDIX 5

Wages: "Dual Basis" Wording – Sum Insured Basis

"DUAL BASIS" WORDING – SUM INSURED BASIS

This wording should only be used in addition to an item insuring gross profit.

Item No.
On Wages

Sum Insured
£
_____
–

Item No.
The insurance under this item is limited to loss in respect of wages and the amount payable as indemnity thereunder shall be:-
(a) IN RESPECT OF REDUCTION IN TURNOVER
  (i) during the initial period
    the sum produced by applying the rate of wages to the shortage in turnover during such period
      less any saving during such period through reduction in consequence of the damage in the amount of wages paid
  (ii) during the remaining portion of the indemnity period
    the sum produced by applying the rate of wages to the shortage in turnover during such period
      less any saving during such period through reduction in consequence of the damage in the amount of wages paid

  but not exceeding

    the sum produced by applying the remainder percentage of the rate of wages to the shortage in turnover during the said remaining portion of the indemnity period increased by such amount as is deducted for savings under the terms of clause (i);

  NOTE: At the option of the Insured the alternative period may be substituted for the initial period provided that the amount arrived at under the provisions of clause (a)(ii) shall not exceed such amount as is deducted under clause (a)(i) for savings effected during the alternative period.

(b) IN RESPECT OF INCREASE IN COST OF WORKING

    so much of the additional expenditure described in clause (b) of the relative gross profit item as exceeds the amount payable thereunder
    but not more than the additional amount which would have been payable in respect of

reduction in turnover under the provisions of clauses (a)(i) and (ii) of this item had such expenditure not been incurred;

provided that if the sum insured by this item be less than the sum produced by applying the rate of wages to the annual turnover (or to a proportionately increased multiple thereof where the maximum indemnity period exceeds twelve months) the amount payable under this item shall be proportionately reduced.

DEFINITIONS

INITIAL PERIOD: The portion of the indemnity period beginning with the occurrence of the damage and ending not later than   weeks thereafter.

REMAINDER PERCENTAGE: per cent

ALTERNATIVE PERIOD: The portion of the indemnity period beginning with the occurrence of the damage and ending not later than   weeks thereafter.

WAGES: The remuneration (including national insurance, bonuses, holiday pay or other payments pertaining to wages) of all employees (other than those whose remuneration is treated as salaries in the Insured's books of account) (See permitted variations overleaf).

RATE OF WAGES: The rate of wages to turnover during the financial year immediately before the date of the damage to which such adjustments shall be made as may be necessary to provide for the trend of the business and for variations in or other circumstances affecting the business either before or after the damage or which would have affected the business had the damage not occurred, so that the figures thus adjusted shall represent as nearly as may be reasonably practicable the results which but for the damage would have been obtained during the relative period after the damage.

SHORTAGE IN TURNOVER: The amount by which the turnover during a period shall in consequence of the damage fall short of the part of the standard turnover which relates to that period.

Note
  (a) When an index of activity other than turnover is used as the basis for the gross profit item, it may be substituted for "turnover" in this wording.
  (b) The words "(including national insurance, bonuses, holiday pay or other payments pertaining to wages)" may be varied suitably to specify other payments pertaining to wages.
  (c) Alternative definitions of "wages". The definition of wages may be varied (although 'skilled employees' and similar inexact terms should not be used) provided that the remuneration of all employees is insured under the policy with the possible exception of
    (i) outworkers paid solely on an output basis
    (ii) agents or employees paid solely on a commission basis
    (iii) casual employees
    (iv) employees engaged in activities not covered by the policy.
  (d) "Wages" may be amended to "payroll" or any other suitable term.

APPENDIX 6
"Dual Basis": Example of Loss Settlement

DB.01 WAGES AS A SEPARATE ITEM

For the purpose of the demonstration loss settlement, we will assume that the same facts and figures as were used in Chapter 8 apply, but that Wages have been insured as a separate item. Since they are insured separately, they will become an Uninsured Working Expense in respect of the item on Gross Profit and, therefore, are not insured under the Gross Profit item.

DB.02 DATA SHEET

The loss adjuster will have arranged for the accountant to monitor the Turnover in the first 13 weeks, the first 19 weeks and the total period of the interruption. The accountant will also be responsible for drawing up the total of the Savings for the three periods.
The details are as follows:

Item 2.   Wages   Sum insured (1) 475 000
                                                       (2) 450 000
Cover -
   Dual Basis Wages –
   100% for 13 weeks/25% remainder
   Consolidation – 19 weeks.
   Indemnity Period – 12 months.

Turnover in last financial year   1 500 000
Wages in last financial year   420 000

	13 weeks	Remainder	19 weeks.
Standard Turnover	345 000	235 000	519 000
Achieved	160 000	250 000	350 000
Savings	19 000	2 000	20 000

Trend   10%
Increase in Cost of Working -
   Expenditure of 35,000 saved Turnover of 55,000.
   Rate of Gross Profit   32% (excluding Wages)
Annual Turnover   1 538 600

The complete wording will be found in the Appendix – the relevant parts will be included in the explanation of the settlement.

Appendices 197

DB.03 NORMAL SETTLEMENT – INITIAL PERIOD

The wording begins –

> **Item No.** **Sum Insured**
> On Wages £...................
>
> **Item No.**
> The insurance under this item is limited to loss in respect of wages and the amount payable as indemnity thereunder shall be
> (a) IN RESPECT OF REDUCTION IN TURNOVER
> (i) during the initial period
>   the sum produced by applying the rate of wages to the shortage in turnover during such period ...

As we found when dealing with the loss of Gross Profit, there are definitions to help us and "rate of wages" is defined as "The rate of wages to turnover during the financial year immediately before the date of the damage, followed by the 'other circumstances' (Trend) clause".

So, from the Data sheet, the calculation of the loss commences with ascertaining the rate of wages, that is, the proportion of wages to turnover in the last financial year. For the purpose of this demonstration, it will be assumed that the rate brought out in the accounts has been maintained.

$$\frac{\text{Wages}}{\text{Turnover}} \times \frac{100}{1}$$

$$\frac{420\,000}{1\,500\,000} \times \frac{100}{1} = 28\%$$

This percentage is now applied to the Shortage in Turnover, the shortage being ascertained in exactly the same way as in the loss of Gross Profit calculation –

(Standard Turnover + Trend) – (Achieved Turnover)

From the Data sheet we get

Initial Period –
Standard Turnover	345 000
+ Trend 10%	34 500
	379 500
Achieved	160 000
Shortage	219 500

28% x 219 500 =   61 460

198 *Business Interruption Insurance: Theory and Practice*

The wording continues

> ...less any saving during such period through reduction in consequence of the damage in the amount of wages paid...

The Data sheet states that there were Savings of 19 000,
so this amount must be deducted   19 000

Loss payable in respect of Initial Period   42 460

DB.04 NORMAL SETTLEMENT – REMAINDER PERIOD

The wording continues

> (ii) during the remaining portion of the indemnity period the sum produced by applying the rate of wages to the shortage in turnover during such period less any saving during such period through reduction in consequence of the damage in the amount of wages paid

From the Data supplied, the figures are

Remainder period Standard Turnover	235 000
+ Trend 10%	23 500
	258 500
Achieved	250 000
Shortage	8 500
28% × 8,500 =	2 380
less Savings	2 000
	380

The wording now goes on to reflect the fact that the Insured elected to restrict the cover to 25% of the Wage roll in the Remainder Period, as follows:

> but not exceeding
> the sum produced by applying the remainder percentage of the rate of wages to the shortage in turnover during the said remaining portion of the indemnity period, increased by such amount as is deducted for savings under the terms of clause (i);

So the amount is *limited to*
  25% × 28% × 8 500 =   595
  increased by the savings in the
    Initial Period   19 000

    So the LIMIT is   19 595
But the actual loss was 380. This does
not exceed the limit, so pay   380

SUMMARY

Loss in Initial Period	42 460	
Loss in Remainder Period	380	
		42 840

DB.05 CONSOLIDATION – ALTERNATIVE PERIOD

In Section 14.05 we said that the Insurers were ready to make the insurance flexible and that, if it would be to the advantage of the Insured, an **Alternative Period,** representing 100 per cent of the total cover paid for, could be substituted for the Initial Period.

From the tables in current use, 100 per cent for 13 weeks and 25 per cent of the Remainder of the Indemnity Period will convert into 100 per cent cover for 19 weeks. Anything beyond this will depend on the level of Savings in the Alternative Period (19 weeks).

The wording is

> NOTE: At the option of the Insured the alternative period may be substituted for the initial period provided that the amount arrived at under the provisions of clause (a) (ii) (*Remainder Period*) shall not exceed such amount as is deducted under clause (a) (i) (*Initial Period*) for savings effected during the alternative period.

To ascertain then, if the consolidation will be to the advantage of the Insured, it is necessary to re-work the calculation on the basis that the "Initial Period" is now 19 weeks and the "Remainder Period" is the balance of the Indemnity Period (in this case about 2 weeks).

The necessary details are shown on the Data sheet and we follow just the same pattern as before. The Rate of Wages is 28 per cent and the calculation is

Alternative Period –		
Standard Turnover	519 000	
+ Trend 10%	51 900	
	570 900	
Achieved	350 000	
Shortage	220 900	
28% x 220,900 =	61,852	
Less Savings	20 000	
		41 852

DB.05 CONSOLIDATION "REMAINDER" PERIOD

Now follows the calculation of the loss in the "Remainder Period" under the Alternative Period wording.

If the Insured is suffering a loss during this "Remainder Period", the Insurers will pay up to the amount of the Savings in the "Initial Period", in this case, a maximum of 20 000. Figures for the balance of the Indemnity Period are not supplied, but they are readily obtainable by deducting, from the total of 13 weeks plus Remainder, the total of 19 weeks' thus –

200 *Business Interruption Insurance: Theory and Practice*

Remainder Period
Standard Turnover
13 weeks		345 000	
Remainder		235 000	
		580,000	
less 19 weeks		519 000	
Balance		61 000	
+ Trend 10%		6 100	
		67 100	

Achieved
13 weeks	160 000		
Remainder	250 000		
	410 000		
19 weeks −	350 000	60 000	
Shortage		7 100	

28% × 7 100   1 988
Does not exceed Savings
in Initial Period
of 20 000   Pay   1988

SUMMARY

Loss in Alternative Period	41 852	
Loss in 'Remainder' Period	1 988	
		43 840

Comparison

Loss under normal wording	42 840		
Loss under Consolidation	43 840	Pay	43 840

DB.06 INCREASE IN COST OF WORKING

The wording continues

> (b) IN RESPECT OF INCREASE IN COST OF WORKING
> so much of the additional expenditure described in clause (b) of the relative gross profit as exceeds the amount payable thereunder

This means that any amount of I.C.W. disallowed under the gross profit section of the policy can be brought forward for consideration under the wages item. This is only equitable, since turnover embraces both gross profit and wages and any money spent on I.C.W. reduces the amount of turnover lost. If turnover is maintained then there is more production to pay the wages and the Insured and the Insurer benefit.

In addition, any amount disallowed under Gross Profit when that insurance is subject to average can also be brought in for consideration.

Wages represent a major part of the cost of production. If wages are not included in the gross profit item, the rate of gross profit is greatly reduced and it is likely that, when this reduced percentage is applied to the turnover saved by spending on I.C.W. to produce the "Economic Limit", part of the expenditure will be disallowed.

The Data sheet shows the Insured spent 35 000 on I.C.W. and this expenditure saved turnover of 55 000, the rate of Gross Profit being 32 per cent. The Economic Limit under the gross profit item would be

32% × 55 000 = 17 600

Insured spent	35 000
Economic Limit under gross profit item	17 600
Balance to be considered under wages	17 400

The "Economic Limit" under the Wages item is contained in the following wording:

> but not more than the additional amount which would have been payable in respect of reduction in turnover under the provision of clauses (a) (i) and (ii) of this item had such expenditure not been incurred.

When there is a fairly lengthy period of delay in the recovery of the turnover, the economic limit under the Wages item is usually based on the Remainder percentage, on the grounds that expenditure on I.C.W. benefits the last part of the Indemnity Period rather than the beginning. The argument is that if the Insured chooses to insure Wages on a partial basis, it is only fair that the cost of the I.C.W. should be met on the same basis.

If the Insured can demonstrate a reduction in the Shortage in Turnover in the Initial Period due to expenditure of I.C.W., then it will be seen that the wording provides for this and a calculation for each of the Initial and the Remainder Periods must be made.

In the case before us, the Indemnity Period lasted approximately 21 weeks and the Consolidation (19 weeks) is to the advantage of the Insured. It could fairly be argued that as the bulk of the I.C.W, expenditure benefitted both Insured and Insurer during the first 19 weeks, there is a case to treat the bulk of the expenditure as repayable at the full rate.

If the first week of the 19 weeks is ignored, since there will have been very little expenditure on I.C.W. in this week, that leaves 18 out of the 21 weeks during which 100 per cent of wages would have been incurred.

The Data sheet shows that the expenditure of I.C.W. saved 55 000 of turnover. Applying the Rate of Wages to this figure gives

28% × 55000 = 15 400.

If it is agreed that the Economic Limit is 18/21 of this figure, the amount payable is 13 200. (Note that under Consolidation there is no Remainder Period as such – all the cover is in the Alternative Period – and therefore only I.C.W. in the Alternative Period can be considered.)

The loss payable in respect of Wages on the normal basis of 100 per cent for 13 weeks and 25 per cent of the Remainder would be 42 480, but "Consolidation" provides a better settlement for the Insured, so the amount of the claim so far is

202 *Business Interruption Insurance: Theory and Practice*

Loss under Wages item	43 840
Increase in Cost of Working	13 200
Total	57 040

DB.07 PROPORTIONATE REDUCTION (AVERAGE)

As was explained in Chapter 9, Section 9.03, where the insurance is not Declaration Linked there will be the check that the sum insured is adequate.

For Dual Basis Wages, the following wording is used:

> provided that if the sum insured by this item be less than the sum produced by applying the rate of wages to the annual turnover (or to a proportionately increased multiple thereof where the maximum indemnity period exceeds twelve months) the amount payable under this item shall be proportionately reduced.

The definition of Annual Turnover does not appear in the Dual Basis wording as Wages are usually item 2 of the B/I policy. Readers are reminded that Annual Turnover is the turnover in the 12 months immediately preceding the date of the Damage, with Trend applied, and in this case, the Data sheet shows that the annual Turnover was 1 538 600.

To check whether proportionate reduction will apply, the calculation is

Annual Turnover	1 538 600
+ Trend 10%	153 860
	1 692 460

Rate of Wages × Annual Turnover (adjusted for Trend) =

28% × 1 692 460 = 473 889.

To obtain a full recovery of the loss, Insured needs a sum insured in excess of 473 889.

The sum insured on the Data sheet is shown as

(1) 475 000, which is in excess of 473 889. The loss of 57 040 is therefore paid in full.
(2) 450 000, which is less than 473 889. Proportionate reduction therefore applies and the claim payable will be

$$\frac{450\ 000}{473\ 889} \times \frac{57\ 040}{1} = 54\ 164.58$$

DB.08 SUMMARY OF LOSS CALCULATION

A statement of the calculation of the loss under Dual Basis is as follows:

Rate of Wages − $\dfrac{\text{Wages}}{\text{Turnover}} \times \dfrac{100}{1}$

$$\frac{420\,000}{1\,500\,000} \times \frac{100}{1} \times = 28\%$$

Initial Period –
 Standard turnover   345 000
 + Trend 10%   34 500

            379 500
 Achieved   160 000

 Shortage   219 500

 28% × 219 500 =   61 460
 less Savings   19 000

                 42 460

Remainder Period –
 Standard turnover   235 000
 + Trend 10%   23 500

            258 500
 Achieved   250 000

 Shortage   8 500

 28% × 8 500 =   2 380
 less Savings   2 000   380

 Limit
 25% × 28% × 8 500 =   595
 + Savings from
 Initial Period   19 000

 Limit   19 595   Pay   380

                 42 840

Consolidation –
 Alternative Period –
  Standard turnover   519 000
  + Trend 10%   51 900

            570 900
 Achieved   350 000

 Shortage   220 900

 28% × 220 900   61 852
 less Savings   20 000

                 41 852

204 Business Interruption Insurance: Theory and Practice

"Remainder Period" –
Standard turnover –

13 weeks	345 000
Remainder	235 000
Total turnover	580 000
less 19 weeks	519 000
Balance	61 000
+ Trend 10%	6 100
	67 100

Achieved –

13 weeks	160 000	
Remainder	250 000	
	410 000	
19 weeks	350 000	60 000
Shortage		7 100

28% × 7 100 =   1 988
Does not exceed
Savings in Initial
Period of 20 000   pay   1 988
                                                                              43 840

COMPARISON

Loss under normal wording	42 840
Loss under Consolidation	43 840

Pay   43 840

Increase in Cost of Working –
Insured spent 35 000 which saved turnover of 55 000.

Insured spent	35 000
Limit under G.P. item	
32% × 55 000	17 600
	17 400

Balance to be considered
Economic Limit –

$$28\% \times 55\,000 \times \frac{18}{21}$$ Pay   13 200

57 040

Proportionate reduction –
Annual turnover 1 538 600
+ Trend 10% 153 860

1 692 460

28% × 1 692 460 = 473 889.

Sum insured (1) 475 000 exceeds 473 889 Pay 57 040

Sum insured (2) 450 000 less than 473 889

$$\frac{450\,000}{473\,889} \times \frac{57\,040}{1} =$$ Pay 54 164.58

APPENDIX 7

Fines or Damages; and Premium Adjustment Clauses

FINES OR DAMAGES

Item No £ ———————————

On Fines or Damages for breach of contract

Item No

The insurance under this item is limited to fines or damages for breach of contract and the amount payable as indemnity thereunder shall be such sums as the Insured shall be legally liable to pay and shall pay in discharge of fines or damages, incurred solely in consequences of the Incident, for non-completion or late completion of orders.

PREMIUM ADJUSTMENT CLAUS4ES

Note: When "Gross Revenue" specification applies, substitute "Revenue" for "Profit" wherever it occurs.

PROVISIONAL PREMIUM – SUM INSURED BASIS ONLY

> The first and annual premiums are provisional being (75%) of the premiums payable at the commencement of the period of insurance with the balance of (25%) to be paid within 6 months of the expiry of that period except that –
>
> > in respect of any item(s) on Gross Profit the premium paid shall be adjusted on receipt by the Insurer of a declaration of Gross Profit earned during the financial year most nearly concurrent with such period of insurance, as reported by the Insured's auditors
> >
> > if any Incident shall have occurred giving rise to a claim for loss of Gross Profit the above mentioned declaration shall be increased by the Insurer for the purpose of premium adjustment by the amount by which Gross Profit was reduced during the financial year solely in consequence of the Incident
> >
> > if the declaration (adjusted as provided for above and proportionately increased where the Maximum Indemnity Period exceeds 12 months)
> >
> > > (a) is less than (75%) of the sum insured on Gross Profit for the relative period, the Insurer will allow a pro rata return of premium not exceeding (33.3%) of the provisional premium paid

(b) is greater than (75%) of the sum insured on Gross Profit for the relative period, the Insured shall pay a pro rata additional premium not exceeding (33.3%) of the provisional premium paid.

In the event that no declaration is received within 6 months of the expiry of such period of insurance the balance of (25%) shall be paid.

NON-PROVISIONAL PREMIUM – SUM INSURED BASIS ONLY

The premium paid hereon may be adjusted on receipt by the Insurer of a declaration of Gross Profit earned during the financial year most nearly concurrent with the period of insurance, as reported by the Insured's Auditors.

If any Incident shall have occurred giving rise to a claim for loss of Gross Profit the above mentioned declaration shall be increased by the Insurer for the purpose of premium adjustment by the amount by which the Gross Profit was reduced during the financial year solely in consequence of the Incident.

If either declaration (adjusted as provided for above and proportionately increased where the Maximum Indemnity Period exceeds 12 months) is less than the sum insured on Gross Profit for the relative period of insurance the Insurer will allow a pro rata return of premium not exceeding 50% of the premium paid.

DECLARATION-LINKED BASIS

The first and annual premiums (in respect of Item No. 1) are provisional and are based on the Estimated Gross Profit.

The Insured shall provide to the Insurer not later than six months after the expiry of each period of insurance a declaration confirmed by the Insured's auditors of the Gross Profit earned during the financial year most nearly concurrent with the period of insurance.

If any Incident shall have occurred giving rise to a claim for loss of Gross Profit the above mentioned declaration shall be increased by the Insurer for the purpose of premium adjustment by the amount by which the Gross Profit was reduced during the financial year solely in consequence of the Incident.

If the declaration (adjusted as provided for above and proportionately increased where the Maximum Indemnity Period exceeds 12 months)

(a) is less than the Estimated Gross Profit for the relative period of insurance the Insurer will allow a pro rata return of the premium paid on the Estimated Gross Profit (but not exceeding 50% of such premium)
(b) is greater than the Estimated Gross Profit for the relative period of insurance the Insured shall pay a pro rata addition to the premium paid on the Estimated Gross Profit.

APPENDIX 8

Special Perils

SPECIAL PERILS (Including Limited Engineering Perils) – BUSINESS INTERRUPTION

SUB-SECTION 1 – SPECIAL PERILS (Other than as provided for in SUB-SECTION 2)

Notes: The following wordings are designed for use with the Standard Fire Policy (B/I). When used with earlier versions of the Standard Fire Policy

1 the following addition should be made at the head of the extension –

Note: The words "CONSEQUENTIAL LOSS" in capital letters, shall mean loss resulting from interruption of or interference with the Business carried on by the Insured at the Premises in consequence of loss or destruction of or damage to property used by the Insured at the Premises for the purpose of the Business.

2 omit "Exclusions and" from Part A

Use Part A of the Master Wording and incorporate the Special Conditions from Part B as indicated in Part C. Special Condition 4 should also be included where a deductible applies under the Material Damage insurance.

MASTER WORDING

Part A

The insurance by (item(s) . . . of) this policy shall subject to all the Exclusions and Conditions of the policy (except in so far as they may be hereby expressly varied) and the Special Conditions set out below extend to include:–

> Here insert the wording(s) from the boxes in Part C appropriate in the peril(s) selected

Part B

SPECIAL CONDITIONS

1 The liability of the Insurer shall in no case under this extension and the policy exceed the liability of the Insurer stated in the policy.
  Note: If a lower limit of liability applies in respect of specific perils the wording should be amended.

2   This insurance does not cover
    (a) CONSEQUENTIAL LOSS occasioned by
        (i) riot or civil commotion (except to the extent they may be specifically insured hereby)
        (ii) war invasion act of foreign enemy hostilities (whether war be declared or not) civil war rebellion revolution insurrection or military or usurped power

    (b) loss destruction or damage occasioned by or happening through or occasioning loss or destruction of or damage to any property whatsoever or any loss or expense whatsoever resulting or arising therefrom or any consequential loss directly or indirectly caused by or contributed to by or arising from

        (i) ionising radiations or contamination by radioactivity from any nuclear fuel or from any nuclear waste from the combustion of nuclear fuel
        (ii) the radioactive toxic explosive or other hazardous properties of any explosive nuclear assembly or nuclear component thereof

    (c) CONSEQUENTIAL LOSS in Northern Ireland occasioned by or happening through
        (i) civil commotion
        (ii) any unlawful wanton or malicious act committed maliciously by a person or persons acting on behalf of or in connection with any unlawful association

        For this purpose of this Condition –

        "unlawful association" means any organisation which is engaged in terrorism and includes an organisation which at any relevant time is a proscribed organisation within the meaning of the Northern Ireland (Emergency Provisions) Act 1973

        "terrorism" means the use of violence for political ends and includes any use of violence for the purpose of putting the public or any section of the public in fear

        In any action, suit or other proceedings where the Insurer alleges that by reason of the provisions of this Condition any CONSEQUENTIAL LOSS is not covered by this policy the burden of proving that such CONSEQUENTIAL LOSS is covered shall be upon the Insured

    (d) loss resulting from pollution or contamination but this shall not exclude loss resulting from destruction of or damage to property used by the Insured at the Premises for the purpose of the Business, not otherwise excluded, caused by
        (i) pollution or contamination at the Premises which itself results from a peril hereby insured against
        (ii) any peril hereby insured against which itself results from pollution or contamination

3   The Insured shall at his own expense deliver to the Insurer within 7 days of its happening full details of loss destruction or damage caused by riot civil commotion strikers locked-out workers persons taking part in labour disturbances or malicious persons.

4   It shall not be a condition precedent to liability in respect of CONSEQUENTIAL LOSS that payment shall have been made or liability admitted under the insurance covering the interest of the Insured in the property at the Premises against such loss destruction or damage if no payment shall have been made nor liability admitted solely owing to the operation of a proviso in that insurance excluding liability for losses below a specified amount.

5 For the purpose of peril(s) (15 to 20) only:–

(a) EXPLOSION shall mean the sudden and violent rending of the permanent structure of the plant by force of internal steam pressure causing bodily displacement of any part of the structure together with forcible ejectment of the contents.

The undernoted defects do not themselves constitute explosion even though repair or replacement may be necessary but explosion arising from any such effect is not excluded.

(b) COLLAPSE shall mean the sudden and dangerous distortion (whether or not attended by rupture) of any part of the plant caused by crushing stress by force of steam gas air or liquid pressure.

The undernoted defects do not themselves constitute collapse even though repair or replacement may be necessary but collapse arising from any such defect is not excluded.

The defects referred to above are:

(i) wearing away or wasting of the material of the plant by leaking corrosion action of fuel or otherwise
(ii) slowly developing deformation or distortion of any part of the plant
(iii) cracks fractures blisters laminations flaws or grooving even when accompanied by leakage
(iv) failure of joints.

(c) OVERHEATING shall mean the sudden and accidental damage to any part of the plant caused by overheating consequent upon general deficiency of water therein and which immediately prevents or makes unsafe its continued use.

6 It shall not be a condition precedent to liability arising from loss destruction or damage caused by explosion or collapse of steam pipes that there shall be in force an insurance covering the interest of the Insured in the property at the Premises against the loss destruction or damage giving rise to the claim.

7 In so far as this insurance relates to CONSEQUENTIAL LOSS caused by Subsidence Ground Heave or Landslip

(a) The Insured shall notify the Insurer immediately they become aware of any demolition, groundworks, excavation or construction being carried out on any adjoining site;
(b) The Insurer shall then have the right to vary the terms or cancel this cover

Part C

1 EXPLOSION

CONSEQUENTIAL LOSS caused by EXPLOSION excluding
(a) CONSEQUENTIAL LOSS caused by the bursting of any vessel machine or apparatus (not being a boiler or economiser on the Premises) in which internal pressure is due to steam only and belonging to or under the control of the Insured
(b) CONSEQUENTIAL LOSS by pressure waves caused by aircraft or other aerial devices travelling at sonic or supersonic speeds

---

and Special Condition 1 (or 1 and 2 if written on earlier Standard Fire Policy form).

Note: Where the FIRE risk is not covered by the same policy, add the following exclusions –

"(c) CONSEQUENTIAL LOSS caused by fire resulting from explosion
(d) CONSEQUENTIAL LOSS caused by explosion
  (i) of boilers used for domestic purposes only
  (ii) of any other boilers or economisers on the Premises
  (iii) of gas use for domestic purposes only."

2 AIRCRAFT

> CONSEQUENTIAL LOSS (by fire or otherwise) caused by AIRCRAFT or other aerial devices or articles dropped therefrom excluding CONSEQUENTIAL LOSS by pressure waves caused by aircraft or other aerial devices travelling at sonic or supersonic speeds

and Special Condition 1 (or 1 and 2 if written on earlier Standard Fire Policy Form).

Note: Where the FIRE risk is not covered by the same policy, amend the words in brackets to "(other than by fire)".

3 RIOT

> CONSEQUENTIAL LOSS (by fire or otherwise including explosion) caused by RIOT CIVIL COMMOTION STRIKERS LOCKED-OUT WORKERS or persons taking part in labour disturbances or malicious persons acting on behalf of or in connection with any political organisation excluding CONSEQUENTIAL LOSS
>
> (a) arising from confiscation requisition or destruction by order of the government or any public authority
>
> (b) arising from cessation work
>
> (c) arising from deliberate erasure loss distortion or corruption of information on computer systems or other records programs or software

and Special Conditions 1 and 3 (or 1, 2 and 3 if written on earlier Standard Fire Policy form).

Note: Where the FIRE risk is not covered by the same policy add the following exclusion –
"(d) by fire caused by Strikers Locked-out Workers or persons taking part in labour disturbances or malicious persons"

4 RIOT (FIRE ONLY)

> CONSEQUENTIAL LOSS (by fire only) caused by RIOT OR CIVIL COMMOTION excluding CONSEQUENTIAL LOSS arising from
>
> (a) confiscation requisition or destruction by order of the government or any public authority
>
> (b) cessation of work

and Special Conditions 1 and 3 (or 1, 2 and 3 if written on earlier Standard Fire Policy form).

5 RIOT AND MALICIOUS DAMAGE

> CONSEQUENTIAL LOSS caused by RIOT CIVIL COMMOTION STRIKERS LOCKED-OUT WORKERS or persons taking part in labour disturbances or MALICIOUS PERSONS excluding CONSEQUENTIAL LOSS
>
> (a) arising from confiscation requisition or destruction by order of the government or any public authority
>
> (b) arising from cessation of work
>
> (c) caused (other than by fire or explosion) by Malicious Persons (not acting on behalf of or in connection with any political organisation) in respect of any building which is empty or not in use
>
> (d) arising from deliberate erasure loss distortion or corruption of information on computer systems or other records programs or software

and Special Conditions 1, 3 and 4 (or 1, 2, 3 and 4 if written on earlier Standard Fire Policy form).

Note: Where the FIRE risk is not covered by the same policy add "if insured hereby" to the words in brackets in exclusion
(c) and the following exclusion

"(e) by fire caused by Strikers Locked-out Workers or persons taking part in labour disturbances or Malicious Persons."

6 (a) EARTHQUAKE – FIRE RISK ONLY

> CONSEQUENTIAL LOSS (by fire only) caused by EARTHQUAKE

(b) EARTHQUAKE – SHOCK RISK ONLY

> CONSEQUENTIAL LOSS caused by EARTHQUAKE (other than fire)

(c) EARTHQUAKE – FIRE AND SHOCK RISKS

> CONSEQUENTIAL LOSS caused by EARTHQUAKE

and Special Condition 1 (or 1 and 2 if written on earlier Standard Fire Policy form).

7 SUBTERRANEAN FIRE

> CONSEQUENTIAL LOSS caused by SUBTERRANEAN FIRE

and Special Condition 1 (or 1 and 2 if written on earlier Standard Fire Policy form).

8 SPONTANEOUS FERMENTATION

> CONSEQUENTIAL LOSS (by fire only) resulting from any property's own SPONTANEOUS FERMENTATION OR HEATING

Appendices 213

and Special Condition 1 (or 1 and 2 if written on earlier Standard Fire Policy form).

9 STORM

CONSEQUENTIAL LOSS caused by STORM excluding CONSEQUENTIAL LOSS

(a) (i) caused by the escape of water from the normal confines of any natural or artificial water course lake reservoir canal or dam
 (ii) caused by inundation from the sea whether resulting from storm or otherwise

(b) attributable solely to change in the water table level

(c) caused by frost subsidence ground heave or landslip

(d) in respect of movable property in the open, fences and gates

and Special Conditions 1 and 4 (or 1, 2 and 4 if written on earlier Standard Fire Policy form).

Note: Where the FIRE risk is not covered by the same policy "lightning" should be added to exclusion (c).

10 STORM AND FLOOD

CONSEQUENTIAL LOSS caused by STORM or FLOOD excluding CONSEQUENTIAL LOSS

(a) attributable solely to change in the water table level

(b) caused by frost subsidence ground heave or landslip

(c) in respect of movable property in the open, fences and gates

and Special Conditions 1 and 4 (or 1, 2 and 4 if written on earlier Standard Fire Policy form).

Note: Where the FIRE risk is not covered by the same policy "lightning" should be added to exclusion (b).

11 ESCAPE OF WATER

CONSEQUENTIAL LOSS caused by ESCAPE OF WATER FROM ANY TANK APPARATUS OR PIPE excluding CONSEQUENTIAL LOSS

(a) caused by water discharged or leaking from any automatic sprinkler installation

(b) in respect of any building which is empty or not in use

and Special Conditions 1 and 4 (or 1, 2 and 4 if written on earlier Standard fire Policy form).

12 IMPACT (THIRD PARTY)

CONSEQUENTIAL LOSS caused by IMPACT by any road vehicle or animal not belonging to or under the control of the Insured or any occupier of the premises or their respective employees

and Special Condition 1 (or 1 and 2 if written on earlier Standard Fire Policy form).

13 IMPACT (THIRD PARTY AND OWN VEHICLES)

> CONSEQUENTIAL LOSS caused by IMPACT by any road vehicle or animal

and Special Conditions 1 and 4 (or 1, 2 and 4 if written on earlier Standard Fire Policy form).

14 SPRINKLER LEAKAGE

> CONSEQUENTIAL LOSS caused by ACCIDENTAL ESCAPE OF WATER FROM ANY AUTOMATIC SPRINKLER INSTALLATION in the Premises not caused by
>
> (a) freezing whilst the building in so far as it is in the Insured's ownership or tenancy is empty or not in use
> (b) explosion earthquake subterranean fire or heat caused by fire

and Special Condition 1 (or 1 and 2 if written on earlier Standard Fire Policy form).

15 EXPLOSION AND COLLAPSE OF STEAM PIPES

> CONSEQUENTIAL LOSS caused by EXPLOSION OR COLLAPSE OF STEAM PIPES at the Premises

and Special Conditions 1 and 5(a) (or 1, 2 and 5(a) if written on earlier Standard Fire Policy form).

17 EXPLOSION AND COLLAPSE OF VESSELS

> CONSEQUENTIAL LOSS caused by EXPLOSION OF VESSELS (other than boilers or economisers) under steam pressure or COLLAPSE OF VESSELS (other than boilers or economisers) under steam gas air or liquid pressure at the Premises

and Special Conditions 1, 5(a) and 5(b) (or 1, 2, 5(a) and 5(b) if written on earlier Standard Fire Policy form).

18 COLLAPSE OF BOILERS

> CONSEQUENTIAL LOSS caused by COLLAPSE OF BOILERS OR ECONOMISERS at the Premises

and Special Conditions 1 and 5(b) (or 1, 2 and 5(b) if written on earlier Standard Fire Policy form).

19 OVERHEATING OF TUBES

> CONSEQUENTIAL LOSS caused by OVERHEATING OF TUBES consequent upon general deficiency of water in boilers at the Premises

and Special Conditions 1 and 5(c) (or 1, 2 and 5(c) if written on earlier Standard Fire Policy form).

Appendices 215

20 OVERHEATING OF BOILERS AND ECONOMISERS

> CONSEQUENTIAL LOSS caused by OVERHEATING OF BOILERS OR ECONOMISERS at the Premises

and Special Conditions 1 and 5(c) (or 1, 2 and 5(c) if written on earlier Standard Fire Policy form).

21 SUBSIDENCE, GROUND HEAVE, LANDSLIP

> CONSEQUENTIAL LOSS caused by SUBSIDENCE or GROUND HEAVE of any part of the site on which the property stands, or LANDSLIP excluding
>
> (a) CONSEQUENTIAL LOSS in respect of yards car-parks roads pavements walls gates and fences unless a building at the same premises used by the Insured for the purpose of the Business is also damaged thereby
>
> (b) CONSEQUENTIAL LOSS caused by or consisting of
>
> (i) the normal settlement or bedding down of new structures
> (ii) the settlement or movement of made-up ground
> (iii) coastal or river erosion
> (iv) defective design or workmanship or the use of defective materials
> (v) fire subterranean fire explosion earthquake or escape of water from any tank apparatus or pipe
>
> (c) loss resulting from destruction or damage which originated prior to the inception of this cover
>
> (d) CONSEQUENTIAL LOSS resulting from
> (i) demolition construction structural alteration or repair of any property or
> (ii) groundworks or excavation
> at the same premises

and Special Conditions 1, 4 and 7 (or 1, 2 4 and 7 if written on earlier Standard Fire Policy form).

SUB-SECTION 2 – NOTIFIABLE DISEASE, VERMIN, DEFECTIVE SANITARY ARRANGEMENTS, MURDER AND SUICIDE

Note: The following wordings are designed solely for use with the Standard Fire Policy (B/I). When used with earlier versions of the Standard Fire Policy omit "Exclusions and" from Part A, and add Special Conditions 2(a),(b) and (c) from Part B of Sub-Section 1 substituting "loss" for "CONSEQUENTIAL LOSS".

Use Part A of the Master Wording and incorporate the Special Conditions from Part B as indicated in Part C.

MASTER WORDING

Part A
The insurance by (item(s) . . . of) this policy shall subject to all the Exclusions and Conditions of the policy (except in so far as they may be hereby expressly varied) and the Special Conditions set out below extend to include loss resulting from interruption of or

interference with the Business carried on by the Insured at the Premises in consequence of:–

> Here insert the wording(s) from the boxes in Part C appropriate to the peril(s) selected

Part B

SPECIAL CONDITIONS

1 Notifiable Disease shall mean illness sustained by any person resulting from –
   (a) food or drink poisoning, or
   (b) any human infectious or human contagious disease [excluding Acquired Immune Deficiency Syndrome (AIDS)], an outbreak of which the competent local authority has stipulated shall be notified to them.

2 For the purpose of this memorandum

Indemnity Period shall mean the period during which the results of the Business shall be affected in consequence of the occurrence discovery or accident, beginning –

(a) in the case of 1 and 4 above, with the date of the occurrence or discovery
(b) in the case of 2 and 3 above, with the date from which the restrictions on the Premises are applied and ending not later than the Maximum Indemnity Period thereafter.
Maximum Indemnity Period shall mean . . . . . . months.

Premises shall mean only those locations stated in the Premises definition; in the event that the policy includes an extension which deems loss destruction or damage at other locations to be an Incident such extension shall not apply to this memorandum.

3 For the purpose of this memorandum

Indemnity Period shall mean the period during which the results of the Business shall be affected in consequence of the occurrence discovery or accident, beginning with the date from which the restrictions on the Premises are applied (or in the case of 4 above, with the date of the occurrence) and ending not later that the Maximum Indemnity Period thereafter.

Maximum Indemnity Period shall mean . . . . . . months.

Premises shall mean only those locations stated in the Premises definition; in the event that the policy includes an extension which deems loss destruction or damage at other locations to be an Incident such extension shall not apply to this memorandum.

4 The Insurer shall not be liable under this memorandum for any costs incurred in the cleaning, repair, replacement, recall or checking of property.

5 The Insurer shall only be liable for the loss arising at those Premises which are directly affected by the occurrence discovery or accident.

6 The Insurer's liability under this memorandum shall not exceed £ . . . . in any one period of insurance, after the application of all other terms and conditions of this policy.

Part C

Hotels, Restaurants and Public Houses

1. (a) any occurrence of a Notifiable Disease (as defined below) at the Premises or attributable to food or drink supplied from the Premises
   (b) any discovery of an organism at the Premises likely to result in the occurrence of a Notifiable Disease
   (c) any occurrence of a Notifiable Disease (in the town/borough of . . .)(within a radius of 25 miles of the Premises)

2. the discovery of vermin or pests at the Premises which causes restructions on the use of the Premises on the order or advice of the competent local authority

3. any accident causing defects in the drains or other sanitary arrangements at the Premises which causes restrictions on the use of the Premises on the order of the competent local authority

4. any occurrence of murder or suicide at the Premises.

and Special Conditions 1, 2, 4 and 5

Schools, Private Hospitals etc.

1. (a) any occurrence of a Notifiable Disease (as defined below) at the Premises or attributable to food or drink supplied from the Premises
   (b) any discovery of an organism at the Premises likely to result in the occurrence of a Notifiable Disease
   (c) any occurrence of a Notifiable Disease (in the town/borough of . . .)(within a radius of 25 miles of the Premises)

2. the discovery of vermin or pests at the Premises

3. any accident causing defects in the drains or other sanitary arrangements at the Premises

   which causes restrictions on the use of the Premises on the order or advice of the competent local authority

4. any occurrence of murder or suicide at the Premises.

and Special Conditions 1, 3, 4 and 5.

218 Business Interruption Insurance: Theory and Practice

Food Processors and Distributors

> 1 (a) any occurrence of a Notifiable Disease (as defined below) at the Premises or attributable to food or drink supplied from the Premises
> (b) any discovery of an organism at the Premises likely to result in the occurrence of a Notifiable Disease
>
> 2 the discover of vermin or pests at the Premises
>
> 3 any accident causing defects in the drains or other sanitary arrangements at the Premises
>
> which causes restrictions on the use of the Premises on the order or advice of the competent local authority
>
> 4 any occurrence of murder or suicide at the Premises.

and Special Conditions 1, 3, 4 and 6.

Notes: 1 Use only those parts of the wordings in the boxes as are appropriate.

2 Where cover is to be given for decontamination etc. add the following memorandum:–

Notwithstanding Special Condition 4 the insurance by this memorandum extends to include the costs and expenses necessarily incurred with the consent of the Insurer in –

(i) cleaning and decontamination of property used by the Insured for the purpose of the Business (other than stock in trade),
(ii) removal and disposal of contaminated stock in trade,

at or from the Premises, the use of which has been restricted on the order or advice of the comptent local authority solely in consequence of the loss as defined above, provided that the Insurer's liability in respect of (i) and (ii) above shall not exceed £ . . . . . . in any one period of insurance after the application of all other terms and conditions of the policy.

APPENDIX 9
Special Clauses

SPECIAL CLAUSES

PROFESSIONAL ACCOUNTANTS CLAUSE modifying the Insurer's rights under Claims Condition 1

> Any particulars of details contained in the Insured's books of account or other business books or documents which may be required by the Insurer under Claims Condition 1 of this policy for the purpose of investigating or verifying any claim hereunder may be produced by professional accountants if at the time they are regularly acting as such for the Insured and their report shall be prima facie evidence of the particulars and details to which such report relates.
>
> The Insurer will pay to the Insured the reasonable charges payable by the Insured to their professional accountants for producing such particulars or details or any other proofs, information or evidence or evidence as may be required by the Insurer under the terms of Claims Condition 1 of this policy and reporting that such particulars or details are in accordance with the Insured's books of account or other business books or documents
>
> provided that the sum of the amount payable under this clause and the amount otherwise payable under the policy shall in no case exceed the liability of the Insurer as stated.

Notes: (1) "Auditors" may be substituted for "professional accountants"
       (2) the second paragraph and the proviso may be omitted
       (3) substitute "Condition 4", "Condition 14" or Condition 15" as appropriate for "Claims Conditions 1" when used with earlier versions of policy forms.

DEPARTMENTAL CLAUSE incorporating a departmental basis into specifications

> If the Business be conducted in departments the independent trading results of which are ascertainable, the provisions of clauses (a) and (b) of the item on Gross Profit shall apply separately to each department affected by the Incident [except that if the sum insured by the said item be less than the aggregate of the sums produced by applying the Rate of Gross Profit for each department of the Business (whether affected by the Incident or not) to its relative Annual Turnover (or to a proportionately increased multiple thereof where the Maximum Indemnity Period exceeds twelve months) the amount payable shall be proportionately reduced].

Note: For insurances on the declaration-linked basis the words in square brackets should be omitted.

SALVAGE SALE CLAUSE

> If, following any Incident giving rise to a claim under this policy, the Insured shall hold a salvage sale during the Indemnity Period, clause (a) of the item on Gross Profit shall, for the purpose of such claim, read as follows:–
> (a) **In respect of Reduction in Turnover**: the sum produced by applying the Rate of Gross Profit to the amount by which the Turnover during the Indemnity Period (less the Turnover for the period of the salvage sale) shall, in consequence of the Incident, fall short of the Standard Turnover, from which sum shall be deducted the Gross Profit actually earned during the period of the salvage sale.

NEW BUSINESS CLAUSE for businesses which have not completed a full year's working

> **Rate of Gross Profit:–** The Rate of Gross Profit earned on the Turnover during the period between the date of the commencement of the Business and the date of the Incident
>
> **Annual Turnover:–** The proportional equivalent, for a period of twelve months, of the Turnover realised during the period between the commencement of the Business and the date of the Incident
>
> **Standard Turnover:–** The proportional equivalent, for a period equal to the Indemnity period, of the Turnover realised during the period between the commencement of the Business and the date of the Incident
>
>) to which such adjustments shall be made as may be necessary to provide for the trend of the Business and for variations in or other circumstances affecting the Business either before or after the Incident which would have been affecting the Business had the Incident not occurred, so that the figures thus adjusted shall represent as nearly as may be reasonably practicable the results which but for the Incident would have been obtained during the relative period after the Incident

Note: Where "Gross Revenue" specification applies omit "Rate of Gross Profit" definition and substitute "Gross Revenue" for "Turnover" wherever it occurs.

MATERIAL DAMAGE PROVISO WAIVER for use with earlier version of Standard Fire Policy form.

> It shall not be a condition precedent to liability in respect of interruption or interference in consequence of destruction or damage (as within defined) that payment shall have been made or liability admitted under the insurance covering the interest of the Insured in the property at the Premises against such destruction or damage if no such payment shall have been made nor liability admitted solely owing to the operation of a proviso in such insurance excluding liability for losses below a specific amount.

ACCUMULATED STOCKS CLAUSE

> In adjusting any loss account shall be taken and an equitable allowance made if any reduction in Turnover due to the Incident is postponed by reason of the Turnover being temporarily maintained from accumulated stocks of finished goods in warehouses or depots.

Notes: The only combination of circumstances in which it is envisaged such a clause would operate are:–
 1 if a manufacturer's stock of finished goods
   (a) be depleted in keeping down the reduction in Turnover during the Indemnity Period, and
   (b) cannot be made good by the end of the Maximum Indemnity Period

and

 2 after the end of the period the manufacturer suffers loss because of the deficiency.

In such circumstances, provided that the Maximum Indemnity Period is not less than 12 months, it is equitable that within the limit of the benefit the Insurer has obtained under 1(a) an allowance should be made for the loss under 2.

It is recommended that the clause should not operate except in the above combination of circumstances.

APPENDIX 10
Business Interruption Extension Wordings

BUSINESS INTERRUPTION EXTENSION WORDINGS

SUB-SECTION 1 – EXTENSIONS (other than as provided for in Sub-Section 2)

> Any loss as insured by (items nos of) this policy resulting from interruption of or interference with the Business in consequence of loss destruction or damage at the undernoted situations or to property as undernoted shall be deemed to be an Incident provided that after the application of all other terms conditions and provisions of the policy the liability under this memorandum in respect of any occurrence shall not exceed
>
> (a) the percentage of the total of the sums insured (or 133.3% of the Estimated Gross Profit) by (item nos of) the policy or
> (b) the amount
> shown below against such situations or property as the limit
> (Here insert the appropriate wordings shown below including the limit required)

Notes: 1 If a lower limit of liability applies in respect of specific perils the wording must be amended.
2 For "All Risks" policies add "accidental" before "loss" in line 2.
3 For Standard Fire and Standard Fire and Specil Perils policies on earlier versions of policy forms delete "loss" in line 2.
4 Where "Gross Revenue" specification applies, substitute "Revenue" for "Profit" in (a)

SPECIFIED SUPPLIERS –

> The premises (situate in Great Britain or Northern Ireland) of the following supplier(s) (situate):–

Note: This extension should not include public utilities, telecommunications services or customers.

UNSPECIFIED SUPPLIERS AND STORAGE SITES –

The premises of any (other) of the Insured's suppliers manufacturers or processors of components, goods or materials but excluding the premises of any supply undertaking from which the Insured obtains electricity gas or water or telecommunications services and premises not in the occupation of the Insured, where property of the Insured is stored all in Great Britain or Northern Ireland	Limit .... but in no case exceeding £

Note: This extension should not include public utilities, telecommunication services or customers.

MOTOR VEHICLE MANUFACTURERS –

The premises of ....
(and any manufacturer supplying them with components or materials) all in Great Britain or Northern Ireland.

Note: This extension applies to the insurance of motor garage proprietors and motor traders.

PROPERTY STORED –

Property of the Insured whilst stored anywhere in Great Britain or Northern Ireland elsewhere than at premises in the occupation of the Insured.

PATTERNS, ETC –

Patterns, jigs, models, templets, moulds, dies, tools, plans, drawings and designs, the property o the Insured or held by them in trust for which they are responsible, whilst at the premises of any machine makers, engineers, founders or other metal workers (excluding any premises wholly or partly occupied by the Insured) or whilst in transit, all in Great Britain or Northern Ireland.

TRANSIT –

Property of the Insured whilst in transit in Great Britain or Northern Ireland.

Notes: 1 This extension should not apply to the insurances of: –
   (a) the business of any haulage contractor bus coach or taxi proprietor, private hirer furniture storer or remover
   (b) any other business where the turnover is dependent wholly or mainly on the operation of motor vehicles of any kind
   The Motor Vehicles extension should be used for such businesses.

2 The wording should be amended if members do not wish to provide impact cover for the conveying road or rail vehicle of waterborne craft.

MOTOR VEHICLES –

> Motor vehicles of the Insured in Great Britain or Northern Ireland elsewhere than at premises in the occupation of the Insured.

Note: The wording should be amended if members do not wish to provide cover in respect of impact and accidental damage.

CONTRACT SITES –

> Any situation in Great Britain or Northern Ireland not in the occupation of the Insured where the Insured is carrying out a contract.

PREVENTION OF ACCESS –

> Property in the vicinity of the Premises, loss or destruction of or damage to which shall prevent or hinder the use of the Premises or access therto, whether the Premises or property of the Insured therein shall be damaged or not, but excluding loss or destruction of or damage to property of any supply undertaking from which the Insured obtains electricity, gas or water, or telecommunications services which prevents or hinders the supply of such services, to the Premises.

Note: Delete "loss or" in line 1 when used with earlier versions of the Standard Fire or Standard Fire and Special Perils policy forms.

PUBLIC UTILITIES –

	Limit
Property at any [generating station or sub-station of the public electricity supply undertaking]	....
[land based premises of the public gas supply undertaking or of any natural gas producer linked directly therewith]	....
[water works or pumping station of the public water supply undertaking]	....
[land based premises of the public telecommunications undertaking]	.... but in no case exceeding £.............................
from which the Insured obtains (electricity) (gas) (water) or (telecommunications services) all in Great Britain or Northern Ireland.	

PROFESSIONAL INSURED – DOCUMENTS –

> Documents belonging to or held in trust by the Insured whilst temporarily at premises not in the occupation of the Insured or whilst in transit, all in Great Britain or Northern Ireland.

Appendices 225

SPECIFIED CUSTOMERS –

The premises (situate in Great Britain or Northern Ireland) of the following customer(s) (situate):–

UNSPECIFIED CUSTOMERS –

The premises of any (other) of the Insured's) Limit ....
customers situate in Great Britain or) but in no case
Northern Ireland) exceeding £

Provided that for the purposes of this extention the term 'customers' means those companies, organisations or individuals with whom, at the time of the Incident, the Insured has contracts or trading relationships to supply goods or services.

Note: When used with earlier versions of policy forms substitute 'Damage' for 'Incident' in line 5.

BUSINESS INTERRUPTION EXTENSION WORDINGS

SUB-SECTION 2 – ACCIDENTAL FAILURE OF THE PUBLIC SUPPLY OF ELECTRICITY GAS WATER OR TELECOMMUNICATIONS SERVICES

Note This wording is a wider alternative to the Public Utilities extension.

Any loss as insured by (items nos of) this policy resulting from interruption of or interference with the Business in consequence of the Contingencies specified below shall be deemed to be an Incident provided that after the application of all other terms, conditions and provisions of the policy and liability under this memorandum in respect of any one occurrence shall not exceed –

(a) the percentage of the total of the sums insured (or 133.3% of the Estimated Gross Profit) by (item nos of) the policy
or
(b) the amount

shown below against such Contingencies as the limit

	Limit
The Contingencies	
The accidental failure of –	
[the public supply of electricity at the terminal ends of the supply undertaking's service feeders at the Premises]	....
[the public supply of gas at the supply undertaking's meters at the Premises]	....
[the public supply of water at the supply undertaking's main stop cock serving the Premises]	....
[the public supply of telecommunications services at the incoming line terminals or receivers at the Premises resulting from –	
i) failure of satellites	.... but in no case exceeding £
ii) failure from any other cause]	.... but in no case exceeding £

in Great Britain or Northern Ireland

but excluding any failure –
i) which does not involve a cessation of supply for at least .... consecutive minutes/hours
ii) due to an Excluded Clause

Excluded Causes

1) Loss resulting from –
   a) failure caused by –
      i) the deliberate act of any supply undertaking or by the exercise by any such undertaking of its power to withhold or restrict supply or services
      ii) strikes or any labour or trade dispute
      iii) drought
      iv) other atmospheric or weather conditions, but this shall not exclude failure due to damage to equipment caused by such conditions

   b) failure of any satellite prior to its attaining its full operating function or whilst in or beyond the final year of its design life

   c) temporary interference with transmissions to and from satellites due to atmospheric, weather solar or lunar conditions

   d) failure due to the transfer of the Insured's satellite facility to another party.

2) Loss resulting from loss destruction or damage occasioned by war invasion act of foreign enemy hostilities (whether war be declared or not) civil war rebellion revolution insurrection military or usurped power nationalisation confiscation requisition seizure or destruction by the government or any public authority

3) Loss resulting from loss destruction or damage occasioned by or happening through or occasioning loss or destruction of or damage to any property whatsoever or any loss or expense whatsoever resulting or arising therefrom or any consequential loss directly or indirectly caused by or contributed to by or arising from –
   i) ionising radiations or contamination by radioactivity from any nuclear fuel or from any nuclear waste from the combustion of nuclear fuel
   ii) the radioactive toxic explosive or other hazardous properties of any explosive nuclear assembly or nuclear component thereof

4) Loss resulting from loss destruction or damage in Northern Ireland occasioned by or happening through –
   i) riot civil commotion and (except in respect of loss destruction or damage by fire or explosion) strikers locked-out workers or persons taking part in labour disturbances or malicious persons
   ii) any unlawful wanton or malicious act committed maliciously by a person or persons acting on behalf of or in connection with any unlawful association

   For the purpose of this exclusion –

   "unlawful association" means any organisation which is engaged in terrorism and includes an organisation which at any relevant time is a proscribed organisation within the meaning of the Northern Ireland (Emergency Provisions) Act, 1973

   "terrorism" means the use of violence for political ends and includes any use of violence for the purpose of putting the public or any section of the public in fear

In any action suit or other proceedings where the Insurer alleges that by reason of the provisions of this exclusion any loss resulting from such loss destruction or damage is not covered by this policy the burden of proving that such loss is covered shall be upon the Insured

Except as expressly varied hereby, the insurance by this extension is subject to all the terms and conditions of the policy.

Notes 1. **Gross Revenue**
Where "Gross Revenue" specification applies, substitute "Revenue" for "Profit" in (a).

                                                                                                              Limit

        2. **Failure of Telecommunications**
If cover in respect of satellites is not required amend wording as follows:
i) substitute
[the public supply of telecommunications services (other than satellite services) at the incoming line terminals or receivers at the Premises]   .... but in no case exceeding £

ii) amend the first two lines of Excluded Cause 1) to read –
"Loss resulting from failure caused by ....."
and delete b) c) and d)

        3. **Time/Monetary Excess**
If a time excess is required the wording should be suitably amended.
Similar action should be taken where a monetary excess is required in addition to or substitution for a time excess.

        4. **Deliberate Act Exclusion**
Excluded Clause 1a) i) may be qualified by adding –
"not performed for the sole purpose of safeguarding life or protecting the supply undertaking's system."

        5. **Standard Exclusions**
Excluded Causes 2), 3) and 4) are wider in application than those applying in the recommended Standard Business Interruption policies.

APPENDIX 11

Book Debts Insurance Wording

Item 1. On outstanding Debit Balances £

The insurance under Item 1 is limited to the loss sustained by the Insured in respect of Outstanding Debit Balances directly due to the damage and the amount payable in respect of any one occurrence of damage shall not exceed
   (i) the difference between
      (a) the Outstanding Debit Balances and
      (b) the total of the amounts received or traced in respect thereof;
   (ii) the additional expenditure incurred with the previous consent of the Company in tracing and establishing customers' debit balances after the damage;
provided that if the Sum Insured by this Item be less than the Outstanding Debit Balances the amount payable shall be proportionately reduced.

Item 2. On Auditors' Charges

£

The insurance under Item 2 is limited to the reasonable charges payable by the Insured to their Auditors for producing and certifying any particulars or details contained in the Insured's books of account or other business books or documents or such other proofs, information or evidence as may be required by the Company under the terms of Condition No. 4 of this Policy

Total Sum Insured ———

£ ————

Definitions

THE BUSINESS:

THE PREMISES:

OUTSTANDING DEBIT BALANCES: The total declared in the statement last given under the provisions of Memo. I adjusted for
   (a) bad debts

(b) amounts debited (or invoiced but not debited) and credited (including credit notes and cash not passed through the books at the time of the damage) to customers' accounts in the period between the date to which said last statement relates and the date of the damage, and

(c) any abnormal condition of trade which had or could have had a material effect on the business.

so that the figures thus adjusted shall represent as nearly as reasonably practicable those which would have obtained at the date of the damage had the damage not occurred.

CUSTOMERS' ACCOUNTS

WARRANTY: It is warranted that the Insured's books of account or other business books or records in which Customers' Accounts are shown shall be kept in fire resisting safes or fire resisting cabinets when not in use.

MEMO. 1: The insured shall within thirty days of the end of each month deposit with the Company a signed statement showing the total amount outstanding in Customers' Accounts as set out in the Insured's Accounts as at the end of the said month. On the expiry of each period of insurance the actual premium shall be calculated at the rate per cent per annum on the average amount insured, i.e., the total of the sums declared divided by the number of declarations. If the actual premium shall be less than the First Premium (or in the case of the second and subsequent periods of insurance the Annual Premium) the difference shall be repaid to the Insured, but such repayments shall not exceed one half of the First or Annual Premium respectively.

If the amount of a declaration exceeds the sum insured applicable at the date of such declaration, then for the purposes of this memorandum only the Insured shall be deemed to have declared such a sum insured.

In consideration of the insurance not being reduced by the amount of any loss the Insured shall pay the appropriate extra premium on the amount of the loss from the date thereof to the date of the expiry of the period of insurance.

APPENDIX 12

Research Expenditure Wording

Specification referred to in Policy No.
in the name of

Item No
1. On research establishment
   expenditure ....
   Total sum insured

Sum insured
£

—

—

The indemnity under this item is limited to the loss sustained by the insured in consequence of the damage in respect of (*a*) the *research establishment expenditure* and (*b*) *increase in cost of working*, and the amount payable as indemnity thereunder shall be:
   (*a*) *In respect of research establishment expenditure*. For each working week in the *indemnity period* during which the activities of the business are, in consequence of the damage,
      (i) *Totally interrupted* or totally given over to the re-working of projects affected by the damage – *the insured amount* per week;
      (ii) *Partially interrupted* or partially given over to the re-working of projects affected by the damage – an equitable proportion of the *insured amount* per week based upon the time rendered ineffective by reason of the damage;
   (*b*) *Increase in cost of working* reasonably and necessarily incurred solely in consequence of the damage in order to minimise the interruption but the amount payable under this heading shall not exceed the additional amount that would have been payable under (*a*) for loss of *research expenditure* if no such *increase in cost of working* had been incurred,
less any sum saved during the *indemnity period* in respect of such of the *research establishment* expenses as may cease or be reduced in consequence of the damage,
provided that if the *sum insured* hereby is less than the *annual research expenditure (see below)* the amount payable under (*a*) and (*b*) hereof shall be proportionately reduced.

Note 1: To the extent that the Insured is accountable to the tax authorities for Value Added Tax, all terms in this policy shall be exclusive of such tax.
Note 2: For the purpose of these definitions, any adjustment implemented in current cost accounting shall be disregarded.

Definitions

Research Establishment Expenditure. The total expenditure on research by the insured at the premises less the relative cost of raw materials consumed.

Insured Amount per week. One fiftieth part of the *research establishment expenditure* incurred during the financial year immediatley before the date of the damage

Annual Research Establishment Expenditure. The aggregate amount of the *research establishment expenditure* incurred during the twelve months immediately before the date of the damage

to which such adjustments shall be made as may be necessary to provide for the trend of the business and for variations in or other circumstances affecting the business either before or after the damage or which would have affected the business had the damage not occurred, so that the figures thus adjusted shall represent as nearly as may be reasonably practicable the results which but for the damage would have been obtained during the relative period after the damage.

Indemnity Period. The period beginning with the date of the damage and ending not later than 12 months thereafter during which the activities of the business shall be interrupted in consequence of the damage.

Note: If an indemnity period of other than twelve months is required the proportionate weekly amount is suitably amended.

APPENDIX 13

Gross Revenue Wording – Declaration-Linked Basis

GROSS REVENUE WORDING – DECLARATION-LINKED BASIS

Item No.		Estimated Gross Revenue
1	On Gross Revenue	£
		–

The insurance under Item No. 1 is limited to (a) **Loss of Gross Revenue and** (b) **Increase in Cost of Working** and the amount payable as indemnity thereunder shall be:–
(a) **in respect of Loss of Gross Revenue:** the amount by which the Gross Revenue during the Indemnity Period shall fall short of the Standard Gross Revenue in consequence of the Incident
(b) **in respect of Increase in Cost of Working:** the additional expenditure necessarily and reasonably incurred for the sole purpose of avoiding or diminishing the reduction in Gross Revenue which but for that expenditure would have taken place during the Indemnity Period in consequence of the Incident, but not exceeding the amount of reduction in Gross Revenue thereby avoided

less any sum saved during the Indemnity Period in respect of such of the charges and expenses of the Business payable out of Gross Revenue as may cease or be reduced in consequence of the Incident

Notwithstanding proviso 2 on the face of this policy

(i) the liability of the Insurer shall in no case exceed, in respect of Gross Revenue 133.3% of the Estimated Gross Revenue stated herein, in respect of each other item 100% of the sum insured stated herein, nor in the whole the sum of 133.3% of the Estimated Gross Revenue and 100% of the sums insured by other items, or such other amounts as may be substituted therefor by memorandum signed by or on behalf of the Insurer
(ii) in the absence of written notice by the Insured or the Insurer to the contrary the Insurer's liability shall not stand reduced by the amount of any loss, the Insured undertaking to pay the appropriate additional premium for such automatic reinstatement of cover.

DEFINITIONS

Notes: 1 To the extent that the Insured is accountable to the tax authorities for Value Added Tax, all terms in this policy shall be exclusive of such tax.
2 For the purpose of these definitions, any adjustment implemented in current cost accounting shall be disregarded.

Appendices   233

Incident: Loss or destruction of or damage to property used by the Insured at the Premises for the purpose of the Business.

Indemnity Period: The period beginning with the occurrence of the Incident and ending not later than the Maximum Indemnity Period thereafter during which the results of the Business shall be affected in consequence thereof.

Maximum Indemnity Period: months.

Gross Revenue: The money paid or payable to the Insured for services rendered in the course of the Business at the Premises.

Estimated Gross Revenue: The amount declared by the Insured to the Insurer as representing not less than the Gross Revenue which it is anticipated will be earned by the Business during the financial year most nearly concurrent with the period of insurance (or a proportionately increased multiple thereof where the Maximum Indemnity Period exceeds twelve months).

| Standard Gross Revenue:– The Gross Revenue during that period in the twelve months immediately before the date of the Incident which corresponds with the Indemnity Period |)))))))))))) | to which such adjustments shall be made as may be necessary to provide for the trend of the Business and for variations in or other circumstances affecting the Business either before or after the Incident which would have affected the Business had the Incident not occurred, so that the figures thus adjusted shall represent as nearly as may be reasonably practicable the results which but for the Incident would have been obtained during the relative period after the Incident |

Alternative Trading Clause: If during the Indemnity Period goods shall be sold or services rendered elsewhere than at the Premises for the benefit of the Business either by the Insured or by others on his behalf the money paid or payable in respect of such sales or services shall be brought into account in arriving at the Gross Revenue during the Indemnity Period.

Renewal Clause: The Insured shall prior to each renewal provide the Insurer with the Estimated Gross Revenue for the financial year most nearly concurrent with the ensuing year of insurance.

Premium Adjustment Clause: The first and annual premiums (in respect of Item 1) are provisional and are based on the Estimated Gross Revenue.

The Insured shall provide to the Insurer not later than six months after the expiry of each period of insurance a declaration confirmed by the Insured's auditors of the Gross Revenue earned during the financial year most nearly concurrent with the period of insurance.

If any Incident shall have occurred giving rise to a claim for loss of Gross Revenue the above mentioned declaration shall be increased by the Insurer for the purpose of premium adjustment by the amount by which the Gross Revenue was reduced during the financial year solely in consequence of the Incident.

If the declaration (adjusted as provided above and proportionately increased where the Maximum Indemnity Period exceeds 12 months)

(a) is less than the Estimated Gross Revenue for the relative period of insurance the Insurer will allow a pro rata return of premium paid on the Estimated Gross Revenue (but not exceeding 50% of such premium)
(b) is greater than the Estimated Gross Revenue for the relative period of insurance the Insurer shall pay a pro rata addition to the premium paid on the Estimated Gross Revenue.

APPENDIX 14

Collective Policies

A *Any of the policy wordings can be converted into a Collective policy as follows:*

1 **Face of Policy**
   (a) For "The Insurer agrees" in line one substitute "The Insurers severally agree each for the proportion set against its name"
   (b) Add penultimate paragraph as follows:–
       "The liability of each of the Insurers individually shall be limited to the proportion set against its name."
   (c) Amend "signature" to read
       "Signed by a representative of the Leading Office on behalf of the Insurers".

2 **Elsewhere**
   Substitute "Insurers" for "Insurer" and, where necessary, amend verb appropriately.

3 **Schedule**
   (a) Against "THE INSURER" insert "As detailed within"
   (b) Amend "Insurer's liability" to "Insurers' liability"
   (c) Continue the Schedule as follows:–

THE SCHEDULE (continued)

The Insurers	Proportion of Specification	Reference Numbers
(Leading Office)		

B *As an alternative to "A" a normal policy form can be used with the following conversion page.*

THE SCHEDULE (continued)

1 The opening words, "The Insurer agrees" on the face of this policy are amended to read "The Insurers severally agree each for the proportion set against its name".

2 "Insurers" is substituted for "Insurer" wherever else it appears in this policy.

3 The liability of each of the Insurers individually shall be limited to the proportion set against its name.

4 The undernoted signature replaces that appearing on the face of this policy:

(insert signature here)

Signed by a representative of the Leading Office on behalf of the Insurers listed below.

The Insurers	Proportion of Specification	Reference Numbers
(Leading Office)		

Note: Add "S" to "THE INSURER" on the Schedule and insert "As detailed within".

APPENDIX 15

City Tailors Ltd v. Evans (1921)

CITY TAILORS LTD *v.* EVANS

Court of Appeal before Lords Justices Bankes, Scrutton and Atkin
(9th December, 1921)

Type of Policy – Valued amount per working day

LORD JUSTICE BANKES: "... The respondents, the plaintiffs, in this action, carried on business as manufacturing tailors at 226/228, Old Street, E.C. At these premises garments were made which were distributed to shops belonging to the respondents at various places. The respondents insured the profits of the Old Street business against fire at Lloyd's. The policy ... is on a 'profits insurance form' – by which the agreement of the underwriters is expressed to be subject to the conditions and definitions expressed in and (or) endorsed on the policy. In the body of the policy it is expressed to be a valued policy upon loss of profits ... those profits are valued at £100 per working day ... a fire occurred in the month of April, 1920, as a result of which the premises at Old Street were almost entirely destroyed and work was partially but not entirely stopped there for the full period covered by the policy. The respondents were able to secure and did secure temporary premises at Craven Street in the near vicinity to their Old Street premises, and there they continued the manufacturing business which, owing to the fire, they could not continue at Old Street ... Disputes arose between the parties as to whether in ascertaining the amount due to the respondents any account should be taken of the output from the temporary premises at Craven Street ... I have considerable doubt whether condition 3" (*The assured shall use due diligence and do and concur in doing all things reasonably practicable to minimise any interruption of or interference with the business and to avoid or diminish any loss*) "ought or ought not to have any effect given to it. I do not think that the condition can be read as imposing an obligation upon the assured in the event of a fire to continue their business in fresh premises in order to reduce the underwriters' loss; on the other hand there is room for contending that if the assured do continue their business in fresh premises they ought not as against the underwriters, and under a contract which is in its nature a contract of indemnity, to be allowed to retain both the profits of the business in the new premises and the valued loss of profits of the business in the old premises, and that a term should be implied in the contract that the former should be taken into account in diminution of the loss. I hardly think the facts warrant such an implication and I am, therefore, not prepared to accept the appellant's contention with regard to the effect of Condition 3."

LORD JUSTICE SCRUTTON: "... It may be that the result gives the assured more than an indemnity. Valued policies often do and the rules of English law assist the process ... I entirely agree ... that this was a local insurance and a valued total loss of local profits and that profits made elsewhere need not be brought into account."*

---

* Policies issued after this decision give the insurers the right to take credit for business transferred to other premises. See Alternative Trading Clause.

APPENDIX 16

Overseas Wording: Model Fire and Special Perils Policy

INTRODUCTION

The Association of British Insurers has published a Model Fire and Special Perils Policy (Business Interruption) wording for use Overseas.
The policy wording and the layout of the document follow a similar pattern to that used in the UK.
The policy wording breaks new ground by providing a definition of "DAMAGE" and the word is used in connection with the Fire and Special Perils wording and in the Specification. The Definition reads "The word 'DAMAGE', in capital letters, shall mean loss or destruction of or damage to property used by the Insured at the premises for the purpose of the business".
The Special Perils wording follows that used in the Overseas Market and the Specification outlining the loss settlement follows the UK. wording, substituting the word "DAMAGE" for "Incident".
As in the UK policy document, there are General Exclusions. General Conditions and Claims Conditions with slight modifications to meet the needs of the Overseas market.
One important point to note is that, unlike the practice in the UK, the policy does NOT automatically cover DAMAGE caused by own boiler, except boilers used for domestic purposes only. It is essential, therefore, if there is a steam raising boiler on the premises, for additional cover to be arranged for this Explosion hazard.
The policy wording reproduced in this Appendix is limited to the Perils and Conditions. The full Model wording also includes the wording for Dual Basis Wages and the various clauses and extensions as found in the UK. These have not been reproduced, but the wording for Dual Basis Wages will be found in Appendix 5.

MODEL FIRE AND SPECIAL PERILS POLICY

(BUSINESS INTERRUPTION)

THE COMPANY AGREES (subject to the terms, definitions, exclusions and conditions of this Policy) that if after payment of the First Premium any building or other property used by the Insured at the Premises for the purpose of the Business be destroyed or damaged by any of THE PERILS specified in the Schedule during the Period of Insurance (or any subsequent period for which the Company accepts the renewal premium) and in consequence the business carried on by the Insured at the Premises be interrupted or interfered with then the Company will pay to the Insured in respect of each item in the Schedule the amount of loss resulting from such interruption or interference

PROVIDED THAT –

1. at the time of the happening of the loss destruction or damage there shall be in force an insurance covering the interest of the Insured in the property at the Premises against such loss destruction or damage and that

    (a) payment shall have been made or liability admitted therefor

    or

    (b) payment would have been made or liability admitted therefor but for the operation of a provision in such insurance excluding liability for losses below a specified amount

2. the liability of the Company under this Policy shall not exceed

    (a) in the whole the total sum insured or in respect of any item its sum insured at the time of the loss destruction or damage
    (b) the sum insured remaining after payment for any other interruption or interference consequent upon loss destruction or damage occurring during the same period of insurance, unless the Company shall have agreed to reinstate any such sum insured

Signed on behalf of the Company

Policy No.

THE SCHEDULE

THE COMPANY	
THE INSURED	
THE BUSINESS	
THE PREMISES	
THE PERILS	Perils .... are operative
ITEMS INSURED	As detailed in the attached specification
ADDITIONAL CLAUSES AND EXTENSIONS	Clauses/extensions .... are operative
TOTAL SUM INSURED	
PERIOD OF INSURANCE	From:
	To: 16.00 hours on
RENEWAL DATE	
FIRST PREMIUM	
ANNUAL PREMIUM	

DEFINITION

The word "DAMAGE", in capital letters, shall mean loss or destruction of or damage to the Property Insured at the Premises.

PERILS

A. FIRE (whether resulting from explosion or otherwise)
excluding

(a) earthquake, volcanic eruption or other convulsion of nature

(b) DAMAGE occasioned by
   (i) its own spontaneous fermentation or heating, or
   (ii) its undergoing any process involving the application of heat;

(c) any DAMAGE occasioned by or through or in consequence of the burning, whether accidental or otherwise, of forests, bush, prairie, pampas or jungle, or the clearing of lands by fire.

LIGHTNING

EXPLOSION

(a) of boilers
or
(b) of gas
used for domestic purposes only but excluding DAMAGE caused by earthquake, volcanic eruption or other convulsion of nature.

B. EXPLOSION

excluding DAMAGE

(a) to boilers, economisers, or other vessels, machinery or apparatus in which pressure is used or to their contents resulting from their explosion,

(b) occasioned by or though or in consequence, directly or indirectly, of acts of terrorism committed by a person or persons acting on behalf of or in connection with any organisation.

For the purpose of this exclusion "terrorism" means the use of violence for political ends and includes any use of violence for the purpose of putting the public or any section of the public in fear.

C. AIRCRAFT and other aerial devices and/or articles dropped therefrom.

D. RIOT, STRIKERS, LOCKED-OUT WORKERS: DAMAGE directly caused by

(a) the act of any person taking part together with others in any disturbance of the public peace (whether in connection with a strike or lock-out or not);

(b) the action of any lawfully constituted authority in suppressing or attempting to suppress any such disturbance or in minimising the consequences of any such disturbance;

(c) the wilful act of any striker or locked-out worker done in furtherance of a strike or in resistance to a lock-out;

(d) the action of any lawfully constituted authority in preventing or attempting to prevent any such act or in minimising the consequences of any such act;

excluding

1. DAMAGE occasioned by or through or in consequence, directly or indirectly, of

   (a) acts of terrorism committed by a person or persons acting on behalf of or in connection with any organisation;

   For the purpose of this exclusion "terrorism" means the use of violence for political ends and includes any use of violence for the purpose of putting the public or any section of the public infear.

   (b) civil commotion assuming the proportions of or amounting to a popular uprising;

   (c) the malicious act of any person (whether or not such act is committed in the course of disturbance of the public peace) not being the wilful act of any rioter striker or locked-out worker in furtherance of a riot or strike or in resistance to a lock-out;

   (d) malicious erasure loss distortion or corruption of information on computer systems or other records programs or software.

2. (a) DAMAGE resulting from total or partial cessation of work or the retarding or interruption or cessation of any process of operation;

   (b) DAMAGE occasioned by permanent or temporary dispossession resulting from confiscation, commandeering or requisition by any lawfully constituted authority;

   (c) DAMAGE occasioned by permanent or temporary dispossession of any building resulting from the unlawful occupation by any person of such building;

PROVIDED nevertheless that the Company is not relieved under 2(b) or (c) above of any liability to the Insured in respect physical damage to the Property Insured occurring before dispossession or during temporary dispossession.

E. MALICIOUS DAMAGE: DAMAGE to the Property Insured directly caused by the malicious act of any person (whether or not such act is committed in the course of a disturbance of the public peace) other than DAMAGE arising out of theft or any attempt threat.

The cover provided under this peril is subject to the cover under Peril D being in force and to the application of the exclusions under that Peril other than 1(c).

F. EARTHQUAKE OR VOLCANIC ERUPTION, including flood or overflow of the sea occasioned thereby.

G. STORM AND TEMPEST

   excluding

   DAMAGE
   (i) caused by
   (a) the escape of water from the normal confines of any natural or artificial water course or lake canal or dam or any water tanks apparatus or pipes

(b) inundation from the sea
whether resulting from storm or otherwise
(ii) caused by frost, subsidence or landslip
(iii) to awnings, blinds, signs or other outdoor fixtures and fittings, gates and fences and moveable property in the open
(iv) to premises in course of construction, alteration or repair except when all outside doors, windows and other openings are complete and protected against storm or tempest
(v) by water or rain other than by water or rain entering the building through openings made in its fabric by the direct force of the storm or tempest

H. STORM, TEMPEST AND FLOOD

excluding DAMAGE
(i) caused by frost, subsidence or landslip
(ii) to awnings, blinds, signs or other outdoor fixtures and fittings, gates and fences and moveable property in the open
(iii) to premises in course of construction, alteration or repair except when all outside doors, windows and other openings are complete and protected against storm or tempest
(iv) by rain except rain entering the building through openings made in its fabric by the direct force of the storm or tempest
(v) resulting from the escape of water from any tank apparatus or pipe

I. ESCAPE OF WATER FROM ANY TANK, APPARATUS OR PIPES excluding

(i) DAMAGE by water discharged or leaking from an installation of automatic sprinklers
(ii) DAMAGE in respect of any building which is empty or not in use

J. IMPACT BY ANY ROAD VEHICLE OR ANIMAL

GENERAL CONDITIONS

1. **Identification**
This Policy and the Schedule and Specification (which form an integral part of this Policy) shall be read together as one contract and words and expressions to which specific meanings have been attached in any part of this Policy or of the Schedule or Specification shall bear such specific meanings wherever they may appear.

2. **Policy Voidable**
This Policy shall be voidable in the event of misrepresentation misdescription or non-disclosure by the Insured in any material particular.

3. **Alteration**
This Policy shall cease if after the commencement of this insurance
(a) the Business is wound up or carried on by a liquidator or receiver or permanently discontinued or
(b) the interest of the Insured ceases other than by death or
(c) any alteration is made either in the Business or in the Premises or property therein whereby the risk of DAMAGE is increased

unless admitted by the Company in writing.

4. Cancellation

This Policy may be terminated at any time at the request of the Insured, in which case the Company will retain the customary short period rate for the time the Policy has been in force. This Policy may also be terminated at any time at the option of the Company, on notice to that effect being given to the Insured, in which case the Company shall be liable to repay on demand a rateable proportion of the premium for the unexpired term from the date of the cancellation.

GENERAL EXCLUSIONS TO THE PERILS

This Policy does not cover loss resulting from DAMAGE

(a) occasioned by
   (i) riot, civil commotion, strikers or locked-out workers unless Peril D is specified in the Schedule and then only to the extent stated.
   (ii) war, invasion, act of foreign enemy, hostilities or warlike operations (whether war be declared or not), civil war,
   (iii) mutiny, military or popular uprising, insurrection, rebellion, revolution, military or usurped power, martial law or state of siege or any of the events or causes which determine the proclamation or maintenance of martial law or state of siege,

(b) to any property whatsoever or any loss or expense whatsoever resulting or arising therefrom or any consequential loss directly or indirectly caused by or contributed to by or arising from
   (i) any nuclear weapons material
   (ii) ionising radiations or contamination by radioactivity from any nuclear fuel or from any nuclear waste from the combustion of nuclear fuel. Solely for the purpose of this exclusion 'combustion' shall include any self-sustaining process of nuclear fission.

(c) caused by pollution or contamination but this shall not exclude loss resulting from DAMAGE to property used by the Insured at the Premises for the purpose of the Business, not otherwise excluded, caused by
   (i) pollution or contamination at the Premises which itself results from a Peril hereby insured against
   (ii) any Peril hereby insured against which itself results from pollution or contamination.

CLAIMS CONDITIONS

1. Action by the Insured
   (a) In the event of any DAMAGE in consequence of which a claim is or may be made under this policy the Insured shall

   – notify the Company immediately

   – with due diligence carry out and permit to be taken any action which may be reasonably practicable to minimise or check any interruption of or interference with the Business or to avoid or diminish the loss.

   (b) In the event of a claim being made under this policy the Insured at his own expense shall

   – not later than 30 days after the expiry of the Indemnity Period or within such further time as the Company may allow, deliver to the Company in writing particulars of his claim together with details of all other insurances covering the DAMAGE or any part of it or any resulting consequential loss

- deliver to the Company such books of account and other business books vouchers invoices balance sheets and other documents proofs information explanation and other evidence as may be reasonably required by the Company for the purpose of investigating or verifying the claim together with, if demanded, a statutory declaration of the truth of the claim and of any matters connected with it.

2. **Forfeiture**
    (a) All benefit under the Policy shall be forfeited if any claim made is in any respect fraudulent or if any fraudulent means or devices are used by the Insured or any one acting on his behalf to obtain benefit under this Policy or if any DAMAGE is caused by the wilful act or with the connivance of the Insured.

    (b) Benefit under the Policy shall also be forfeited in respect of any claim
       (i) made and rejected if an action or suit be not commenced within twelve months after such rejection,
       (ii) where arbitration takes place in pursuance of Claims Condition 5 of this Policy and an action or suit be not commenced within twelve months after the arbitrator or arbitrators or umpire shall have made their award.

3. **Contribution**
    If at the time of any DAMAGE resulting in a loss under this policy there be any other insurance effected by or on behalf of the Insured covering such loss or part of it, the liability of the Company hereunder shall be limited to its rateable proportion of such DAMAGE.

4. **Subrogation**
    Any claimant under this Policy shall at the request and at the expense of the Company do and concur in doing and permit to be done all such acts and things as may be necessary or reasonably required by the Company for the purpose of enforcing any rights or remedies or of obtaining relief or indemnity from other parties to which the Company shall be or would become entitled or subrogated upon its paying for or making good any loss under this policy, whether such acts and things shall be or become necessary or required before or after his indemnification by the Company.

5. **Arbitration**
    If any difference shall arise as to the amount to be paid under this Policy such difference shall be referred to the decision of an arbitrator to be appointed in writing by the parties in difference, or, if they cannot agree upon a single arbitrator, to the decision of two disinterested persons as arbitrators, of whom one shall be appointed in writing by each of the parties within two calendar months after having been required so to do in writing by the other party. In case either party shall refuse or fail to appoint an arbitrator within two calendar months after receipt of notice in writing requiring an appointment, the other party shall be at liberty to appoint a sole arbitrator; and in case of disagreement between the arbitrators, the difference shall be referred to the decision of an umpire who shall have been appointed by them in writing before entering on the reference and who shall sit with the arbitrators and preside at their meeting. The costs of the reference and of the award shall be in the discretion of the arbitrator, arbitrators or umpire making the award. It is hereby expressly stipulated and declared that it shall be a condition precedent to any right of action or suit upon this Policy that the award by such arbitrator, arbitrators or umpire of the amount of the loss or damage if disputed shall be first obtained.

APPENDIX 17

Standard Policy (Pre-October 1989)

STANDARD POLICY – COLLECTIVE
(BUSINESS INTERRUPTION)

IN CONSIDERATION of the Insured paying the premium to the Insurers named herein or to Insurers whose names are, with the consent of the Insured, substituted therefor by memorandum hereon or attached hereto signed by or on behalf of all the Insurers concerned (such Insurers or substituted Insurers, as the case may be, being hereinafter called "the Insurers").

THE INSURERS SEVERALLY AGREE each for the proportion set against its name (subject to the conditions contained herein or endorsed or otherwise expressed hereon which conditions shall so far as the nature of them respectively will permit be deemed to be conditions precedent to the right of the Insured to recover hereunder) that if after payment of the premium any building or other property or any part thereof used by the Insured at the premises for the purpose of the business be destroyed or damaged by
    (1)   Fire (whether resulting from explosion or otherwise) not occasioned by or happening through
          (a) its own spontaneous fermentation or heating or its undergoing any process involving the application of heat,
          (b) earthquake, subterreanean fire, riot, civil commotion, war, invasion, act of foreign enemy, hostilities (whether war be declared or not), civil war, rebellion, revolution, insurrection or military or usurped power;

    (2)   Lightning

    (3)   Explosion, not occasioned by or happening through any of the perils specified in (b) above,
          (i) of boilers used for domestic purposes only,
          (ii) of any other boilers or economisers on the premises,
          (iii) in a building not being part of any gas works, of gas used for domestic purposes or used for lighting or heating the building;

(destruction or damage so caused being hereinafter termed Damage) at any time before 4 o'clock in the afternoon of the last day of the period of insurance or of any subsequent period in respect of which the Insured shall have paid and the Insurers shall have accepted the premium required for the renewal of this policy and the business carried on by the Insured at the premises be in consequence thereof interrupted or interfered with

THEN THE INSURERS WILL PAY TO THE INSURED in respect of each item in the schedule hereto the amount of loss resulting from such interruption or interference in accordance with the provisions therein contained

PROVIDED THAT –

(1) at the time of the happening of the damage there shall be in force an insurance covering the interest of the Insured in the property at the premises against such damage and that payment shall have been made or liability admitted therefor under such insurance

(2) the liability of the Insurers shall in no case exceed in respect of each item the sum expressed in the said schedule to be insured thereon or in the whole the total sum insured hereby or such other sum or sums as may be substituted therefor by memorandum signed by or on behalf of the Insurers

(3) the liability of each of the Insurers individually in respect of such loss shall be limited to the proportion set against its name or such other proportion as may be substituted therefor by memorandum hereon or attached hereto signed by or on behalf of the Insurers

IN WITNESS WHEREOF I being a representative of the Leading Office which is duly authorised by the Insurers have hereunto subscribed my name on their behalf

The Insurers	Proportion of the Specification	Reference Numbers

(Leading Office)

Policy No.

THE SCHEDULE

THE INSURED

THE BUSINESS

THE PREMISES

ITEMS	As detailed in the specification attached hereto which is declared to be incorporated in and to form an integral part of the schedule
TOTAL SPECIFICATION ESTIMATED GROSS PROFIT AND SUM INSURED	£
THE ESTIMATED GROSS PROFIT AND SUM INSURED HEREBY	£
	being % of the total specification estimated gross profit and sum insured
PERIOD OF INSURANCE	from
	to
	at four o'clock in the afternoon

RENEWAL DATE	
FIRST PREMIUM	£
ANNUAL PREMIUM	£

Note: For insurance solely on a Sum Insured basis references to Estimated Gross Profit should be deleted

CONDITIONS

1. This policy shall be voidable in the event of misrepresentation or non-disclosure in any material particular

2. This policy shall be avoided if:-
   (a) the business be wound up or carried on by a liquidator or receiver or permanently discontinued or
   (b) the Insured's interest cease otherwise than by death or
   (c) any alteration be made either in the business or in the premises or property therein whereby the risk of damage is increased at any time after the commencement of this insurance, unless its continuance be admitted by memorandum signed by or on behalf of the Insurers.

3. This policy does not cover:-
   (a) loss resulting from damage occasioned by or happening through explosion (whether the explosion be occasioned by fire or otherwise) except as stated on the face of this policy
   (b) loss resulting from damage occasioned by or happening through or occasioning loss or destruction of or damage to any property whatsoever or any loss or expense whatsoever resulting or arising therefrom or any consequential loss directly or indirectly caused by or contributed to by or arising from –
      (i) ionising radiations or contamination by radioactivity from any nuclear fuel or from any nuclear waste from the combustion of nuclear fuel.
      (ii) the radioactive, toxic, explosive or other hazardous properties of any explosive nuclear assembly or nuclear component thereof.
   (c) loss resulting from damage in NORTHERN IRELAND occasioned by or happening through –
      (i) civil commotion
      (ii) any unlawful, wanton or malicious act committed maliciously by a person or persons acting on behalf of or in connection with any unlawful association
   For the purpose of this condition –
   "Unlawful association" means any organisation which is engaged in terrorism and includes an organisation which at any relevant time is a proscribed organisation within the meaning of the Northern Ireland (Emergency Provisions) Act, 1973.
   "Terrorism" means the use of violence for political ends and includes any use of violence for the purpose of putting the public or any section of the public in fear.
   In any action, suit or other proceedings where the Insurers allege that by reason of the provisions of this condition any loss resulting from such damage is not covered by this policy the burden of proving that such loss is covered shall be upon the Insured.

4. On the happening of any damage in consequence of which a claim is or may be made under this policy the Insured shall forthwith give notice thereof in writing to the first named of the Insurers, and shall with due diligence do and concur in doing and permit to be done all things which may be reasonably practicable to minimise or check any interruption of or interference with the business or to avoid or diminish the loss and in the event of a claim being made under this policy shall not later than thirty days after the expiry of the indemnity period or within such further time as the Insurers may in writing allow at his own expense deliver to the Insurers in writing a statement setting forth particulars of his claim together with details of all other insurances covering the damage or any part of it or consequential loss of any kind resulting therefrom. The Insured shall at his own expense also produce and furnish to the Insurers such books of account and other business books, vouchers, invoices, balance sheets and other documents, proofs, information, explanation and other evidence as may reasonably be required by the Insurers for the purpose of investigating or verifying the claim together with (if demanded) a statutory declaration of the truth of the claim and of any matters connected therewith. No claim under this policy

shall be payable unless the terms of this condition have been complied with and in the event of non-compliance therewith in any respect, any payment on account of the claim already made shall be repaid to the Insurers forthwith.

5. If the claim be in any respect fraudulent or if any fraudulent means or devices be used by the Insured or anyone acting on his behalf to obtain any benefit under this policy or if any damage be occasioned by the wilful act or with the connivance of the Insured, all benefit under this policy shall be forfeited.

6. If at the time of any damage resulting in a loss under this policy there be any other insurance effected by or on behalf of the Insured covering such loss or any part of it, the liability of each of the Insurers hereunder shall be limited to its rateable proportion of such loss.

7. Any claimant under this policy shall at the request and at the expense of the Insurers do and concur in doing and permit to be done all such acts and things as may be necessary or reasonably required by the Insurers for the purpose of enforcing any rights and remedies, or of obtaining relief or indemnity from other parties to which the Insurers shall be or would become entitled or subrogated upon their paying for or making good any loss under this policy, whether such acts and things shall be or become necessary or required before or after his indemnification by the Insurers.

8. If any difference shall arise as to the amount to be paid under this policy (liability being otherwise admitted) such difference shall be referred to an arbitrator to be appointed by the parties in accordance with the statutory provisions in that behalf for the time being in force. Where any difference is by this condition to be referred to arbitration the making of an award shall be a condition precedent to any right of action against the Insurers.

9. This policy and the schedule annexed (which forms an integral part of this policy) shall be read together as one contract and words and expressions to which specific meanings have been attached in any part of this policy or of the schedule shall bear such specific meaning wherever they may appear.

NOTE 1   For an insurance relating solely to premises not in the occupation of the Insured, the following should be omitted:–

the words "used by the insured for the purpose of the business" in line 7
the words "at the premises" in line 21
Condition 2(c)

NOTE 2   The following may be substituted for proviso (2) with the schedule amended accordingly:–
"(2) the liability of the Insurer in any one period of insurance shall in no case exceed –
  (i) in respect of each item the sum expressed in the schedule to be insured thereon or in the whole the total sum insured hereby,
  (ii) any limit of liability shown in the schedule,
or such other sum or sums as may be substituted therefor by memorandum hereon or attached hereto signed by or on behalf of the Insurer".

Index

References in this index are to numbers of sections within the text.

Accidental Failure of Public Supply   12.12
Accountants –
  Charges   9.06
  Clause   9.06, App. 9
Accounts –
  Profit and Loss   2.03
  Trading   2.02
Additional Increase in Cost of Working   8.20, 13.02
Additional perils   10.01
Adjustment proviso   8.14
Advance profits insurance   13.03
Advertising   3.07
Agents   15.01
Aircraft   10.03
"All Risks"   14.10
Alterations   7.10
Alternative –
  Basis of Settlement   9.08
  Period – Dual Basis   14.05
  Trading Clause   8.19
Annual turnover   9.02
Arbitration   7.19
Associate companies   6.02
Association of British Insurers   6.01
Attraction, loss of   12.11
Auditors' fees   3.07
Average   9.02

Bad debts   3.07
Bad debts reserve   3.07

Basis rate 11.12
"Blundell Spence" letter 11.05
Bomb scares 12.16
Book debts 13.04, App. 11
Brokers 15.01
Burst pipes (escape of water) 10.09
Business Interruption – Title 1.01

Carry-over proviso 14.04.
City Tailors v *Evans*(1921) 8.19, App. 15
Claims –
  action by adjuster 8.03
  action by Insured 8.03
  Condition 7.14
  discontinuance of business 7.15
  due diligence 7.14
  final settlement 8.06
  increase in cost of working 8.16
  notification of 8.01
  settlement 8.06, 8.07
  Clauses –
  accumulated stocks 11.04, App. 9
  departmental 11.01, App. 9
  Material Damage Proviso waiver App. 9
  new business 11.03, App. 9
  salvage sale 11.02, App. 9
  special circumstances 8.14.
Closure due to bomb scares etc. 12.16
Collapse and overheating of boiler 10.12
Collective policies 6.15, App. 14
Computer virus 10.04
Computers 13.07
  corruption of material 10.04
Consequential Loss –
  Committee 6.01
  definition 7.02
  engineering cover 13.06
  List of Rating Adjustments (CLORA) 11.13
Contamination (pollution and) 7.07
Contract, law of 17.02
Contract sites 12.10
Contribution 7.17, 17.06

Customers –
   Specified   12.14

Damage –
   away from Insured's own premises   12.01
   to office premises   11.05
Declaration Linked   5.04
Deductibles   11.20
Defective sanitary arrangements   10.14
Denial of access   12.11
Dentists   13.01
Depreciation   3.07
Deterioration of undamaged stock   10.17
Difference wording   4.04, App. 3
Disaster planning   16.05
Doctors   13.01
Dual Basis Wages   14.01, App. 5
   Loss settlement   App. 6
   Due diligence   7.14

Earthquake   10.05.
Economic Limit   8.17.
Employment Protection (Consolidation) Act 1978   11.16.
Engineering –
   basic perils 13.06
   breakdown   13.06
   computers   13.07
   excesses and franchises   13.06
   modified cover   13.06
Escape of Water   10.09
Exclusions to the policy   7.03
Exhibition covers   13.08/13.14
Explosion   10.02
Extension wordings   App. 10

Failure, accidental, of supply   12.12, 13.06
Fines or damages   10.16, App. 7
Fire Protection Association   16.06
First Loss Gross Profit policy   5.06
Fraud   7.16

Gas leaks (closure)   12.16
Gross profit –
    definition   4.02
    difference basis   4.03
    makeup   4.02
    rate of   8.14
    without average   5.04
Gross rentals   11.06
Gross Revenue   13.15
 – wording   App. 13
Ground heave   10.13

Heat light and power   3.08
Heave, ground   10.13
Hotels   10.14

Impact   10.10
Inception hazard   11.12
Income loss   13.01
Increase in cost of working   1.04, 8.04
    economic limit   8.17
Increase in cost of working only   13.01
Indemnity   17.06
Indemnity period   3.11
Initial period – wages   14.02
Insurable interest   17.04
Insurer's liability   6.12
Insurance concepts   17.01
Intention of a policy   1.03
Interest   2.03

Landslip   10.13
Legal contract   7.01
Lloyd's   15.01
Long term agreements   11.20
Loss Adjuster   8.02
Loss Assessor   8.09
Losses not covered   1.05
Loss settlement   8.11
    Ex gratia   6.10

Proportionate reduction   9.02
Savings   9.01

Malicious persons   10.04
Material Damage Proviso   6.09
Material Damage Proviso Waiver   6.11, App. 9
Maximum Indemnity Period   11.14
Memo 1 Alternative Trading Clause   8.19
Memo 2 Uninsured Standing Charges Clause   8.16
Minimisation of loss   7.14
Motor vehicles   12.09
Motor manufacturers   12.05
Murder, suicide, food poisoning etc   10.14.

Net Profit   3.05
Notifiable Diseases etc.   10.14

Office –
    premises   11.05
    records   13.01
One contract   6.13
Option to Consolidate – Dual Basis   14.05
Overheating of boilers   10.13
Overseas wording   App. 16

Patterns   12.07
Payments on account   9.07
Payroll   3.04, 11.16
Payroll Dual Basis   14.08
Policy –
    alterations   7.10
    conditions   7.08, 7.11/13
    general exclusions   7.03
    preamble   6.02
    schedule   6.02, 7.21
    standard perils   6.05
    utmost good faith   7.09
Pollution and contamination   7.07
Premises not in the occupation of the Insured   7.20

Premium adjustment   4.01, App. 7
Premium calculation   11.21
Prevention of Access   12.11
Professional Accountants Clause   9.06, App. 9
Professional Insured – documents   12.13, 13.01
Professional people   13.01
Property stored   12.06
Proportionate reduction   9.02
Proposal forms   15.03
Proximate cause   17.07
Provisional premium   5.03
Public utilities   12.12

Radioactive contamination   7.05
Rate calculation – example   11.21
Rating   11.11
  of perils   11.17
  of payroll   11.16
  Scale table   11.14
  special   11.19
Reinstatement of sum insured   5.05
Remainder percentage – Dual Basis   14.02
Rent   11.06/11.10
Research Establishments   13.05, App. 12
Residual value   8.18
Return of premium   5.03
Riot and civil commotion   10.04
  Northern Ireland   7.06
Risk management   16.01

Salaries   3.04
Savings   9.01
Semi-Variables   3.08
Special circumstances clause   8.14
Special Perils wording   App. 8
Specification   8.10
Spontaneous fermentation or heating etc.   6.05, 10.07
Sprinkler leakage   10.11
Standard "All Risks" policy   App. 2
Standard Fire Policy (Business Interruption)   App. 1 and App. 17
Standard perils   6.05, 6.07

Standard Turnover   8.14
Standing Charges   3.03
Stored property   12.04
Storm, flood etc.   10.08
Subrogation   7.18, 17.06
Subsidence   10.13
Subsidiary companies   6.03
Subterranean fire   10.06
Sum insured   4.01
   basis   4.05
   projection   5.02
   reinstatement   5.05
Suppliers –
   named   12.02
   suppliers   12.03
   unnamed   12.04

Theft   10.15
Transit   12.08
Trend   8.14
Turnover   1.04

Uninsured Standing Charges   8.16.
Utmost good faith   17.05.

Variables   3.02
Value added tax   3.10

Wages   3.04
   definition   14.03
Wordings –
   recommended   6.01
   previous to Oct. 1989   App. 17